Routledge Revivals

Preface to Action

First published in 1934, *Preface to Action* was written to provoke thought on society and its structure and to enable readers to make a considered judgement at election, particularly those with less time to make their decision.

The book discusses the conflict between wanting to make an informed political decision, and not having the time or all the information to do so. In light of this, Catlin brings together what he considers useful points to help guide readers towards a decision. He outlines his personal opinions and explains his reasons for them. Divided into three parts, the book first explores psychology and considers what institutional forms would best satisfy what he identifies as the major human instincts or impulses. The second part considers the community, whether it is state or nation, and what the best form of it is. The third part is a detailed exploration of the religions of Catholicism, Toryism, Fascism, and Communism.

Preface to Action will be of great appeal to those with an interest in twentieth century British and European history, the history of politics, the history of political thought, and political psychology.

Preface to Action

By George E. G. Catlin

First published in 1934
by George Allen & Unwin Ltd

This edition first published in 2021 by Routledge
2 Park Square, Milton Park, Abingdon, Oxon, OX14 4RN
and by Routledge
605 Third Avenue, New York, NY 10017

Routledge is an imprint of the Taylor & Francis Group, an informa business

© 1934, George E. G. Catlin

All rights reserved. No part of this book may be reprinted or reproduced or utilised in any form or by any electronic, mechanical, or other means, now known or hereafter invented, including photocopying and recording, or in any information storage or retrieval system, without permission in writing from the publishers.

Publisher's Note
The publisher has gone to great lengths to ensure the quality of this reprint but points out that some imperfections in the original copies may be apparent.

Disclaimer
The publisher has made every effort to trace copyright holders and welcomes correspondence from those they have been unable to contact.

A Library of Congress record exists under LCCN: 34027240

ISBN 13: 978-0-367-67883-8 (hbk)
ISBN 13: 978-1-003-13991-1 (ebk)

A PREFACE TO ACTION

Books by the Author

POLITICAL THEORY

THOMAS HOBBES
SCIENCE AND METHOD OF POLITICS
PRINCIPLES OF POLITICS
PREFACE TO ACTION
BRITAIN MUST CHOOSE
In preparation

SOCIAL LEGISLATION

J. S. MILL ON THE SUBJECTION OF WOMEN:
AN INTRODUCTION
LIQUOR CONTROL

GEORGE E. G. CATLIN

PREFACE
TO
ACTION

LONDON
GEORGE ALLEN & UNWIN LTD
MUSEUM STREET

FIRST PUBLISHED IN 1934

All rights reserved

TO
VERA BRITTAIN

CONTENTS

	PAGE
Foreword	11

PART I

SECTION
i. Introductory	15
ii. The Erotic Impulse	29
iii. The Economic Impulse	57
iv. The Power Impulse	94
v. The Religious Impulse	127

PART II

| i. Is the State the Community? | 149 |
| ii. Is the Nation the Community? | 177 |

PART III

i. The Religion of Catholicism	203
ii. The Religion of Toryism	215
iii. The Religion of Fascism	231
iv. The Religion of Communism	259
v. The Conclusion of It All	283

FOREWORD

This book is a preface. It is not designed to provide any detailed plan of what politicians ought to do or even to give any dogmatic advice upon how voters ought to vote. It is intended as a provocation to thought on our society and its structure, and not as a tractate for the next election. Its purpose will have been served if, by dissolving certain preconceptions, it prepares the ground for a reasonable and independent judgement.

It is, however, "a preface to action," although not "a plan for action." It is designed for ordinary folk who have no time, before they reach a decision in political conduct, to wait for complete scientific evidence on every point. Were there any pretension in this book to such scientific certainty, I should not have had the temerity to write it.

I recall a passage in Lord Oxford's *Life*, in which Mr. Desmond MacCarthy expresses his opinion of that statesman. "He had a great aversion from stuffing the blanks in his convictions with provisional thinking." . . . "His reluctance, in private as well as public, to discuss what was not yet clear to him seems to me the manifestation of a fundamental characteristic—one which I personally admire more than any other—a perfect integrity of mind." Were we so fortunate as to be privileged never to act until the direction of action was entirely clear to us in all its bearings, no prudent man would ask for better than to be permitted to suspend judgement upon most of the vexed issues of this present age. As Mr. Lloyd George has commented upon his great colleague and opponent, we should then have the merit of correctitude, if not of rectitude.

Minds, however, have to be made up on the balance of probability, in the hope that we shall reach a right practical decision. We should think before we act. But we are under a compulsion, whether we have finished thinking or not, to act. Politics does not move in terms of geological time. A useful purpose seems to be served by assembling considerations which may guide that action.

Much of this book is a matter, not of academic refinement, but of prejudice and taste. What follows is submitted as the prejudices of the writer. It is, in part, the record of a personal pilgrimage among political ideas. He has sought merely to give some reasons for the faith that he holds.

The author, while taking full responsibility, owes his thanks to his friends, Messrs. R. H. S. Crossman, H. Lehrman, Owen Papineau, and Allan Young, for their aid and suggestions, and to his friend, Professor Bronis Paw Malinowski, for assistance in the second chapter (Part I, sect. ii), when the writer would be the first to confess to trespass "outside his own field."

PART I

§ i

Introductory

When I began to write this book, in 1931, the General Election in England had been over for three days. The party candidates as barristers had stated their cases. The jury of the nation had delivered its verdict. The Ministry and Government were empowered to carry out the decision. It was the most momentous election since the War. The public, however, for two days past, had already turned back to its customary interests. The news-placards of a great popular daily carried, as headlines, the tips for the Newmarket Races. The human mind once more showed itself resistant to interests associated, not with a pleasant irresponsibility, but with trouble and vexation of spirit.

If, surveying the Anglo-Saxon world, one turned, in this same winter of 1931, from the Eastern monarchy to the great Western republic, the news was of the conversations between the President and M. Laval, which bade fair to determine the diplomacy and finance of the next decade, and—no less—of whether Signor Alphonse Capone should be imprisoned as an income-tax defaulter. Three years had elapsed before anyone had taken the trouble to show that criminal aspersions on the character of an American President, Warren Harding, and his wife were a venal hoax. Apparently, it was not of sufficient public interest. The good citizen went on his way moneymaking, proving to himself and the world that he was an efficient business man, and left politics alone. Or he walked the streets without bread. Anyhow, Chicago continued to grow: evidence of material grandeur struck the mind at the same time as the miseries of human society.

Messrs. Post and Gatty circumnavigate this world in their aeroplane in eight days and some hours. Meanwhile the sixty-odd sovereign nations of the world, scientifically armed, preserve their sixty-odd sovereign self-sufficiencies, and the hope of the world is seen in tariff barriers to protect the standard of living and the manufactures of the sixty-odd states. The standard of living is so protected; the cost of living, however, rises, and the average wage-rate falls. Professor Gustav Cassel explains that the world's rate of productivity rises annually by 3 per cent and he sees that it is good.

Science has enabled us to invent astonishing new machines for the production of wealth. In Detroit, Michigan, 14,500 sets of motor lamps can be manufactured in a day. The lamp reflectors are nickel-plated by a conveyor-belt process which only requires the supervision of two men. Actually, however, markets are shut off by tariffs, and inventions for the increase of wealth mean, in the export trade, increase of unemployment on a contracted market. In Britain, automatic electric substations are being established which require no attention whatsoever save that of one man to check the instruments. This is no unparalleled phenomenon: it has its counterpart in America in the rayon silk industry. It is a great manifestation of progress; but, while community wealth remains unrelated to the well-being of the citizen, no multiplication of these stations will decrease poverty. It will rather aggravate unemployment and misery.

A few years ago two thousand men were required to turn out ten thousand motor-chassis a day; now two hundred can do the work. Steel plants have been able to cut the number of men required in unloading pig-iron

INTRODUCTORY

from 128 to 2. In Czechoslovakia, in one branch of glass making, it has been found possible to increase production by 100 per cent and to decrease the number of employees by 60 per cent. In the United States, in 1933, the same production as in 1932 required 12 per cent less labour. The *New Survey of London Life and Labour* illustrates the almost miraculous powers of the modern machine. Mr. Fred Henderson, in his illuminating *Economic Consequences of Power Production*, draws the conclusions.

I do not wish, for a moment, to imply that this increase of production, if well balanced, is not good or that the masses of mankind could not well use far larger quantities of certain commodities. I do not mean that, hitherto, "technological unemployment" exists on a large scale under the conditions of an expanding market. What I mean I can put in the words of Professor Lionel Robbins. "In the world at large at any given moment, there are definite limits to the extent to which the mass production of any one type of commodity to the exclusion of other types is in conformity with the demands of consumers." ... "It is one of the paradoxes of the history of modern thought that, at a time when the disproportionate development of particular lines of production has wrought more chaos in the economic system than at any earlier period of history, there should arise the naïve belief that a general resort to mass production, whenever and wherever it is technically possible, regardless of the conditions of demand, will see us out of our difficulties."

In South America they burn coffee and in North America they throw away corn; in Japan they burn pearls; in Java they burn tea; and in Malaya they utilize parasites to destroy the rubber trees. The *Manchester Guardian* announces: "Cotton Plan's Success:

10,000,000 acres for destruction." Unemployment and population alike increase, the first to the distress, and the second by the encouragement, of statesmen. High-speed machinery mills out, as its chief product, poverty in days of a restricted market and a money shortage. In America, where most of the gold is, 1932 has seen a quarter of the working population out of jobs, queues of hungry men, starvation and suicides from despair. In Britain, the Governor of the Bank of England explains, like the Psalmist, that the problem is too great for him.

Distinguished economists have now told us that there is so much potential wealth that we all ought to be as happy as kings; or, again, that municipalities should wisely spend; or, contrariwise, that municipalities should not spend money, but that tariffs should be abolished. From these contributions *The Times* has selected the thesis that municipalities should not spend money and that tariffs should not be abolished. Ratepayers' associations maintain that the direction of expenditure in a fashion consonant with a planned rational economy is patently an affair for the private individual. The workless tighten their belts.

Professor Cassel argues that the natural economic order, allowing time and world-space for its operations, will regain its benevolent sway and that the present economic system is remarkably sane and strong. About the political system, indeed, he entertains a scintilla of doubt. Meanwhile, in one year (1931) the nations of the world spent on armaments one gold pound for every minute of time since the birth of Christ.

A couple of centuries ago the Peace of Utrecht, which gave England an effective monopoly of the slave trade with America, was celebrated in St. Paul's Cathedral by a *Te Deum* especially composed for the occasion by

INTRODUCTORY

Handel. Mr. Hartley Withers, who cites this incident in his *Case for Capitalism*, continues: "About a hundred years ago, at the end of a war which had shaken and strained England almost as much as the one which we have just gone through, the Income Tax, on the declaration of peace, was immediately abolished, and the whole burden of a heavy debt-charge was thrown on to indirect taxation of articles of consumption, which pressed most wickedly upon the poorer classes." "Our ancestors who committed this economic crime were at least as good, according to their lights, as the statesmen of today, but they did not understand what they were doing." It seems to me not unreasonable to suggest that we enquire just how many similar offences, cases of what will seem to our grandchildren obvious folly, we are committing socially today without "understanding what we are doing."

It is not my object here to write a pamphlet of political propaganda. Empty criticism does not aid an understanding of matters too grave for verbal victories. Nor is alarmism a qualification for making constructive proposals. On the other hand, it is not enough to supply what I have seen termed, by one perturbed critic of an earlier book of mine, "a bloodless theory without a flicker of passion." It was Mr. Bernard Shaw who said that political science was "the science by which alone civilization can be saved." If so, it is certainly necessary to decide accurately what the science is all about and how one goes about developing it, that is to say, its methodology. Elsewhere I have spent time on these matters and I have not regretted this as wasted time. Nevertheless, methodology and dialectic, Hegelian or Marxist, are not enough.

What also matters is the understanding of human nature, of the constants of human behaviour, and the laws of psychology—the natural law of man's conduct to man—in order that we may be able to interpret the confused phenomena of economics and politics. Here is our rock of salvation. Every solid addition that we can make here is an enlargement of the body of scientific knowledge and a permanent capture for truth. Even systematic deductions from hypothetical premises, based on practical experience but only partially true psychologically, have their value by introducing plan and understanding into the confusion of human affairs. That is why, abstract although their methods necessarily were and endowed although they were with inadequate psychological understanding in what they took for the premises of their study, we are indebted to such economists as Adam Smith and Ricardo and Marshall, as well as to biologists and psychologists, Darwin and Mendel and James.

The departmental scientist, indeed, can do no more than expound the principles of his subject and indicate the technically best means consonant with them. The politicians at Versailles, on nationalistic and political grounds, could defy the counsels of theoretical economists. The principles of economics, certainly, were not to be, with impunity, defied. Inevitably the consequences befell the nations—sovereign though they might call themselves till the crack of doom—as a nemesis. There is nothing to prohibit men from defying psychological or biological laws of their own nature any more than, in defiance of gravitation, there is anything to prohibit the man who conscientiously chooses to do so from walking over precipices. The only consequences will be, as a probability, in the one case madness or disease, and, in the other case, human pulp.

INTRODUCTORY

Admittedly, however, it is not the task of the scientist to prohibit men, individually or collectively as sovereign peoples, from disregarding the laws of biology or psychology or economics, if they so choose. His is not the task of deciding what men *should* do: he must leave that to the moralist—or to the common sense of the plain man. Yet, when all available technical and departmental scientific knowledge has been brought to bear, this question of what men should purpose and do is one that cannot be avoided. Ultimately political decisions turn on the ends we are aiming at. A discussion of those ends against the background of what we know of human nature is part of our problem. It will be the main task of this book.

Much nonsense is talked about the expert. Frequent expression is given to sentimental longings for some non-party expert form of government where competent men get ahead with their job without wrangling in Parliament on factitious issues. No one acquainted with the actual work of government will underestimate the technical work of the Civil Service as administrators. General Smuts is entirely right when he indicates, as one of the tests whether democracy can remain a successful system of government, its answer to the problem of finding for the expert an organic rôle in the working of democracy. No issue is more important in politics in this present age of a complicated civilization than how to make detailed or fundamental knowledge—technical or scientific knowledge—carry its full weight in that work of social control which is politics.

When, however, all this has been said, it remains true that no collection of those "facts, facts, facts" which Lord Bryce demanded, of itself, will decide action. What men do actually want will decide that; and what men think they should want or are entitled to want is the most universal and permanent factor in the chaos of what they do want. Those who seek for reasonable principles have but this comfort, that what men think they want, in its turn, in large part rests upon their nature, and upon the general characteristics of human nature. Here perhaps we may find solid ground amidst the whirl and flux of contemporary experience and problems.

Such a study of whatever fundamental human nature there may be and of its desires may still appear to many people very remote from what they have always regarded as politics. The only politics, however, is not that of parliament or parish council, congress or township. The General of the Society of Jesus and Commander Evangeline Booth are as truly among the rulers of men as are Mr. Lloyd George and Senator Borah or even Signor Mussolini, and their concerns are as truly political. The methods of managing men and affairs adopted by Mr. Green, of the American Federation of Labor, are not so sharply different from those of a Congressman. Mr. Ernest Bevin, trade unionist, is not in conduct and function a remarkably distinct person from Mr. Ernest Bevin who will in due course be Member of Parliament. To the province of the science of politics belongs the discussion of all means by which some men in society seek and succeed in controlling others. Within the province of the philosophy of politics, on the other hand, lies, for example, the determination of whether we should look for the remodelling of the social order in the direction of Socialism or for its reinforcement by Conservatism.

Do I believe in Property? Do I believe in it so much that I would see men starve rather than compromise on

INTRODUCTORY

my right? Do I believe in Citizenship? Or do I believe in inherited ability and its privileges more? Do I believe in Nationality? Even so much that I would see men burned to death by *flammenwerfers* for the sake of it? Do I believe in Liberty—so much that I am willing, rather than limit it, to see disease and corruption spread? Do I believe in Communism—even at the cost of bloodshed and famine? Do I believe in Democracy, white, yellow, black—or in the choice culture of the favoured few, such as does not flourish on the New York Subway? A consistent answer to these most practical questions can only be given in terms of a considered philosophy based on the conclusions of conscientious enquiry.

When I was a child of eleven I read Charles Kingsley's *Hypatia* and re-read it five times. Philosophy and Theon's daughter became identified in my mind. The effect so far lasted that the pursuit of philosophy became something almost sensuous, and philosophic truth something like a golden city, to be indicated by some friend, as it were, just the other side over the hill or like lights in water falling in a fountain, which can only be seen by those who have learned where to stand. These things are not so. Philosophy and the apperception of truth is not something absolute: philosophy has a history. Philosophy is made of the fustian of common experience, a little better tested than ordinarily. It is a final survey of significant experience which embraces both science and poetry. Its appreciation may enable a man to live his individual life more rationally and with greater love of the civilized and reflective virtues of justice and mansuetude—with more quiet happiness to himself. Pythagoras was right when he called it the highest music.

However, this theoretical understanding of things is not merely an adornment in the life of honest individuals, making them more fully rational men; it is a very practical and indispensable requirement when the question at issue is that of the control of a multitude of men, prompted by their animal passions and only to be held in order by the still voice of reason in the midst of the tempest. Here, in positions of control, men with a wrong philosophy, by which especially I mean a false estimate of values (which I shall endeavour to explain later), may do incalculable and almost irreparable harm. That is why the issue of moral philosophy cannot be evaded in politics.

Any philosophy which we can map out cannot transcend the necessity of appealing to the common sense—which is to say the reasoning on the basis of common experience, direct or imaginative—of other men. Ultimately our philosophies are built upon the prejudices which we seek to tame. We can do more than paint our picture and hope that it may appeal. We can urge no iron necessity of logic, no Athanasian infallibility save to those who accept the premises of our reasonable faith. We set out, as Plato said, to be painters of republics, that and no more. Our passionate faith is not unaware of the background of metaphysical scepticism. It yet hopes to convince people of a reasonable soul and humane experience. At least neither Rome nor Calvin nor Moscow have built on any surer basis.

This book, then, will attempt no pretentious and dogmatic political scheme. Rather it will be the record of a personal enquiry. It will begin by taking each of the major instincts or impulses in the psychological life of man and enquiring what institutional forms would give them satisfaction, at once adequate for the individual and

INTRODUCTORY

tolerable for society—give them, in brief, reasonable satisfaction. These institutions, to be adapted to their function, depend for their form, not only on the possibly permanent nature of man, but also upon the changing environment. Institutions suited to the civilization of the bullock cart and the Indian village, or to the civilization when mediaeval man, in his impoverished world, wore for the most part one single garment day and night, when his cities stank with corruption, and his soul was haunted by the instant presence of death, are not necessarily institutions suited to the metropolitan civilization of industry and of the thousand horse-power turbine, with its entirely different standard of supply and of demand. We retain the old institutions when our contemporary conditions would seem to the men who fashioned these instruments of social purpose as wildly dissimilar and fantastic as the tales of John de Mandeville of Orient lands and of the kingdom of Prester John. It may perhaps be that even the Louis XIV state dates as much as does the Louis XV chair.

In the first part of this book I have discussed the institutional manifestations of, and impediments to, certain impulses of almost universal validity throughout human nature. Any sharp distinction of human vital energy or libido into tabulated instincts must be more expedient than real. The religious and the erotic impulses cannot be sharply divided and many will maintain that the one is but a limited manifestation of the other, or, as Rickert holds, that they are intrinsically connected in the hierarchy of the values which they sustain. The acquisitive impulse and the desire for exclusive possession, although connected with hunger and nutrition, is actually undivorceable from that impulse for power which is based on the need for self-defence. The reader must suffer these artificialities for the sake of clarity of explanation.

What is fundamental is to recognize that the basis for the criticism and reformation of institutions lies in a study of the permanence of human nature. The Sabbath and like institutions are made, not indeed for individuals, but yet for man.

No attempt is here made to assert that "all social conduct can be explained in terms of one or four or twenty fundamental impulses" or even of these impulses as conditioned by permanent factors of the environment. The academic discussion of these matters I leave to another place. What is asserted is that in human life we can recognize certain impulses always at work.

It is true, as Marx writes, that "Hunger is hunger, but the hunger that is satisfied with cooked meat eaten with knife and fork is a different kind of hunger from one that devours raw meat with the aid of hands, nails, and teeth." It is yet true that, in this biological need, we have a solid basis, separate from any private, egotistical opinion or value, whereby we may criticize, let us say, institutions under whose sway men go short of bread. The norm whereby we criticize, as lacking in value, social institutions is a norm distilled by thought from consideration of the basic needs of humanity. These needs are matter for a rational generalization in natural law and are a datum for every philosophy of values that is not committed to that other and more vicious form of rationalism which is sheerly abstract. In this sense (and this alone) we can speak, with Robert Owen, of "the rational state of man's existence, based on the unerring and unchanging laws of nature." We can agree with Mr. Emile Burns that there is a "natural law governing society as well as inanimate nature."

INTRODUCTORY

In this sense we shall agree with Rousseau that "il faudrait, en un mot, connaître l'homme naturel."

In the second part of this book, having arrived at some general indications of the types of institutions which are likely to satisfy human nature, or at least to remove the more irritant causes of discontent, we shall proceed to the examination and criticism of certain existing forms of political life which profess to further these objects of society. In the third part, with a clearer notion of what we are seeking, it will be possible to examine current tendencies which show vitality—Catholicism, Nationalism, Fascism, and Communism—and to shape our political faith. Some may hold that there is no room for free action, since the succession of political forms and social systems is historically predetermined. They develop, like Herr Spengler, some philosophy of history, as did the occultists and astrologers of old, or they are obsessed by a sense of inevitability. We shall, perhaps, reach some other faith than this false determinism. An intelligent conviction of that faith is the necessary preparation for any sustained action.

Before we have finished this Preface, perhaps we shall better understand why the lives of masses of simple men are embittered by an uneven struggle in a property system that should preserve and produce, but which, for them, does nothing of the kind—which system they scarcely understand, but which seems to them inevitable. We shall seek to understand why the same men are periodically taken out and shot or drowned in mud and green putrescence under a system of national governments, instituted for the better order of men—which also seems inevitable and which also they scarcely understand. We shall have to understand and explain why men and women contrive to make each other so wretched under a social system which mankind has itself devised, and to produce defective children when the knowledge is available to produce healthy ones. In brief, we shall have to explain why men and women have established and confirmed authorities which appear, in fact, to be maleficent, and continue to obey them. God and the Devil, all these we have to explore—and to find the answer, unlike Job, not in Heaven or Hell, but within ourselves, collectively the masters of our circumstance.

Men of good will seek for light upon how these contradictions may be removed. Since miseries beat in upon us like a tempest in these days, we are at last prepared to be borne to whatever strange shores the wind of cogent argument may carry us. We declare ourselves of open mind, honest heart and integrity of judgement. We are humbled enough to be content just to understand, not to bluster at obstinate fact and inconvenient logic. We doubt the comfortable conventional explanations which put to sleep. This doubt is the beginning of a valid and courageous understanding.

§ ii

The Erotic Impulse

The most profound of all human instincts, besides those of hunger and self-defence, is the erotic instinct. That instinct, it may be thought, has little to do with any discussion of politics. Any responsible person, aware how little we, at present, have certainty concerning the biological and psychological facts which are determinant in any argument on this matter, may well sympathize with Plato when he explains how he wished to avoid being enticed into dispute on it. It is not, however, possible to discuss the family or, hence, in any satisfactory fashion, the social order without discussing the relation of the sexes. The elementary and fundamental forms of society take shape from the nature of that relation.

Much of present-day political dispute turns on the issues of race and family. Still more is likely to do so in the near future. It is the birth-rate which finally determines frontiers: the final warfare is biological. Here it is, in this connection, that nations—French, Italian, Anglo-Saxon, Chinese—have to decide what they mean by civilization and what by victory.

The Churches, again, have not been guilty of idle folly when they have placed such stress on the control of concupiscence, while preaching a religion of love, as almost to make morals and sexual morals interchangeable words. From this prime impulse streams the generation of the human race, its vitality, its creative power. Upon the character of its control depends the nature of the forms assumed by this creative power of mankind. Upon its inhibition depends the weaning of men away, to the service of idealism (or of cruelty), from interest in this immediate world and from preoccupation with personal or domestic happiness.

It is not our business here to discuss the erotic instinct in psychological abstraction, but in its cultural context. The cultural forms themselves, however, if they are in part dependent upon the laws of the social structure, resting upon other impulses and upon the material environment, are in part dependent upon the permanence of this erotic impulse in humanity.

Further, if Freud is to be believed, no small part of the individual and social disquiet from which we suffer today is due precisely to the ineptitude of the regulations and repressions which civilization has increasingly placed upon this erotic impulse. Some writers would put the more vigorous word "misery" in the place of "disquiet." Substitutes for our affections, it is argued, can be discovered for us in church and nation, but they remain inadequate. The great flame of life may occasionally blaze skywards in a religion of human love, but it is not easily turned to the conventional service of nation or class. These objects of attachment cannot awaken or absorb all of human vital energy. Some more satisfying object is required if there is to be harmony in living.

No person with his eyes open can fail to detect the clash between egoistic lust and another impulse, also related to reproduction, which now acts as check and censor on the first—that of protective affection. Our first social problem is how these two can be harmonized. The suppression of the one is deadness and the extinction of the other is an unlovely anarchy. If, yet, it so happens that both impulses stream from the same source—the drive of race preservation—healthy reconciliation should be possible.

For most animals the two impulses, sexual and parental, are never in conflict. Part of their year is under the star of Aphrodite; part is dedicated to the Great Mother. The mating season and that when the young are dependent remain distinct. For man the period of the dependence of the young outlasts the year, with its natural rotation of courting, conception, birth, suckling, and freedom. That is the outstanding fact in the natural history of man— his long immaturity. For compensation, in mankind apparently alone desire has become perennial and abnormal: it is the original sin of Adam, this carnal concupiscence. Nature has, as it were, protested against this excess and has stigmatized humanity, as distinct from even humanity's nearest kin, with menstruation—which remains for primitive man a thing of sacred dread. Owing to this disturbance of the natural sequence the primary, sexual form of the erotic instinct, as Briffault has shown, is often not the ally, but in active opposition to the secondary, parental impulse. Here we have the beginning of sin. Here also we have the beginning of rivalry, of clash within the community and of individual claims and jealousies.

Sexual satisfaction, turned to satiety, rather dissolves than fortifies any inclination to live quietly in accordance with family obligations. It gives life to the individual, has its by-product in children, and is of itself death to society. Alone among the instincts, the erotic impulse (in a world that has abolished the more intense forms of sex competition and even the duel) can usually be satisfied, in its cruder forms, without bodily peril or disciplined sacrifice. Its satisfaction thus has especial attraction for the degenerate. Such sexual conquest (we can make no complete division between the erotic instinct and the power impluse) has the significance and attraction of a victory. If the passion is indulged, it may, for the better assurance of conquest, mix sadism with its lust. This instinct is a demonic and vital force; but it is also an egoistic, cruel, and uncivilized one which is liable, like drink in weak stomachs, to turn little men into praisers of darkness and power and blood. Especially is this true of inferior-feeling men who, preoccupied with a panacea of masculinity to give them self-pride, cannot afford the luxury of generosity and self-criticism in affection. It is a force, therefore, which must be brought under social control; and a measure of discipline, restraint, and inhibition of it is necessary.

Happy the animals for whom the two major forms of the reproductive or erotic instinct, sexual and maternal, do not come simultaneously into play or into conflict. Happy the may-fly which completes its cycle of eight-day life with a sequence of unbroken regularity: happy the instinctive machine. For the human being this struggle of inclinations has been a major and basal cause of misery. The fascination of the matter for all writers of imaginative literature—I exclude the great field of best-selling novels that are mere aphrodisiacs—from the days of *Daphnis and Chloe*, of the mediaeval romance and of *Manon Lescaut*, to those of Stendhal, Ibsen, and Maugham, shows the torture and the attraction which it holds. That attraction it will continue to hold until the problems of desire, duty, and jealousy are solved.

All disquiet, however, in family life is not to be put down only to this conflict. Other impulses (and immensely complicating ones) besides the parental and the sexual, have contributed to the establishment of the social tradition which regulates marriage and sex relations and which is alleged to be the cause of so much social *malaise* today.

The desire for protection and the love of mutual society can account for the holding together, around the mother, of primitive communities. Again, the community has been held together by the leadership and sense of property of a patriarch, very conscious of the rights of paternity, who kept his wives under jealous control and who brought his daughters-in-law into his own clan in a position akin to privileged slavery. Erotic desire was alloyed by lust of acquisition. "This type of human society," says Myres, "with its state limited to a single family, its government vested in a single elderly man, and its conception of women and children as highly domesticated animals, is simply man's ancient and habitual clothing, in the political sense, against a particular kind of weather."

In the course, however, of the ages the "particular kind of weather" has changed not a little since the days of the Semitic patriarchs. Male jealousy and the expense, under new conditions, of such female property made one wife, exclusive to oneself, the custom of those humbler classes which imposed in later ages their morality on their economic betters. The ancient sacred form of prostitution is supplemented by economic prostitution—the relation of economic superior who buys and economic inferior who sells—which replaces polygamy.

The later, laxer Roman Empire saw an emancipation of women; but the new morality and the Middle Ages brought retrogression. Even until the middle of the last century in England rustics could be found who thought they had a customary right to sell their wives at the cross-roads for cash down. The rustics had at least this excuse that, in the opinion of the legislators and lawyers, women were not fit to be accounted legal persons. Still less were they economically self-sufficient. Economic self-sufficiency is the problem of the present.

Western family organization represents not only the natural expression on the social plane of the parental and sexual instincts springing from the biological urge to reproduction, but also the expression of these instincts as channelled within the dykes of respect for the proprietary sense and for a (predominantly male) social order. In the West, however, and (by imitation) in the East those dykes are disintegrating. To the exact extent to which the dykes hold confined the primitive impulse when in spate, they are subject to constant strain and to a revolutionary impulse moving towards their overturn.

The retaining walls of the structure of tradition—or, rather, traditions, and these the most various, since monogamy is no more the only tradition than polygamy or the ritual prostitution of the East—can only be intelligently reinforced against impulse by such considerations as will gain the support of those persons who are ready to be led by reason. (I immediately add that I deny the antithesis between reason and instinct, since a reasonable reason must also allow due weight to instinct—reason is not mere cerebrality.) The attack upon tradition is slowly massing as popular intuition becomes more articulate and explicitly Rousseauist—unmoved by the sentiment of reverence for antiquity. The attack is massing against a tradition that is suspect of admixing affection and racial duty with considerations of property, superstitious inhibitions, and exploitation for the purposes of national ambition or of class notions of morals. The old tradition must submit to rational revision and justification unless it is to fall before the new interests which do not recognize it. The tradition in significant respects is predestined to be changed if a vital and sane social life is to develop.

It may be urged that *laissez-faire* is best, that too much noise is made about the matter. If all the havoc wrought by the erotic instinct under our Western customs and all the cost of English morals have been a few broken homes and a few unhappy mothers, it is no matter for hysteria. There is, it may be said, no need gravely to perturb ourselves, whether about the theories of Mr. Havelock Ellis or the activities of the late Lord Brentford, whether about Mr. Norman Douglas or Mr. James Douglas. It is not, however, all so simple; nor is the present system at all one of *laissez-faire*. Actually the system has broken down, in America in one way, in France in another—unless we say that in France a partial breakdown was always part of the system. In Britain it is better maintained, but at a cost which demands consideration. A new system is being sought, in the Scandinavia of latitude 60° north in one way and in Russia in a more extreme way.[1]

I agree that, superficially, one honest day's work by a local party secretary, one day's visiting by a parish priest, one day's good craftsmanship—I will not refer to the more heroic work of the great leaders, revolutionaries, martyrs, adventurers—matters more, as an expression of distinctively human values, than all the amours discussed in the last ten popular novels on the publishers' lists, with their dreadful sameness in an act admittedly somewhat circumscribed in possible variation—"sweating palm to palm," as Mr. Aldous Huxley puts it.

I am yet not entirely prepared to agree finally with this judgement, partly for reasons which will appear,

[1] In Scotland, in 1931, the number of births was 92,220; of these 6,661 were registered.

partly because the honest day's work is a thing of value complete in itself, whereas the fascination in the narration of the amour is not complete of itself, but is a symptom of an underlying *malaise* of far greater human significance —of a vital significance deeper than that of the merely civil or economic life. Much of religion, much of art, is connected with the understanding of these emotions here revealed in disorder. And, more obviously, upon rational control of these emotions depends the quality and character of the human stock, and the decencies of everyday civilized life and affections—which matter far more than all the bloody and revolutionary quarrels of the followers of the statesmen and captains of industry and labour.

Women have their own wages; they have their own mind. Slowly women are winning through to the right to retain their employment on marriage, thanks to recognition that, if marriage is to be penalized—not encouraged—by the state and the employer, these women will marry in fact if not in name, and public opinion will only listlessly condemn them. For the moment, at least, the facts laugh at the moral code (for women only) of protection, tutelage, and jealousy. For good or evil, in accordance with the present tendency, the alternative is either that the woman will be jealous of the man, which is called a one-standard morality, or there will be (so it seems) no room for jealousy, but only for a life essay in understanding.

In every class of society, from prince to commoner, this Western system of sexual morals has shown startling signs of strain. The practical challenge here to convention has been conspicuous in the lives, not only or chiefly of slow-moving common folk, "vulgar people," but in those of men of outstanding ability, outstanding vitality, and of great demands for vital stimulus. These men, great poets, great writers, great statesmen, have, almost in the run of cases, declined to accept any strait-jacket for their moral life to cramp their requirements and contentments to those of Mr. Robinson, the grocer who wants as his highest in life the good opinion of his neighbours, or even of Mr. Jackson, the reliable bank-clerk. Where passion transcends the heights of seeking a good housekeeper, especially with imperious men, such results are not unexpected. I do not wish to say that they are good; that is what I propose to examine. Also I do not wish to say that true morality and a sense for civilized restraint have diminished in this age. On the contrary, all the evidence is that men are more sensitive and less brutal in their conduct in sexual morals (a fact resented by some —the would-be neo-barbarians) today than they were two centuries ago. They are, however, more inclined than they were to challenge the principles, as distinct from the practice, of accepted morality than they were— perhaps because they take them more seriously.

There is a second major consideration. The development of mechanical aids is neutralizing the difference in muscular strength between men and women. The women are in the workshops—not only in Russia. That is the major guarantee (precarious at present) of an emancipation—for good or ill. It is a more substantial guarantee than any vote. Perhaps it is cheap labour, but it is a new freedom. Adjustments, however, to the fundamental needs of life have still to be made and must inevitably involve a changed morality. These new work-habits force the moral issue, although many professed "feminists" choose to ignore it. Such great changes in civilization and environment must necessarily have consequences in changes of *mores*. Morals and economic conditions are alike integral and undivorceable parts of the one texture of social life.

Various answers have been suggested to the problem of the clash between the primitive Bacchic lubricity of the forest, too strong for the decorum of modern civilization, and the established tradition of social order and family stability. The most orthodox answer, which has the sanction of Paul, the Apostle, and Augustine, Doctor of the Western Church, insists upon the subordination and effacement of the erotic impulse itself as sensual, irrational, and disgraceful. That orthodox and traditional answer it is incumbent upon us to examine.

The sexual impulse is, in accordance with this orthodox ecclesiastical theory, not merely subordinated, as natural, to reason, which is the crown of nature. It is outlawed from among the legitimate impulses of life as a carnal knowledge intimately connected with the Original Sin; it is hacked apart from the procreative power. In view, however, of the contingent Divine Purpose, until the Day of Judgement come, of maintaining the human race, the concession is made of suffering those who are attracted to each other to marry rather than to burn.

Procreation without concupiscence, if that were possible, and so far as it is possible, is throughout regarded as the ideal. The angels achieved it when they had relations, at the beginning, with the daughters of men. There are more women than men in most countries; but this difficulty can be overcome, not by talking about the right to motherhood, but by recommending celibacy.

The second century, apocryphal (orthodox) "Acts of Paul" says: "Blessed are they that possess their wives as though they had them not, for they shall inherit God." In the "Acts of John," "the nuptial union . . . is the experiment of the serpent . . . the gift of death." As Dr. Burkitt tells us, in his *Early Eastern Christianity*, the orthodox Syrian Church of the fourth century declined to baptize the married, and Bishop Aphraates declared: "The man that wishes to be in holiness, let not his wife dwell with him, lest he turn back to his former nature and be accounted an adulterer." The Latin Church was more temperate and hallowed this union as it hallowed the extreme unction of the sick. Those, indeed, who propose to follow the life of religion are excluded from it. Abstinence, moreover, is possible in marriage itself, which relation becomes merely a limited illustration of the general principle of abstinence. The marital relationship is a concession to the animal for the specific and sole purpose of reproducing the race, and, as a sacrifice to that inscrutable purpose of the Almighty, is sanctified as a lesser sacrament. It is an outpost on the battlefront against lustful desire.

St. Alphonso de Liguori is prepared to countenance what the sentimental moralists of a later age would foolishly blush at as perversions, provided always that the main object of conception is thereby promoted. The orthodox, however, have always rejected the sophism of the Gnostics, by which promiscuity is condoned by the very act of condemning all sensuality alike, in marriage and without—thereby admitting it to be a necessary failing of all but esoteric believers. The concession to marriage is no ground whatsoever for supposing that any further concession to the animal impulse, leading out beyond monogamy, would be approved. The most that could be admitted is that no such sharp line divides the authorized and purposeful sensuality of marriage from the unauthorized and inexcusable indulgence outside marriage as would render those guilty of the sins of the flesh beyond pardon or, as the Gospel says, more grievous offenders than, for example, the Pharisees and hypocrites.

Protestantism, with its procreating bishops and marrying ministers, has never felt very happy about the orthodox doctrine. In the sixteenth century a part of the Western world, in reaction alike against the Papacy, the Erasmists, and the free-thinking Renaissance, returned at the Reformation to patriarchal Judaism and to the primitive Teutonic forest, under the fantastic impression that this was the world of first-century Christian Levantines. After a period of distressful hesitation under the odd moral influence of the Jewish patriarchs (illustrated by Luther's attitude towards bigamy for princes), outside Salt Lake City a moral doctrine hardened which countenanced natural indulgence in men so long only as it is maintained within monogamous marital bonds by the fear of God. It identified virtue in women with attachment to a monogamous sexual relation safeguarded by the jealous indignation of men. Protestant moral bluster is all too frequently substituted for an admission that we have here a reaction of the natural male against the ascetic principles of early Mediterranean Christianity.

In the lay mind this morality has become so far extended that sexual relationship in marriage is recognized as of itself good; civil marriage, divorce, and remarriage are recognized; it is even considered in the courts to be monstrous that the innocent party should oppose the legal remarriage of the guilty; and we are left with the mere assertion of some profound moral difference between those who do, and those who do not, make a statement before a civil registrar. This difference may exist. Civil marriage has its obligations and guarantees. These moral obligations, however, are scarcely comparable with the traditional stern morality of the Church, in accordance with which a man may well be condemned as living in adultery with his (legal) "second wife," whereas some American states would imprison him for adultery if he again lived with the first wife. The difference may exist as more than a police convenience, but the rational ground for much of this layman's morality has yet to be stated.

The objection to the orthodox system, as one whereby we may order society, is that it is valueless and impracticable unless it rests upon inner and passionate acceptance. Discipline may be well in life, but certain kinds of discipline cannot be prescribed from without. This erotic asceticism is one such discipline.

Where the erotic impulse is not killed by sadistic perversion or by the lust of power, and erotic impulse conquers, in some religious form, without becoming specialized upon any transient or animate object, the result is something beautiful as an amethyst. This diffused kindliness, moreover, achieves innocently the wisdom and detachment perpetually retaught by sexual satiety and by the comedy of sexual heroics.

To impose, however, without explanation and by force of fear, this discipline upon young men and women who do not understand their own nature is an irrational interference, destructive of much that is beautiful, and productive of perversions. Instinctively the lay world has turned away from the authoritative imposition of such a morality, which horrifies many natures by its logic, without the lay world being able to replace it by any more than a patched-together morality of its own.

The opposite argument to the ascetic has been put

A PREFACE TO ACTION

forward again recently—it is an old one enough—in Britain and America by a group of writers, among whom it is usual to place as outstanding D. H. Lawrence. In part this position, very definitely allocated to Lawrence by the popular mind, rests, so far as one can judge from study of the material he has left and from some small acquaintance with the already extensive literature, upon a misconception.

At his best Lawrence is a great artist (it is no good writing him down just as that: the man stamps and clamours to be judged as a philosopher), gifted with perception, able to make words quiver with vitality. He has been seized upon by the mass of his readers as preaching a doctrine of emancipation which at least most emphatically requires to be discussed. In part he did preach this doctrine, but, as it were, incidentally to revolt—the revolt to which he was under a compulsion, gnawed by his sense of inferiority. That he wrote about what men in fact do was good, and that he called it pure was, in my opinion (as will appear), right. For the Lawrence of the noon-day sun, the Lawrence spreading Hellenic light and health, the Lawrence of Rebecca West's little gem of a study, I have nothing but respect. Lawrence was an apologist of vitality. But there is also a very un-Hellenic rolling, roaring, maenad Lawrence—and not such an athletic maenad. And there is the complementary Lawrence, with the infantilist motif, who shows himself in certain of the poems. What has not been made clear is the broad thread of cruelty—not the cruelty of a strong man, but the compensatory cruelty of a weak animal, if a strong artist—running throughout his writings. This appeal, in Lawrence's writings, to what grandiloquently he calls "the dark gods" is unutterably mischievous.

THE EROTIC IMPULSE

There is a "criminal" side of human nature which demands recognition and which has its limited tempestuous values—especially values of courage and of personal confidence which a merely utilitarian, democratic civilization tends to crush down. Their reassertion, as Durkheim and Freud have said, is an important task for the enriching of civilization and it is a task of youth which will certainly be denounced as immoral. But cruelty is scarcely to be counted as one among these values, whereas for Lawrence it, not erotic emancipation, is of the texture of his essential gospel. The power-motif appears in its least happy form in his poem on the Prince in Ceylon. Lawrence suggests, as a substitute for that of chivalry, the motto, "Ich nicht dien." Having failed first with men, then with women, and then (as shown in *Kangaroo*) with men again, coveting, although a man, the more passive power of the woman who remains still and draws her conquest into a relation physically subordinate, Lawrence ends by finding satisfaction in preaching the worship, like Huxley's Savage, of the dark, bloody Mexican gods. This gospel has an uncanny fascination for that large mass of humanity (especially, but not exclusively, women) which is fundamentally masochistic.

Emancipation for Lawrence is not an aristocratic emancipation through reason from superstition, an emancipation which is yet subject to the bright control of reason. It is not even a Rousseauistic return to a gilded Utopia of primitive freedom. His word is not of Olympus, but Panic and chthonic. Emancipation is a return to the darkness of primitive instinct because his half-conscious sadism was titillated by these suggestions of barbarism. "Some, having given up their vanity of the light, having died in their own conceit, saw the gleam in the eyes of the wolf and the hyena, that it was the flash of the sword of angels, flashing at the door to come in, that the angels in the darkness were lordly and terrible and not to be denied, like the flash of fangs."

In this passage the whole outlook of Lawrence is epitomized. And the comment must be that it offers neither a healthy nor a constructive philosophy. The comment must be that it is not good—or true. It is not life-giving and, in this true sense, power-giving (I use Spinoza's criteria) but death-giving. Cruelty, although a concomitant of assertion and power, is not itself in any need of development. Blakesque allusions to the jungle do not aid matters. We end in Satanism. "It is Lucifer's turn, the turn of the Son of Morning, to sway the earth of men." The conclusion is diabolism which, in days when the material flames of hell no longer burn, is not even heroic. There are other and no less poetic ways (are these ways so poetic?), mightier ways, of making the pulse beat quick. All of which does not affect, of course, the fact that Lawrence is one of the greatest writers of this country and generation.

If instinctivism, as an infallible standard, and asceticism are alike rejected, we are again forced to consider whether the proper rational check on instinct, which prevents the expression of vitality from becoming Bedlam, is not to be found solely in the utilitarian condemnation of acts which have consequences generally socially injurious and acts which cause specific pain to others.

One objection to any departure from tradition need only be mentioned to be dismissed: that any such licence would lead to an increase of prostitution. Clearly, complete continence outside marriage would exclude prostitution. Such complete continence involves the acceptance of the ascetic ideal—which is also, as has been shown, distrustful of marriage itself. Our problem arises precisely where such entire and absolute continence is not observed because asceticism is not *ex animo* accepted. It is just where the moral code imposed on the majority of women is more rigid than that imposed on the majority of men that prostitution, in the accepted sense of sexual relations primarily for money, is most common. Complete asceticism for both sexes will exclude prostitution. It is not clear that an equal departure from asceticism on the part of both sexes will increase it: it is, indeed, improbable. With the decline of prostitution, one of the greatest blots on the old morality, so abundantly conspicuous in the records of the past, is being removed—along, it may be added, with some of the rigour of this morality itself. The two indeed, as a great authority, Parent-Duchatelet, bluntly says, are joined together as light and shadow.

The Catholic case is, indeed, that, if all danger is removed from unregulated intercourse, the world will relapse into a carnival of sensual lust comparable to that of the world of the Roman Empire in its hey-day before Christianity. The rasher prophets already detect this happening in America. As St. Augustine says: "Remove the prostitutes and everything will be disturbed by lust." This, however, is not construed as any reason for diminishing the dangers of being a prostitute or offering any alleviation—which might be converted into a facility for other women entering into non-pecuniary relationships. The argument appears to carry its own condemnation.

The case against any change of tradition because of its supposed effect upon prostitution it has been shown will not hold. The second argument is one derived from the nature of the family. The contention of Aquinas still

A PREFACE TO ACTION

stands solid that the governing moral consideration in the family is the good nurture of the children. As has been said, this has not by any means been the sole consideration in determining orthodox thought, since the corrupting effect of the "natural sin of concupiscence" has played no small part in fashioning this thought. Aquinas concludes that children can only fitly be brought up under the equal attention of both the parents. Hence alike illegitimacy and polygamy are excluded as short of the ideal of duty and as immoral. He makes the assumption, very natural in his age, that sexual relations must result in offspring. He therefore condemns retrospectively those relations which do not fall within the limits of monogamy.

It is not, however, possible to found a morality upon consideration of mishaps and of avoidable mishaps. The revolutionary change of our age is that children probably will not result from a relationship when children are not willed, and that this probability is apparently capable of indefinite increase, granted social approval and encouragement. This, of course, says nothing whatsoever about the desirability of that relation. It does, however, invalidate the argument of Aquinas. Since the Revolution, in Russia (a country with a rapidly growing population), the control, not solely of conception but of gestation, is made entirely subject to the choice of the prospective parent. What is done in Russia efficiently and by permission of the state and society, in fact takes place, although inefficiently and without the approval of the state, as has been shown by social investigation, throughout the industrial areas of Britain.

The orthodox answer is that, whether or not children result, it is in accordance with nature that they should do so. The frustration of the purpose of nature, whether within

THE EROTIC IMPULSE

or outside marriage, is itself perversion and sin. It is apparently forgotten, in this argument, that concupiscence is itself in accordance with physical nature, whereas, if the "natural" is synonymous with the "rational," then the use of intelligence in the control, in sexual relations, of natural consequences is still, for rational man, natural.

We are now forced back upon the question whether any relation other than the traditional one is possible without the inherent probability of the infliction of pain on third persons. If we are seeking some moral criterion of the healthy social regulation of sexual and marital relationships, we shall not get adequate indications from enquiries into who is aggrieved by this or that system, but only by an enquiry into who has the rational right to be aggrieved in view of the social functions served by these relationships themselves.

Here, in what concerns the race, lies the first moral criterion of what is right and wrong—not in the convenience and happiness of the adult partners or in the traditions of an ascetic morality which, in the last analysis, regards marriage itself as an inferior condition. Those who believe that easy divorce should be granted, thus offering facilities to all the twists and turns of romantic relationships, misunderstand this. The case is strong against any encouragement of the break-up of the family, although not so strong that divorce should not be encouraged where the perpetuation of adult quarrelling may destroy all the happiness of children. The road of courage may here be the road of separation. If, however, the good nature and nurture of the children were taken as the basis of the social conventions governing sexual relations, easy divorce and frequent remarriage would almost certainly be excluded as favouring (probably) childlessness and (certainly) the subordination of the interest of the children to the agreeable companionship or erotic attraction of the adults.

Such a subordination of the more permanent to the more ephemeral interest, whether manifested in the tendency to irresponsible divorce, as in America, or in promiscuity without divorce, as in Europe, is to be condemned. As has been pointed out in America, there is a sharp distinction of moral responsibility between those cases where there are children and those where there are not. Even so, temporary relationships, although they may prevent the humiliation and unhappiness of those who have found no permanent partner or have lost one, cannot alone satisfy the human desire for a relationship of stable affection, support, understanding, and mutual enrichment, completed by the birth of children.

Understanding, indeed, is possible without physical relations, and is all too frequently absent where they exist. Mutual support is a thing of light account for the young, the happy, and the successful. Moreover, something less than the ideal may still be good, and much better than a life of craving and unhappiness, a damping down of vitality, a slowing of the wing in flight. If the ideal be not (as Dante thought) the unobtainable, and Beatrice the ever unobtained, yet something less than even the lyric and mundane ideal need not be cheap or sordid, or unbeautiful—and this even in an age still so imperfectly civilized and full of foolishness and treachery as our own. It may make a sonnet. The sonnet may be better for its maker than a bad epic. There is intelligible meaning to the words when Mr. Noel Coward says:

"Let's look on love as a gay thing." ... "Please let us keep this a casual thing." The fact remains that the beauty does not increase with the casualness; and the philosophic willingness to treasure merely a fair memory is battled against by the urgency of deeper human desire. Passion aroused, then conquered or affronted, leaves a very empty heart. And yet the practice of casualness unrestrained is indeed "the expense of spirit in a waste of shame."

Mr. Aldous Huxley, in his *Texts and Pretexts*, prints the letter of a suicide whose wife had left him, which has as much beauty to it as anything that I recall. One knows the suicide to be a deluded fool, and that his wife who could inflict such pain on him could not truly be "the first love in the world." In a more civilized age maybe he would not have committed suicide. But such things are; and the lyric of love has in itself much of the nature of tragedy. As such its song is not to be played by clumsy or profane, intolerable hands.

The highest love is full of ire and loneliness and fierce hate of what soils the world and the honourable things in it. When, therefore, we place our pleasures of good animals beside her, we should do so with the frank, clean courage of a new vitality, not in sullied and tawdry riot or burlesque indignity. The highest love is a flame which can make molten for us all from which we shall cast a new world; it is not the lust of a night—but still less is it the possession of the Pharisees and Susannah's elders, who have no courage against lust save what is lent by a crawling fear.

The importance of the ritual, control, and severe dignity of life it seems to me very hard to exaggerate. It may yet be doubted whether erotic abstention, any more than abstention from wines, is control, except for the deliberate ascetic who seeks the detachment from life of the ascetic.

It is clear, of course, that abstention is the only proper course so long as we entertain the prohibitionist attitude that the entire erotic relation is better not discussed, as being at best a concession to human frailty and, fundamentally, a manifestation of original sin. Only, however, if we entirely reject this attitude, although with however cautious a temperance, can we advance.

The sensuous, said Hobbes, are the thralls of despotism. Those who live their lives in a tortured conflict between their impulses and their fears are the thralls of death. If an undisciplined appetite for sensuous pleasure is the enemy of a finished perfection in the living of life, fear, since the days of the jungle, is one of the most powerful emotions in the human heart and one of the most inimical to significant life.

All class prohibitions which render shamefaced by snobbery the relations between persons, admirable in themselves, who are of different economic levels or which place a premium on ruses for social advancement by marriage; all proprietary sentiments and other relics of the chattel slavery of the patriarchal period; all superstitions which are to be known by their inability to give a reason for their dogmas beyond mere arbitrary command—these must all be condemned. We are left with the task of the social control of the attraction of human beings in such fashion as does not lead to a bedlam of manners and as promotes the excellence of the race. Human impulses, sexual rather than procreative, are sufficiently strong for the shaping of that control to be no light matter.

So far our argument has justified, against certain advocates of change, the conventional family. The increasing difficulties, however, of the self-sufficient "household-of-two-with-children," as the sole form of family institution, has to be recognized. Apart from the permanent excess of women over men and the disorganization of this institution by the mass employment of women in industry, the achievement by women, with the development of civilization, of full, adult personality creates difficulties for it. It is improbable and undesirable that these changes should be reversed. It is a basic rule that human institutions should be adapted to fundamental human needs and values, and not the converse. Of these institutions the modern European family system is one.

Out of our present experiments may develop, on the one hand, a community prepared to assume responsibility, to a larger extent than is the case now, for desirable children and hence to mitigate the strain imposed on women who have other than exclusively or primarily domestic interests. Neither the frustration nor, alternatively, the barrenness of the able can be held to be socially satisfactory.

On the other hand, it is my belief that we stand on the verge of a reaction against that competitive and commercial form of society which places an intolerable strain upon women who endeavour to adapt themselves to it. Precisely recognition of the personality of women may force forward the development of the non-competitive, co-operative community, instead of the present condition of an individualistic competitive society, entirely unsuitable for married women, conjoined to a private family system entirely unsuited to women of definite personality and non-domestic talent.

I see no other method than experiment in these directions to accommodate, ultimately and satisfactorily, a healthy, erotic impulse without the frustration of ability. Certainly the satisfaction of this impulse—and not, invariably, its satisfaction by ascetic sublimation—is at least as important to the individual, and hence ultimately to society, in the production of balanced personality, as the satisfaction of the exacting demands of ambition and talent.

Beside the family, as the normal institution for parenthood and for the emotional satisfaction of intimate and enduring companionship, ought to stand the community, as a face-to-face friendship group, redeeming the family from its egoistic narrowness, sharing the care and guarding the nurture of the next generation, assisting the individual in the development of his rational personality by offering, not merely material facilities, but a wider mental and emotional life, and providing a protective milieu in which those who cannot be assimilated in the ordinary family system may yet discover a useful and stable social life. This community is not inconsistent with the family, which rests on the normal demand of the fully mature human being for a permanent and rooted emotional relationship, as a condition of pose of personality and subtlety of emotional loyalty—save so far as this family may become a private world, egoistical, jealous and anti-social, even from the point of view of the children and of continuity of tradition.

In the family both sides of the erotic impulse must be satisfied, but they are to be harmonized and satisfied by the recognition of the family in the context of the community and of its subservience to the community. Parenthood is not simply a private satisfaction, still less something imposed upon the woman by the man, but something to be judged by the degree of its conformity, in the production and nurture of children, to standards of public obligation. Complementarily, the parent has rights against the community. It is not just an affair between two partners and a matter of parental duties as against sexual desires.

Likewise, sexual desire, although a matter of private choice, is to be judged morally, in its expressions, first, by whether it does or does not conduce to desirable and disciplined parenthood and the good of the next generation, and, secondly, by whether its satisfaction conduces to the happiness and public usefulness of adults in this generation. Both parental and sexual desire must be placed in the context of community obligation and disciplined by the sense for the community.

This sense for the community is itself a filial sense, sprung from the recognition of the community as the great parent. Duty to the community is rendered easy when there is a certain transference of affection and fixing of it upon the community itself as object. It has been the work of Mr. Gerald Heard to stress and explore this truth in his fascinating book on *The Social Substance of Religion*. Diversion of emotion is possible, indeed, upon many other objects besides the community—personal ambition, art, private salvation—but none of these alternatives is social in the same fashion that the object of the normal erotic sense is social. In the case of these diversions the check of social idealism is removed.

So soon as this erotic attachment to the community, as well as to the natural parents, is lost, the power of the community to command obedience, discipline, and harmony is also lost. And, in a vicious circle, as this power to discipline is lost the riot of immediate erotic satisfaction gains control. This community, as distinct from the family and from larger, more heterogeneous associations, under the form of the *gens* or some similar face-to-face group, is a social form common in primitive life. Its revival or rediscovery, perhaps in the nation, perhaps (as we shall see) elsewhere, is an urgent need of social life today. To rediscover the community and to ascertain its natural form today is our present task.[1]

Only if a double harmony, psychological and social, is effected by the recovery of a sense for the actual community can, not only indefensible and furtive immoralities with their domestic havoc, but a furtiveness corrupting to the soul be avoided. It becomes possible to lay down straightforward, rational principles of moral conduct—principles of trust, respect for personality, and discipline. Otherwise the courageous personality is not developed. The living of life in accordance with these principles, which allow for both reason and emotion, becomes a matter of affirmative vitality, without the weakening trauma of inner conflict. When, however, the erotic self is made criminal by the incubus of the sense of original sin and by superstitious custom, a fearless habit of morality is driven out and a discouragement about achievement sets in, infecting all the fields of life, whether artistic, political, or scientific, or those of adventure and discovery. Along with fearlessness, initiative is depressed and that good vanity which contributes to achievement. The habit of repression suffocates the upspring of confident power. Fear, the great enemy, returns to hold sway.

Deliberate asceticism, as an act of will, with its concentration of desire, can arm with fanatic power. A satisfied, controlled body and adult emotions can give a healthy and resolute soul. But the morality of furtive tension between Artemis and Pan can do neither. Each god may appropriately be worshipped, but each must

[1] Somewhere D. H. Lawrence writes: "None, however, is quite so dead as the man-to-man relationship. I think if we came to analyse to the last what men feel about one another today, we should find that every man feels every other man as a menace."

be worshipped with frankness and clear reason. Nothing is more evil than this kind of inhibited obsession and this preoccupation, not of body but of thought. It results, in physical perversions and the more sullied perversions of the mind. The vitality, the Eros, that strives after perfection, whether spiritual or sensuous, is a sacred god, eldest born of her *hominum divomque voluptas*, to be honoured, not trivialized.

The suggestion, then, here urged in theory is similar to that which we must suppose Plato intended in the rough sketch in his *Republic*. Here he clearly did not contemplate any ban by law on relations without progeny, according to conscience and honour, where no third-party rights were involved. Equally he did contemplate, on the one hand, the exclusion of family jealousy and, on the other, the strictest prohibition of marriage with a view to progeny, except between those truly fitted for this undertaking, and a strong emphasis upon the high social importance of that undertaking.

What, however, is possible in Plato's Republic or in the communist Oneida Community (which existed, in the last century, in New York State as a religious body) is not desirable in Balham and the Bronx. It is noteworthy that at Oneida itself, under Noyes, a working system of monogamy developed as the community matured (although the community care of the children largely remained), probably in answer to the need for emotional stability. Communism, moreover, wherever it has been acceptable, has involved a rigid discipline and subordination of the individual. Its most successful example, monasticism, insisted on celibacy. Certainly any disciplined movement if it is to live must do so by a certain rigour of manners. Anything resembling a preoccupation with relaxation of conventions in sexual morals would be catastrophic for it. That way to disaster went Enfantin, the follower of Comte, and all his group. The danger has been fully appreciated in contemporary Russia. The release of the creative powers of the human individual, of either sex, must be accompanied by the intelligent control of immediate sexual impulse. It must not be the servant of erotic debauch. But the new civilization will be built by an energy that will make a levy upon every vital power and that will require for its service men rationally at harmony with themselves.

An understanding of this function of the erotic impulse, in giving vitality to creative power in and through society, is essential to an understanding of impassioned loyalty, of the nature of the group—the community—and of the modern dissatisfaction with a mechanical civilization as a substitute for the intimate community.

§ iii

The Economic Impulse

The prime instinct is that which makes for the continuation and reproduction of life. To ward off death is the concern of the individual. To maintain life is the concern of the species, and the arrangements of the natural world appear to be more preoccupied with this. The drive towards continuation of life, however, finds in the individual its vehicle. The nourishment of the individual—the satisfaction of hunger, economic production—is the condition of that continuation and reproduction of life. Hunger and love—the economic and the erotic impulses—are the two prime forces.

Man, however, as a provident animal, does more than satisfy his immediate hunger: he endeavours to safeguard himself against being hungry and against all shortage of material needs. The impulse to acquisition, if in part a magpie instinct, a decorative tendency showing itself in conspicuous consumption, is in large part merely the more primitive demand to be free from fear of shortage become autonomous as a desire to acquire wealth for its own sake. It is just with this nightmare fear and then with this desire that we fret our lives and make thin and "economic" our personalities, turning ourselves into cogs and levers for money-getting.

Somewhere here, in this fear, we must seek the explanation of the appalling drabness, the baulked and damped-down vitality in the lives of the bulk of middling folk, from small business men to the fustian masses of clerks, who were healthy animals enough in the hopeful twenties of their youth. Until this irrepressible desire in each, for security, is adjusted to the like desire in all, that "social unrest," which threatens revolution and in this age is predominantly economic, will not abate, any more than a malady of the body physical abates when the deep-set causes remain unremoved. A social system that perpetuates insecurity of livelihood is "unnatural"—more so than a primitive society or a rural economy in which some balance has been found between demand and what the environment has to offer—in the sense that it involves this permanent state of fear.

The acquisition of wealth acquires new importance as a motive as civilization advances. Human demands become more elaborate; the satisfaction of those demands grows to be a more calculated affair and less a matter for the direct action of the hunter. The growth of civil order permits this work of acquisition of goods to supplant for the fortunate and powerful few, as the ordinary centre of attention, the more vital and basic considerations of security of life, as distinct from livelihood. In the earlier stages of civilization the acquisition of large wealth is by piracy and raiding. Life itself is involved in the issue. In the later phases wealth is acquired by trade and industry. Although poverty, shortage, and, for most of the centuries of the world's history, starvation have been rife enough, the threat and fear of sudden death recedes. The economic and the power motives become distinguishable, although they remain intertwined—as in Persia at this hour, from whose oil-fields the British Navy draws supplies. The trader no longer comes literally with sword as well as balances. Moreover, change of standard of demand comes with change of culture. But the fear of material insecurity, of poverty and its humiliations, if not the fear of being short of food and houseless, continues to lurk (however overlaid by the adventure of great speculations) beneath the acquisitive desire, where that is not a misnomer for desire for power.

I do not say that all men are moved by this acquisitive desire and, still less, that all are influenced by particular cultural standards of demand. Nothing is more amazing than the indifference of masses of men to provident calculations of pecuniary advancement. It is further true that much economic activity is due to variants of those sentiments that Kropotkin emphasized. The personal pride of the craftsman is bound up with doing a good job; the monotony of idleness is tedious; much work is a form of exercise, of play, stabilized by a purpose; probably even more of the work that is done is just habit. The habit, however, is formed, the play maintained, for a purpose that is not habit or play, that may itself compel the acceptance of monotony, that is more commonplace and insistent than pride. That purpose is the maintenance of economic security, which even the improvident desire in the present, although they may be too light-headed or heavy-headed to guarantee it in the future. That purpose to acquire is the obverse side of an impulse arising from experience of restriction of means—of hunger in a "hunger situation" (which those who have experienced it never forget) or of shortage, real or imaginary. What each man understands by shortage and deprivation will depend, of course, upon the standards of his civilization, upon the conditions of good living (so far as they are buyable) in his time and place, and upon his own material expectations in life. The universality, however, of the impulse is to be explained by these more basic considerations. Concurrent with this acquisitive impulse, moreover, is the power impulse, and the two converge where the vital love of display and even sexual vanity and rivalry are converted into a passion for conspicuous consumption and into love of wealth as a condition of display.

Were the fear of grave insecurity once quite killed by social co-operation, and the power impulse satisfactorily canalized (which is another problem), the other motives that operate in economic activity, not excluding healthy vitality and pride of work and person, would inversely increase in importance. The desire for acquisition and adverse possession, deprived of the militant vigour lent to it by fear and habits founded on centuries of fear, would undergo change and domestication.

Here, then, is our problem: to give to this desire for goods (which is a natural and ineradicable desire) a social and civilized form, instead of forms in which it will impel men to trample over their neighbours, ignore suffering, condone an hypocritical identification of the poor with the worthless, sap citizen obligations and disrupt society, rather than sacrifice the main chance of money at any cost—money by spoiling the rich or money by spoiling the poor. If we cannot solve this problem, then we are condemned to a condition of society where "there are two parties at war with each other," and, "hating and being hated, plotting and being plotted against, they pass the whole of their life, much oftener and more afraid of the enemies from within than from without, they and the rest of the state hastening speedily to its destruction."

If the social structure, the economic system, of civilization is the work of man, by man it can deliberately be changed—although subject, if the change is to be successful, to limits imposed by a power greater than the will of any individual man, namely, man's own nature and its demands. It may be that it can be changed so that some at least of all this misery of poverty, this monotony of indigence can be removed in a world so marvellously equipped by intelligence for production that it might seem—it does seem to Mr. Keynes—that we all should be as happy as kings. So far as command of material goods is concerned, thanks to machinery, a coster from Whitechapel should fare as well as the first Edward Plantagenet or the second Richard. Something, however, has happened; something seems to have gone wrong. The coster is still not so far above the economic Plimsoll line: he may be below it.

Let us consider, for a moment, the history and structure of society on its pecuniary side. During a long period of the world's history the wealth and power motives are so far intermixed that it is taken for granted that those who have superior power should have superior wealth, and (somewhat secondarily) that superior wealth will exercise superior power. Status implies wealth, and, conversely, wealth gives status. The Semitic patriarchs had great herds of cattle. The wealth basis is clear in the early constitutions of Hellas and Rome. On the other hand, as late as the Middle Ages it is assumed that those holding the higher political dignity should have the larger wealth and broader acres. The lord is land-lord; the land-lord is lord. There is resentment against the trader who amasses sufficient wealth to bring him into competition with the prestige of the baron and to constitute him a potential threat to the older baronial privilege. Thus St. Thomas develops the doctrine that no interest should be taken on capital loans, save as safeguard against loss, and that no profits should be made in trading, save such as enable a man to maintain his status in life. The ranks of the people are to be stabilized.

As late as the end of the eighteenth century this sentiment persists concerning the immutability of status, although it has undergone the sea-change that the man of wealth, unlike the old landowner, no longer feels himself under the obligation to assume magisterial responsibilities. Mr. Leonard Woolf quotes Arthur Young as saying: "All these things imply a different order of beings; let these things, and all the folly, foppery, expense, and anxiety that belong to them remain among gentlemen; a wise farmer will not envy them." By this date the habits of the gentlemen are regarded as not beyond criticism—just as the Church had earlier denounced mundane pomp—but the attitude adopted in viewing these habits in gentlemen is regarded as naturally enough entirely different from that adopted to the same habits in farmers. Unequal distribution of wealth, all ability or virtue apart, appears natural and carries with it inequality of power and social position. Even when a peerage and a politically privileged class fall into the background, the notion of an economically unequal society (now unjustified by performance *ex officio* of feudal or of public obligations) persists unimpaired. The demand for economic security, so that each man (to use the old definition of a freeman) knows on the day what he shall do on the morrow, is not satisfied. The ineradicable demand for recognition of the right to acquire through work the material conditions of a minimum of good health, decency of surroundings, and dignity of living as a citizen is, for masses, a demand unsatisfied.

The democratic movement has challenged this entire division of human beings into social "orders" naturally enjoying privileged powers, pecuniary and political, to the exclusion and suppression, economic and psychological, of others.

The first wave, indeed, of this movement was Liberalism. It came from the commercial and middle classes themselves. Their concern, however, was not truly for equality —much as they talked about it—save as a weapon to destroy aristocratic privilege and that landed power that shut out, from equality with itself, the power of wealth. Certainly they were not interested in equality with the manual workers. The conflict between the class interest of the traders, for whom the phrase about equality was merely used as a destructive argument against the holders of privilege, and the idea of equality itself to which nominal allegiance was demanded, is overcome by the aid of the Jeffersonian and Liberal theory of equality of opportunity. The mental reservation here is that oneself and one's friends have ability, and indeed ought to occupy a more lofty position than at present they do among the squires and junkers, with their undeserved privileges, but that the manual workers, except for a few thrifty apprentices, were a test of ability applied, would mostly remain in their existing stations in life.

The Liberal argument of equality of opportunity readily merges itself, for those interested in providing a justification for the capitalist system, into one in favour of natural selection of ability and one of *laissez-faire* in order to enable this natural selection to operate. The appeal, however, to natural selection is specious. There is no practical probability that strict natural selection will be permitted to operate under civilized conditions, and if this appeal to the lion and the fox, to physical strength and to cunning, were in fact made, the results would be very surprising to some of the supporters of *laissez-faire*

"Darwinism." The results would probably issue in something far more similar to conditions in the underworld of Chicago or perhaps in the November Revolution in Russia than the Thrasymachi and Callicleides of our modern world, the exponents of the survival of the fittest, imagine. Actually the needs of civil peace are such that *laissez-faire* means unlimited competition only within the limits of certain rules which are, in fact, drawn up with a view to the protection, not only of property, but of the existing owners of property. (The taxing power is, under universal suffrage, the great exception to this statement.) A society, however, which embodies this principle, of so-called "free competition" which yet has a bias, is an unsatisfactory form of society in structure.

A social structure organized primarily—as Locke said the state was organized—for the protection of property is an unsatisfactory form of society even when its new Liberal test of opportunity for ability is applied. The boy of ability born into a poor family has, even today, in no wise the same opportunity as one born into a wealthy family. He will probably be worse nourished. That difference of nourishment may, as Mr. Tawney has shown, actually result in difference of physical size. There is abundance of evidence to show that it will result in the difference of capacity to put up a competitive fight. He will be brought up surrounded by people normally with little leisure for ideas. He will, at an early age, have to assume responsibilities for the upkeep of the family; bread and butter will be the chief mental, as well as physical, pabulum. He will probably be unable as a child to command quite the best education, just as his parents will be unable to command the best medical or legal services. He will, too often, be brought up with a psychological sense of inferiority among people conscious of playing a small part in the world. He will go through life cursed, not by his genuine and innate biological inheritance, but by his social and cultural inheritance. That is neither just nor useful.

When all allowance is made for the legislative removal of specific handicaps or objective social restraints, such inequality must always be the case when the sons of poor men compete with the sons of the rich—as distinct from that competition of natural ability alone that was contemplated by Plato. If indeed the sons of the poor compete, their best chance is themselves to compete for riches. The handicap of the rules in a pecuniarily preoccupied society is most heavy upon those not interested in commercial gains, or who do not desire to live a competitive life of ambition.

Let us assume that the men of the wealthy class hold their position neither by hereditary wealth nor by speculation; and never by such speculation as that of a Hatry or Kreuger, but only by thrift. It is quite false, but let us assume it. Let us assume that Henry Ford is quite wrong when he declared that no lad who does not start as a spendthrift ever will end as a millionaire. Let us assume, as the middle-class, "Self-Help" argument requires, that we live in the small trader's nineteenth century and not in the large-scale, advertising twentieth century, with its quite different kinds of business ability. Except for the merely technical difficulty of finding a suitable social structure, it is still not clear why Plato's argument is not better and why talent should not find its immediate place, instead of compelling a musician to make money in order that his grandson may make the attempt, thanks to proper early training, to become a great musician. It may, of course, be argued that it is more important to have good citizens, ambitious for their grandchildren, than to have great musicians, ambitious for their art; but, by the logic of this civic argument, it would be better still if they were ambitious for the community.

The fault, assuredly, of the traders and commercial men—the Ernest Benns of their day—who elaborated the *laissez-faire* ideal is that, like good grocers, they thought purely in terms of pecuniary competition. Such competition offers no steady positive relationship between effort, ability, and social character, on the one hand, and success or even security, recognition or even freedom from fear of poverty, on the other hand.

Competition in those fields in which thrift and prudence play little part in the making of a master—where rather the leisured mind is required—although perhaps understood by the clergy and by the feudal gentleman, was beyond the ken of the commercial mind. Here a *carrière ouverte*, to be no sham, involves an ample provision from an early age of scholarships for the child of talent, and similar socialistic schemes, whether effected by private or by public benefaction—provision such as is anathema to the strict business men and cash-down individualists. It involves a society which fosters sound values. It does not spell a pecuniarily competitive society in which it is not true that the most socially valuable work is pecuniarily rated highest, but where it is more really true that what creates the greatest vulgar demand is pecuniarily rated highest—and will be rated higher as bourgeois democracy becomes, with the entire collapse of feudalism, more dominant and clamant.

Ability is not so entirely the victor in competition as business men imagine. It is not like a pound of butter, either there or not there. It needs to be developed by an appropriate environment and is easily stifled by obligations and duties in too barbarously harsh a world. A system of economic competition, superimposed on a world where social duties are still supposed to be performed that can wreck the competitive chances of the humble, means that only the coarser kind of ability—which easily thrives under competition or which goes with characters capable of ignoring duty—comes to the top. For one who seizes the main chance and insists on the right to develop ability, five are sacrificed to the needs of parents or kin. In an acquisitive society generosity of temperament is a heavy handicap. A socially minded ability can be developed only by competition with its like. It will not be developed, thanks to the commercialization of civilization, where all competition is equated with competition in which specifically business ability—the ability to seize the pecuniary main chance—counts first and dictates the rules of the game. How, then, are we to remedy this commercialization and effect a change to a psychologically more satisfactory and healthy order?

The recognition of the control of the field of power and personal satisfaction by wealth and a (less adequate) recognition of the perversion of values by a commercial civilization, are the ground causes of the Socialist movement for the social control of wealth and for the revision of the rules of the competitive game. The second wave of the democratic movement is Social Democracy. Each man is thought of as demanding his modicum of security, his modicum of liberty and opportunity for the pursuit of happiness free from the external control of money-barons for no social good end that he can detect. So-called "free contract" of the unequal is only a mockery of that liberty. When the worker says "liberty" he means the kind of socially organized liberty that assures, at least, security—not the liberty to go as one pleases, of lawyers and small farmers. Equality of opportunity must spell, not merely the abolition of those privileges of hereditary titles which the merchants viewed with jealousy, but also of the privileges of hereditary wealth and of the use of wealth as an instrument of power to sway, for personal benefit, the lives of others.

This development of the doctrine of equality of opportunity to its thorough conclusion was the work of Marxist Socialism. In its determination to destroy the privileged power of wealth it advocated a proletarian equality. As the theory was developed by Lenin, for tactical reasons, the claims even of the inequality of ability were little tolerated (as M. Chaliapin complains), save the claim of that ability which was of service in advancing the policy of the movement. M. Chaliapin did not realize that the class war was also war. The special talents of the scientist and musician could be tolerated so far as they were otherwise in accord with the ethos of the commonwealth, but only so far. Communist morality—as once upon a time Catholic orthodoxy—came first and all else was ancillary. Ultimately, however, a free condition is visualized where, with class barriers removed even from the very minds of men, ability may, it is supposed, take its natural pre-eminence in the fulfilment of social functions.

Let us consider more closely this Socialist solution. In dealing with the problem of how to gratify the acquisitive impulse in each man, so far as it is legitimately concerned with adequate facilities of living and of consumption ordered in such a way as not to lead to frustration and injustice between man and man, the Socialist remedy has hitherto assumed, along with the classical economists, a certain quantum of wealth. The question arises whether this assumption and the deductions made therefrom are sound. The portion which was allocated to capital as profits was regarded by Marx as subtracted from the portion allocated to labour out of a total at least approximately fixed. There was perpetual warfare between capital and labour for their portion of the cake of profit—with the iron law of wages, as it operated under a capitalist régime, favouring capital, especially in a flooded labour market.

There can be little reasonable dispute concerning the large measure of truth in the Marxist analysis. The relation between supply and wage rate is an every-day matter of business practice and the peculiar conditions of high-paid labour in the United States are in large measure to be explained in terms of labour shortage. The Fordian philosophy of high wages results from the enforced meditations of employers on the possible merits of paying well workers who anyhow must be paid well. Especially has the Marxist analysis force at a time of trade depression and of a contracting market when employers rediscover their old conviction that the cutting of labour costs is the merest common sense.

It is, however, possible to argue that the road of progress for civilization lies in another direction than that plotted out by Marx. Here lies the chief defence today of the capitalist social structure. The American philosophy of wealth of 1920–30, accepted alike by some employers and some trade unionists, looks to a continuous increase of *per capita* production of such magnitude that wages and profits alike increase. The task is that of turning energy towards increase of production—the energy of both management and labour. It must be assumed that the proposal here put forward has universal application. If propounded, as by some of the rationalizers, merely for a specific country in competition with others for foreign markets, the end of its beneficial effects is speedily in sight and that end may well be war. The more considered proposal rests on the assumption that human appetite is practically limitless and that, with new machinery and organization, that appetite can be stimulated, and concurrently met, by the production of new goods and wealth. High wages are necessary to create this mass market. Such high wages are held to be not inconsistent with high profits. Cheaper goods result from mass production by machinery for such a mass market.

It may be questioned, not only by exponents of the Simple Life, whether human appetite is in fact so unlimited. The reasonable demand for table salt and stethoscopes is probably fairly inelastic, nor is the unlimited development of luxury production and titillation perhaps desirable. Only a few rich men regard their automobiles as an obvious necessity of good living. It must yet be granted that the realization of this new capitalist scheme would advance us almost the whole way to the solution of the problem of poverty. Its realization, however, it must be noted, would involve the honest adoption of the high-wage policy and such a balanced relation of production to demand that overproduction for the available market would be obviated and the cycle of unemployment, in which labour rates are cut in self-defence by private employers, would be a thing of the past.

Such balanced general production, however, in relation to demand and symmetry in the production of particular goods in relation to specific demand, although possible without planning during a short boom period, can scarcely be expected to endure without a system of conscious planning so comprehensive that, whether it were carried out by the state or under pressure from national industrial associations, private control in business would persist only in name. Only peculiar national conditions, during the opening up of local natural resources, appear to justify the confidence voiced by such bodies as the Amalgamated Clothing Workers of America, with their concentration on production and the ratio of workers' profits rather than on fixed wages, distribution and control. Only such conditions justify the confidence—of which the event was not too happy—expressed by President Hoover in his speech of acceptance in 1928, with its philosophy of a pioneer individualism antithetic to control.

Further, it is a necessary concomitant of power production either that a new mass market (such as is involved concurrently with the removal of real poverty) be found or that machinery replaces men. The latter alternative, in turn, spells either that machinery spreads unemployment and increases poverty or else that its use leads to the adoption of a shortened hours system with the same wage rates.

The choice of the course either of developing a new workers' market or, where this is not immediately possible, of cutting hours and maintaining wage rates, in proportion to the new profits yielded by the new machinery, is something which assuredly would be part of a planned national economy, under any normal conditions of trade, aiming at the benefit of the community. Equally certainly it is no part of a capitalist economy run simply to ensure the maximum profits and the quickest returns for private employers and investors. Capitalist theory has supposed that, if economic law is permitted free play, supply (subject to natural scarcity) will vary with demand. Socialist theory points out that supply, under the profit system, rests not on potential demand but on consumption, and that distribution of consumption power varies with distribution of wealth and speculative *flair*.

The New Capitalism—so antipodal in its assumptions from the Old Capitalism of the individualists and of the Manchester School—demands earnest attention for its philosophy, according to which high wages are, with the aid of tariffs, to be maintained in self-supporting countries (what the great Fichte called "Closed Trade States"); profit-sharing and co-partnership in industry are not excluded; the rights of private property are to be maintained intact in order to stimulate energy and initiative; and attention is to be directed towards yet further production with a view to removing poverty. This goal presumably is what such writers as Mr. St. John Ervine have in mind when they say that capitalism has been on the production side a blazing success and that, although on the distribution side it has been a blazing failure, there is no reason why this condition should persist.

The objection to the New Capitalism advocated by such writers as Adolph Weber and by such practical men as Mr. Owen D. Young (in connection with the Swope scheme for American business planning) and the late Lord Melchett, is that the argument assumes an exceedingly large measure of social disinterestedness in business. The payment of high wages may be considered to be commended on economic grounds as the obviously best method of commanding an extensive market. In time, however, of depression such as may result (*inter alia* and world conditions apart) from asymmetry and misdirection in production, such high wages are no more possible for private industry than is profit-sharing without loss-sharing. Only with (at least national) co-ordination is there guarantee of symmetry.

Such co-ordination, Socialist or Fascist, must almost necessarily be opposed by any system of private capital. As Professor Zimmern has excellently said, one of the main issues today is between the planners and those who believe in individual, unco-ordinated action. Even were nation-wide business trusts, under Chambers of Commerce, established for co-ordination in order to avoid cyclic depression and unemployment, there is no guarantee that, under the pressure of ordinary business considerations, they would use the power which they had acquired in order to improve machinery, reduce prices, and raise the standard of living. Rather it is improbable that they would do this whenever profits—as distinct from wages—were equally high without any such elaborate procedure of central planning.

An acquisitive society will direct the production of real wealth, not to meet the material needs of mankind, but to meet the cash-value demand of the relatively few who have attained outstanding pecuniary success. They, for the trader, are the great consumers who offer the profitable market without involving radical changes of marketing. It is no business of the industrialist to produce for those who need but can't pay—can't win the means to pay. All production is governed, not by any limit of potential demand, but by limit of means—of relative means compared with those of the most successful—in making demand effective. The small wage-earners are no predominant interest of this market and its victories are not for them: they are fortunate if its improved mechanical devices for primary production, for foreign production for the rich and for luxury production do not merely result in the dismissal of manual workers from employment.

The new capitalist philosophy is only realistic where local or temporary conditions exercise that pressure which otherwise social and patriotic opinion, of a non-capitalist kind, must exercise. In the alternative, we have to rely upon an accidental harmony, quite other than an *ordre naturel*, between the acquisitive spirit of the man of business and the economic elevation of the mass, with the concomitant abolition of poverty.

In his extraordinarily fascinating book, *In Defence of Capitalism*, Adolf Weber[1] argues that, contrary to the Marxist analysis, the condition of the labouring poor has greatly improved during the last generation; that the qualities of private enterprise which have built up modern prosperity will disappear under Socialism; that the risk of personal loss is the incentive of progress; that the actual management of business is becoming, in fact, increasingly divorced from the ownership of capital by private shareholders; that, nevertheless, the existence of a wealthy class is necessary for the accumulation of capital; that there is an identity of interests in production between capital and labour; that only the revolutionary energy of the liberated individual can invent; and that social reform defeats its own ends if carried out at the cost of capital accumulation.

The plan which Weber, however, himself sketches out is one which involves the combating of poverty. It supposes that the business man, while responding to the motive of private profit as business man, yet regards himself as a public servant and sinks his personal demands before the technical requirements of the business. He

[1] London: George Allen & Unwin Ltd.

adds: "It is generally admitted today that hardly anywhere has private enterprise been found wanting and become petrified so much as in England." It is, it may be remarked in passing, perhaps odd and shows mental vacillation when the British Liberals, who are peculiarly identified, in their tradition, with the triumphs and failures of classical British Capitalism, advocate in their most recent statements of political policy, non-individualistic, centralizing plans not dissimilar to Weber's.

Weber, in fact, admits that the Old Capitalism—the system of small free private enterprise to which the Victorians pinned their faith as capitalism—has broken down under modern conditions and is flatly to be rejected.

The spirit of enterprise, however, it may be retorted against this New Capitalist argument, in the fields of adventure, science, and technology is not likely to suffer from the restriction of a commercialism from which the inventor and technician have not hitherto profited highly. The private history, not only of great artists and thinkers, but of practical men who had immensely increased the wealth of countries is, all too frequently, a history of unrewarded talent. Trevithick, who made possible our railway system, scarcely escaped a pauper's grave. Sir Ronald Ross, whose researches made vast areas of Africa fit for human habitation, had to sell his manuscripts in order to continue his work. That spirit of enterprise in industry, commerce, and finance which is chiefly directed to profit-making—as distinct from the art of organization which would have abundant scope under great public bodies—clearly will suffer. The cost to be paid for this more banal species of commercial initiative is the existence of a wealthy class which not only receives a salary for its services as distributors of capital (as managers do in an industrial enterprise), proportional to the salaries paid for other social services of equal importance, but which is itself in control of the whole of this capital and of the social power which it carries with it.

There is, as His Grace the Catholic Archbishop of Liverpool has told his radio audience, the possibility that this wealth may be flaunted in the face of the poor. There is the more serious possibility that it may be used to make assured the control of the country's policy by this limited group and to frustrate opposition. As such it holds power, without being accountable to society at large—or in any fashion save, like the Kaiser, to its own conscience—for the power which it holds. Thereby it frustrates the cardinal principle of democracy. We shall see later that it is, as such, an evil.

It is not a necessary evil, since the justification, if there is any, for the feverish enterprise of modern industry lies precisely in the need, not for production or machinery or luxury for its own sake, but to maintain and improve the standard of living of the average. And this is not most usefully attained by putting a profit-pursuing group in power whose interests are not those of the average. The prejudice in favour of doing this is largely mere habit— a prejudice in favour of keeping in power an existing governing group, even when that commercial plutocracy itself rose to power by supplanting the feudal aristocracy.

The serious question is whether the technician who is artist, the inventor, the business manager of technical enterprise, will have scope under a system of social control where they are not running their own private business. The answer to this is that the technician and the inventor have seldom ever had their own private businesses. The man of enterprise, on the other hand, has many fields for his hand to till. Private industry is indeed one. But enterprise as manager of a great public concern—

granted there is not stupid and inefficient popular interference—or adventure on behalf of a nation are not impossible. The real problem is that of the man with a lust for power who wants to feel his power. With that problem we shall be concerned in the next chapter.

It must yet be admitted that indolence is a perpetual factor and that enterprise will not flourish where there is no danger and no possibility of loss in money or prestige. Even the *moral* and discipline of the corporate warfare for civilization on poverty is not enough, by itself alone, to maintain the interest in the everyday detail required for business alertness. That discipline is only enough where a country is swept by a movement religious in its fervour. Such movements, for those who do not share the religion, become moral tyrannies. On these industrial grounds—not on the customary argument of the need for a financial group (save as themselves, not mere leaders, but technicians of finance)—the case for competition in commerce and industry seems to be made out. The case is not, however, made out for private-employer anarchy.

The constitution of a system of public companies in national key industries and even in commerce, like the great seventeenth-century chartered companies, could provide this necessary competition, granted power, subject to safeguards, on the part of the managers to hire and to fire, while accountability would be secured by the power, not primarily of the shareholders, but of the charter-granting social authority, representing consumers and producers alike, to remove the managers and to exercise a financial whip-hand. This could be supplemented by consultation with the workers, as co-operators, not only on labour conditions, but also on policy. In this way industrial democracy would be realized in the only feasible fashion. The workers would have a sense of unity of interest with an enterprise conducted in accordance with plan for the weal and under the control of the community. Competition, but socially co-ordinated competition, subordinate to a central body (as between the state-controlled concerns in Russia), would be maintained such as would supply a comparative standard of achievement, stimulate invention, and reinforce the motives working towards efficiency of *personnel*. The danger of an unduly powerful class, without specific social responsibility and quite unrepresentative of the average man's interests, would be excluded.

I should, I suppose, be comforted to discover that what I here advocate is not entirely dissimilar from the recommendations in favour of large-scale associations and nationally planned co-ordination advocated, after a study of American conditions, by Dean Donham, of the Harvard School of Business, or, again, by Mr. Harold Macmillan in England. It almost appears that this Socialism, politically imperative, is coming to be regarded, even by conservative economists, as offering the most practical route of business progress. The nature of the social control must still be a matter for debate. The solution will be connected with what we may discover to be the appropriate satisfactions of the instinct for power. The extension of social control must, moreover, be correlative with the importance of the industry and the social power which control of it gives. In many cases small businesses may be as efficient in production as large industry—or more efficient. Pseudo-efficiency is to be eschewed. And of such small businesses there is no cogent argument for more than the lightest advisory social control by any central organization, whether or not they themselves should be run locally for private profit or as co-operatives.

The scheme which is sketched above is certainly not the "New Capitalism," since it insists on central supervision by an organization representative of the citizen body; on the industrial democracy involved in social control; and on the consultative position, on policy, of those engaged in the work.[1] How far it will be Socialism depends upon the surrounding political and social organization.

This system should reduce poverty. It should do this with some permanency and not, as under the American system, solely during some period of exceptional prosperity and optimism. It should give a measure of security against fear of shortage and distress. It should give that measure of the material conditions of dignity to the ordinary man which will enable him to live a life of self-respecting independence and to escape from that atmosphere of servility which has been the immemorial curse of the great majority of the children of Adam. It will make provision, by competitive increase of production of goods, for the fact that the standards of the mass of men, and especially those of less ability and experience in the variety of values, are materialistic and are governed by an appetite for things—that is, that it is the poor who especially appreciate what it requires just nothing else than money to acquire.

Those, however, who think of Socialism as principally a plan for equalization of incomes—and not as an

[1] No pretence here is made of elaborating any economic scheme in detail or of providing "A programme of Action." That is not a matter for this book. Details are introduced merely to give concreteness to an argument concerning the general characteristics of a psychologically healthy economic structure.

endeavour to realize in full the democratic movement, in its true sense as a realization of the principle that no human being is entitled to power over another without accountability—will feel that, in what has been said above, the chief issue of Socialism has been side-tracked. This system, indeed, which we have discussed, is not fully socialist in just this sense that it decides nothing on the issue of equality of incomes. That issue is, after all, at present a little academic to the poor.

The primary interest of the workers under Capitalism is not in abstract equality of income, but in concrete sufficiency of bread and material goods. They are like thirsty and hungry men, not normal until this appetite, trivial in a full man, is assuaged. That is where Marx, with his propagandist stress on what he chose to call "materialism," was substantially right. That also is where the banal idealism of middle-class Pecksniffs, with their respectable views, their connivance at the power to command luxury of the rich and lucky, and their horror at the desire for luxury and material goods in the poor and unlucky, is pharisaical and detestable, real though the danger of a culture of democratic sensuality may be. These men deliberately refuse to apply to the poor, as proper rules in living, those standards which seem to them inoffensive and useful when assumed by the powerful and rich. They are flunkeys in their souls. But I shall return to the discussion of these people later.

Control, however, of the abuse of financial power, through social legislation and by the granting of limiting charters, is not the same as the equal distribution of power and of that power which wealth gives.

The issue of equality of income, abstract although it may be at the present, is not one which can be evaded when the problem is faced of the construction of a classless society in which, not only the fear of undeserved and material insecurity is removed, but in which pecuniary rivalry is reduced to an entirely subsidiary position, to be retained only so far as it may be auxiliary to the major purposes of the community. It may, indeed, be argued that if wealth be divorced from dangerous social power, there is no harm in individuals, whether barristers, heiresses, industrialists on a £20,000 per annum salary, comedians or film-stars at £150 a week at par, having great wealth. There is no harm in the junior Mr. Samuel Insull drawing an annual salary of $113,000 as president of one of his father's subsidiary companies. There is no harm at all in Mr. Charles Chaplin, who takes precedence of duchesses at dinners with the Prince of Wales, and who, it appears, treats engagements with the Prime Minister as unimportant, being in a position to refuse £333 a minute—not from mere pride, but as a business matter. We have to decide whether we are to say, with Shaw, that it is a sin to be poor or whether we are (also, paradoxically enough, with Shaw) to aim at the elevation, or reduction, of men to a pecuniary level. At the present time the reduction, such is the mass of poverty, would be more steep than the elevation. Is absolute poverty a sin against every man's health and manhood; and, if so, is relative poverty a duty for the rich in order that a general level may be maintained and that the community may not be shattered by envy and grievance?

No one of spirit and ability—no one who is not already in spirit a failure—is prepared to accept an inferior position so long as any measure of significant prestige attaches to a position of superior wealth. Thus far the discrepancies of wealth produce an irritant diversion of energy from the pursuit of valuable creation to the acquisition of prestige in the struggle for money. Creative artists, as such, must tend to be the enemies of men of money, at least until they have taken the decision to make large money in their turn—which they are fortunate if they do not make to their artistic loss.

The mass of men, however, are not creative artists and enjoy their bit of money and prestige. There are small men who appreciate more a pecuniary superiority over lesser men than they suffer in pride by their inferiority to others. Nor, as G. D. H. Cole has remarked, does pecuniary equality always appeal more to the worker than to any other section of the community—personal privation has not allowed him the luxury of that grand detachment. The most vigorous argument in favour of economic equality would seem to be that the energy of ability can only be harnessed to the relief of poverty and the raising of the general level if it itself is made to experience the restriction of means and facilities consequent upon the lowness of that general level. Otherwise it becomes detached in its interests and we revert to that situation which had its extreme in the France of the great age when a cultured aristocracy lived alongside a brutalized peasantry.

The only certain motive force for improvement seems to be need. The removal of this need disproportionately for a portion—especially if it be the more intelligent or energetic portion—weakens the impulse to remove it for the whole community. A luxury market diverts energy from the development of a more proletarian one. Even the use by the very wealthy, or by private corporations, of highly trained surgeons and lawyers impedes the process by which their services are necessarily reduced nearer to the pecuniary range of the ordinary man. It is healthy that, in the United States (to take no more violent an instance), it is difficult to procure domestic service, but the professional service of chefs and waitresses is being developed. Nothing is more amusing than to read the ingenuous, sad plaint of distress of a distinguished European "progressive," Signor Ferrero, fleeing from Fascist tyranny, when he arrived in a land where personal service is not readily obtainable by the middle classes. The habit of service by one specific section of the community, not for the community at large but for another specific section, stamps the first group with a sense of social inferiority. It is a system something short of completely civilized. The detachment of the few from experience of the needs of the community is no more civilized.

It is necessary that the man of talent, not only shall be able to earn, but even shall be assisted to secure, fully and generously, all the aids and facilities which the practice of his vocation requires. But it does not follow from this that he should be permitted to live in a world where the miseries of poverty, which afflict so many of the community, are without any direct significance in his own experience, any more than that a section of the citizen body should escape the terror of war when it afflicts the rest. Human civilization advances through pain and the men of ability cannot be spared from engineering that advance. Conquest will not be by sectional rushes if some sections leave the others entirely behind as part of a separate army.

So far our argument has been all in favour of making equalization of incomes the complement of a programme of public control of the means of production. A new plea, however, may here be put forward against any large measure of pecuniary equalization if not against any united front of the community in a war on poverty. It is a plea for an hereditary nobility, adequately endowed with wealth, as the trustees of a traditional culture or even for merchant princes who, thanks to wealth and liberality of talents, are prepared to encourage the arts. It is the last line of plutocratic defence. The answer to the entire problem of the desire for acquisition, it may be suggested, is to be found not in the world of industry—which is a world of means—but in the world of leisure. It may well be asked, if this aristocracy of opulence and these means of the wealthy life are removed, what will keep in the world all the beautiful things or promote mansuetude in living? If life is to be reduced for all to one monotonous struggle for bread and butter, what is to happen to creative art in civilization? And will not even the lives of the poor be the poorer if they are never to have a view of people, artists, or princes living a fuller and richer life than their own?

There is an ascetic answer to this question, the answer of Savonarola and Tolstoy, which would declare that a luxury art, not in the service of sympathy with human suffering and toil, is a bad and meretricious art which, like sensuous indulgence, should be rejected and repressed. I do not propose to argue this contention because I do not believe the answer valid. With Spinoza I agree that what makes for life and power is of the sap of virtue. I fairly thoroughly disagree with Principal Jacks, with his judgement of the avocations of leisure by the lugubriously puritanical standards of the poetry of Langland and with his unabashed preference for a rustic civilization, free from all the sophisticated luxuries of our age of machines and of a proletariat avid for escape from drabness. Here, in this rural arcady, the new Piers

Plowman is content "to fling down weary limbs on a straw pallet and snore away the hours of a dreamless sleep, unaffrighted by the spectre of unemployment and unconscious of the fleas that swarmed over his body." Not that I believe that Principal Jacks is doing more than merely exercise his humour.

A much more solid answer may be given. The promotion of art for the common benefit of society is best accomplished through public bodies, as it was so largely in Hellas. These bodies, moreover, can be far more reliable patrons than capricious private benefactors and can give more independence to the artist. Architecture and literature must almost necessarily be of this public nature, music readily is so, and painting loses little by becoming so—however unsatisfactory the obsolescent art gallery may be. The vision of opulent living, if it is so desirable, can as well be met in the inside of a cinema *palace de luxe*, at a modest charge, as by gazing at princes or viscounts. Indeed, actual princes are likely to correspond to the demands of the imagination far less well than does Mr. Adolphe Menjou.

The patronage of art may sometimes be more liberal and more intelligent from a single wealthy man, such as Sir Joseph Duveen or Mr. Otto Kahn, than from a democratic public body. I believe that it frequently is much more intelligent than the popular taste as educated by the newspaper barons. Perhaps, however, the most intelligent form of patronage today comes, not from private patrons, but from the trusts established precisely to encourage certain forms of art.

Much, however, of this argument is mere smoke-cloud, concealing the point of attack. The real issue, in fact, is something quite different: more closely concerned with the patron and less with art itself. It is whether life is not very pleasant for the wealthy; and whether any argument can be constructed why they should abandon this civilized pleasure of living; or any argument be used which can rebut the contention that this refined Mahomedan Paradise is a prize that encourages healthy emulation and ambition. This means that an artistic leisure, at best a speculative life in the ivory tower, at worst a *dolce far niente*, is intrinsically desirable and is a goal of escape from the sweat and swink of affairs, to which goal the pecuniarily successful may hope, and should be encouraged, to aspire. The successful should be permitted to escape from the united front of a common experience in the war on poverty and for community.

It is assumed that a gracious and dignified life must always be an opulent and a leisured one—and, hence, that society must be prepared, cheerfully and without enquiry, to pay the cost of this expensive stateliness. The arguments that wealth does not contribute to happiness or does not command happiness I shall put on one side, the first because it is false and the second because it is irrelevant. All of us desire the facilities now, under Capitalism, provided by money, just because wealth is, as a matter of fact, a part condition of happiness. The wealthy (the tastes of Sardanapolus apart) can enjoy a dignified life and what good art can provide.

Wealth, by this argument, is not the reward of the lovers of art or dignity, but the reward of pecuniarily successful ambition to which art and skill contribute. The ambitious, however, indirectly benefit those who have a true sense for the beautiful life; they are mannequins who display how it may be lived in its more costly forms; artists may be encouraged in the pursuit of art by this contemplation of the leisured life of others. They may even temporarily share it.

THE ECONOMIC IMPULSE

The basic assumption here—which is a very ancient one—is that the object of endeavour should be to attain the life of leisure, which is the only desirable one; and that this life is feasible only for the few. It is proposed to allocate it to the men of money. Some may prefer to allocate it to middle-class landed men. Anyhow, it cannot be allocated to the workers. Servile work has to be done; those engaged upon it may yet be permitted the compensation of viewing the cultivated life of their superiors.

If we accept the leisure ideal, then the civilized life is only possible for those who acquire the means to have complete mastery over their time and avocation and have the self-control so to regulate this avocation as to occupy them seriously, but not disproportionately or to an unbalanced and illiberal degree. In brief, it is the case, as Aristotle said, that first a man must acquire wealth and then occupy himself with virtue. Excellence is for the few; broad-based democracy is wrong; and the endeavour to render civilization a good available to all mankind is quite futile.

The immense difficulties of any alternative recommendation must be recognized. The remoteness from true standards—true by any test—of very many people must be admitted. It can, however, be urged that, whatever the distinction in degree, there is no abrupt and generic distinction between the experience of mason and architect, mechanic and engineer, bank clerk and financier, plain man and philosopher, such that the first is no step or an undesirable step in approaching the more catholic culture of the second. Indeed, the philosopher can often benefit by studying to be rather more plain man and the architect to be good mason. It is not desirable to be one of those who (in the warning words of Mr. Lloyd George about a famous statesman) expect "to find a place on the magisterial bench to sit in judgement upon and above their fellow men, before they ever have any opportunity to make themselves acquainted with the tasks and trials of mankind." "They are remote from the hard work of the community. They take it for granted."

The core of the argument, which we are here urging and to which we shall revert in the last chapter, is that the sound culture is a culture broad-based, catholic in experience, in contact with the hard and disciplined work of the world. The belief in discontinuity between the workers' life and the creative life rests on a false notion of values.

If this democratic position be accepted, then the pursuit of wealth assumes a new colour. The persistent pursuit of wealth becomes merely the sign of a desire for conspicuous consumption and a manifestation of the lust for power. There is no justification for a choice and elect wealthy class from any cultural standpoint. There is only justification for getting on with our job as, and so far as it is a job organic in the life of the community, intelligibly connected with that life and socially recognized as such. The only justifiable course lies in the full provision to every man of the tools of his trade and of the facilities (including rest) for him to win to full development somehow as a craftsman—whether as scientist, poet, physician, or bargeman—in the world's workshop and in the creation of a world under completer human mastery.

In a capitalist system this right to work and these social facilities have perpetually to be fought for against "smart Alecs" who are only interested in cash—to whom it and its enjoyment is end, not means—or against those only interested in personal power. In a socialist world they are correlated with the plain man's personal experience of activity on behalf of the community and sense of the community ownership—which means his own—of industry. There is no cultural justification for wealth above this level of full facilities. Morality can only recognize socially defensible claims to wealth. Likewise there is no defence or excuse on social grounds for poverty below the level required for living life in a fashion consistent with the minimum requirements of dignity and health. Such defence as may remain for great wealth must be placed on the grounds of the desirable distribution of power and dignity in the rule of men. It is open, I suppose, for the Napoleons to argue that they require great wealth, not to act as craftsmen in the world's work, but just to develop limitlessly their own Napoleonic egos as men of destiny. The question then becomes—we shall revert to it—whether we need Napoleons.

If it be true that the idea of a leisure culture is false, that the pre-eminent wealth which alone can guarantee distinctive leisure is not a necessity of any high civilization, then our problem of so stilling the acquisitive instinct that it no longer threatens social unity becomes far simpler. Civilization consists in the actual work of controlling our environment so as to reduce human pain and so as to increase the possibility for every human being of living a full and dignified life. It does not mean detachment from the world of affairs of the most able, but the occupation by the most able of the eminent positions of guidance and control. Those positions can be as well occupied by those who share the poverty of the monastery as by those who live in the palaces of lords. Civilization, then, is consistent with a joint attack on poverty and other human curses—a united front of comradeship—and not in the individual winning by able men of detachment from the immemorial fight against nature's hostility and against material shortage.

The very deep-seated demand for a costly life of high colours or of unusual veneer is natural, not only among those who enjoy it, but fully as much, by reaction, among those whose own lives are reduced to a dulling monotony, who are economically mutilated, who are economic corpses almost incapable of life in themselves. But it is precisely the setting up, in a position which fills others with an initial sense of defeat, of a limited, powerful world of conspicuous leisure—not made up of team-workers with the rest—which suffuses with drab inferiority the outlook of the great mass whose highest hope can be but middling opportunity.

There is no little to be said for Mr. De Valera's thesis (echoed by Herr Hitler) that, in the present condition of civilization and of the poverty of much of the citizenry, an upper limit of private net income might, ethically and politically, be imposed—let us say, Mr. De Valera's £2,000 per year per individual. This seems to me more socially sane than the Bishop of Durham's declaration: "He found it difficult . . . to live in Auckland Castle at all . . . gradually the whole community would tumble to dissolution." As an employer of labour on his estate the Bishop is entitled to consideration, but as a prelate his wealth must be judged in terms of the comparative social good of its possible uses, and as an employer the economist and the state are under obligation to ask whether the labouring occupations he encourages are of the highest comparative economic productivity. Only if the Bishop Palatine emerges unscathed from those judgements can the cogency of his thesis be admitted. I do not, however, say that the upper limit should be absolute at present, in cases of conspicuous public service.

THE ECONOMIC IMPULSE

The demand for the full facilities to develop personal talents is legitimate enough. But the lust for great wealth and the envy of wealth alike spring, as perversions, from a valid desire for heightened vitality which is balked of adequate expression in a social form owing to the lack of any richness and intimacy of community life, with its common satisfaction, in our contemporary world. The conscious demand for an intimate community life, with its social pleasures, is made only by certain temperaments, just as the compensatory conscious demand for solitude is made only by certain temperaments. The unconscious demand, however, is rife enough for social admiration and good opinion, such as an intimate community should satisfy to the full extent that is healthy, as it also can satisfy the more basal demand for security. Under present conditions it makes one of the great driving forces behind acquisition—makes a chief cause of the itch for conspicuous consumption. The disease should be remedied at the source.

If, however, insistence is to be placed upon the sense of common citizenship instead of individual or class self-help, if guarantees are to be given against the extremes of poverty and, for social reasons, the more glittering prizes of the talent for money-making are to be removed, a certain discipline is necessary, unless the indolent are to become parasitic on the energetic. There is grave danger that social ownership without individual conscious risk may not develop civilization, thanks to co-operation and to a new personal pride, but may merely result in collective indifference and material corrupt dealing. That the industry of a country appertains to the people of a country must issue in a new pride and a new aristocracy; not in an irresponsible and sensual idleness. The socialization of wealth means the socialization of industry with a view to allocating to those who work the means to eat and enjoy. It involves the insistence that no one shall live without doing sufficient work to earn such a livelihood as is consistent with the minimum of dignity. It involves the insistence, thanks to a system of death duties and public control of profits, that men shall not be able to maintain—much less to increase—their wealth, as silk-clad unemployed, without themselves performing some social activity. It also means that men who benefit by the restriction of individual wealth shall be under adequate social pressure to increase and maintain the community wealth.

For reasons which will be indicated later, the complete discipline of pure communism and the complete supersession of pecuniary competition—so that all are placed under supervision in order that from each may be extracted according to his ability and in order that to each may be rendered solely according to his needs, labour utility apart—is, in my opinion, undesirable in any compulsive heterogeneous society because it involves an undue infringement of personal liberty. In a compulsive society, such as the present-day state (as distinct from a society based on free choice, such as the party or some free settlement in some social system from which the need for the coercive state had disappeared), the governing consideration must be the merely utilitarian one of the majority advantage. Granted the rigid limitations in wealth already referred to, the case seems to be final for subsidiary variations in wealth according to effort.

Hence, the principle of piece-work, as in contemporary Russia, must be held to be consistent with Socialism, at least in a mixed society, where discipline rests on law. This is expressed with striking vigour by Stalin, in his *New Conditions: New Tasks*. "Who is right, Marx and

Lenin, or our equalitarians? We take it that Marx and Lenin are right. But, if so, it follows that whoever draws up wage scales on the 'principle' of equality, and ignores the difference between skilled and unskilled labour, is at loggerheads with Marxism and Leninism."

What is imperative is that these variations shall correspond to socially useful effort and not to luck. This, of itself, requires a keen social discipline.

So long, however, as men of different ideals are held together in coercive societies, short of a discipline so rigid as to trespass on a reasonable liberty, other motives than the common ideal must be allowed place. Equality, in the greater society, must remain imperfect, governed in its degree by the expediences of the common advantage and by the dangers of disruption by the acquisitive. It may, nevertheless, well be that only those who share a common outlook, in smaller voluntary societies, will, by their monastic *moral* and fanaticism, effect the changes of habit required in the mass, if satisfaction is to be given to the demands of economic justice. Such great changes only take place at fever heat. If so, the task, preconditioning change, is to forge such a limited community of common devotion and purpose which will have the requisite political force and close texture of organization. That community organization may itself be the very condition of scientific Socialism.

§ iv

The Power Impulse

Whatever may be true in the technical field of economic theory, in the field of politics the most influential philosophies today are those that trace, directly or by reaction, from Marx.

If it be true that the universities ignore this, this is probably due to the fact that Marx has not been dead long enough for him to become part of that tradition about which the professors lecture. Only Rousseau has as yet reached that degree of antiquity and remoteness from practical controversy requisite for academic notice. Desire to keep inviolate the ivory tower, where the men of the chair rule, "inclineth to a reverence of antiquity." The disorderly Rousseau is a philosophic writer; Marx, from this point of view, is only a controversialist. The counterpart, by antithesis, of this prejudice on the part of those entrenched in the past is the religious belief frequent among Socialists and Communists in the verbal infallibility of the gospel revealed to Marx and written down by him.

In an able book by Max Eastman a beginning was made of that psychological criticism of Marx which has been continued, independently, by de Man (1926) and Russell. Unsatisfactory although de Man's work in many ways may be, this psychological approach is the line of criticism which alone, by being more radical and fundamental, can carry us beyond economism. Almost all Fascist doctrine has rested upon a philosophy of vitality, élan, and will, and upon a stressing of psychological factors. It has found its maxims in Sorel, Bergson, and Nietzsche.

If that doctrine is to be met, it must be met on the same level of argument.

It would, however, be a grave error if criticism were, in the mood of Sombart, to be developed solely as an attempt to dilute, temper, or negate the truth in Marxism. On the contrary, it should make Marxism more radically effective, because these newer psychological considerations throw a light more brilliant and more convincing than a purely environmental materialism upon the struggle for power. The will of human beings is directed towards a freer life in an environment social as well as economic, in an environment of other human wills as well as of the instruments and processes of production. The determinant material is, not only the economic and material factors, but the assertive drive of life itself. In the newer work on Marx, for example, by Sidney Hook, in accord with the general temper of the Leninist school, full allowance is made for this element of will and creation. This shift in the exposition of Marxism from the economic fatalism of Kautsky is itself of high significance. With the consideration of this impulse of assertion, and of its social consequences in fights for freedom and progress and, again, in hatred and conflicts, this chapter is concerned.

In the general philosophy of the economic interpretation of history Kautskyh ignored the factor of the psychological and biological inheritance of the human race. That does not mean that the practical followers of Marx, turning the blind eye of faith to metaphysical contradiction, have ignored psychological factors or have even abstained from appealing to these factors as a force to outbalance more matter-of-fact material considerations. Mr. Louis Fischer, a sympathetic authority on Russian affairs, complain, that, in pushing forward Communist organization in Russia, "these Marxists" (the supporters of Stalin), "whose philosophy is based on economic determinism, stress only the psychological element." In fact, however, this Stalinist appeal is rather to Communist tradition and sentiment. What is important is to recognize the part played in moulding human civilization by the deeper impulses. If the material environment has determined tradition and the survival of species, what Mr. Shaw chooses to call the life-force has worked through that matter, thrown up variations and developed the hereditary characteristics of human nature.

Further, in the specific interpretation of human conduct, Marx treats all men as engaged in the money game. In fact most men who have enough to eat, clothe themselves, and take their leisure are not engaged in the money game at all except in a symbolical fashion. Possessions have value for them chiefly as a sign of their success—as a means to conspicuous consumption. Marx wrote in the age of the classical economists, in times characterized by the mentality of the cautious banker and the psychological attitude of the counting-house. It was the age of thrift. Now men live in times characterized by the psychological attitude of the advertising office. It is the age of display and of the press-made "legend." Most men who are in any position to plan their lives, instead of living planted out like vegetables with their lives controlled by others, are not playing the money game. They are playing the game for power. The recognition of that is the stage beyond the older German Marxism, and the road to the statement of the fundamental class-struggle problem of Communism. The omission to state it gives quite artificial simplicity to the task of a communist society in controlling human nature.

Men such as Hill and Morgan, the Rothschilds and Sir Basil Zaharoff, in building up their fortunes as industrial magnates or financiers, were not primarily interested in a bank account. They were interested in the defeat of their rivals and in predominance. They were heated by the lust of battle, with power over other men's destinies for the prize. The pursuit of wealth is only incidentally a pursuit concerned with the control of men, although that control of men by money may result in solid evils against which the Socialist democratic movement is directed. But those who pursue power, on the contrary, are concerned in a game directly involving the control of human beings. The gamesters of power, unlike the gamesters of money, inevitably put their fingers into the inner lives of men, to master their wills and to pull the strings of their behaviour.

Of the two games, for money and for power, the game for money is the cleaner. The object is the amassing of tangible possessions or of that less tangible wealth called credit. When Dr. Johnson said that the desire to acquire money appears a very harmless pursuit, he went, unfortunately, beyond the warranty of the facts. This, however, is true that, in the course of time, the rules of the money game have been laid down, however widely some people may depart from them, in what is called "business morality," which receives at least some homage.

Moreover, although poor men may be exploited in order to make a fortune, at least the impress of the millionaire's career on their lives is a contact external, mechanical, pecuniary. The struggle for power deals with intangible advantages of status, prestige, influence, control. It has no such rules—no recognized marts, no stock exchange. There is not much generosity or gratitude in this power game: there is, however, in it scope for much intelligence, hard work, and shrewd judgement—and no little personality. It is played hourly by almost every man of importance and by many women. The significant change in our own age has been from the economic psychology of Manchester, of the counting-house, of the thrifty 'prentice, of the philosophy of "Self-Help" and Samuel Smiles, to the power psychology of Manhattan, of dollars as mere register of energy and success, of advertising and self-advertising, of publicity, and of the power of the Press, operating on public opinion, to make or ruin. Since success in the acquisition of power and publicity is more exclusive, competitive, and relative to the lesser success of others than success either in getting rich or in love, the appetite for it and its frustration are probably the cause of more misery to men and nations than is even the misery caused by the misdirection of the other two great impulses, erotic and economic.

The hope of the more simple-minded Communist has been that, when the wealthy were deprived of their privileges and the means of production were under social control, or even the product distributed equally, the power of class over class would end. For the first time, says even Trotsky, there would emerge a culture that is truly human. In Russia there was to be an end of the power of the few over the many, and even of the many over the few. There was to be "a withering away of the state." That the Communist Party members themselves, or this or that section of the Communist Party, might be interested in retaining power and prestige, and permanently imposing its will on others, was not in the theoretical scheme. It is in the facts.

For ambitious men wealth is but one form of power and a means to more power. Money itself, and what immediately it can buy, is not the only end, once man has quite passed starvation level (any more than it was when primitive man was still literally fighting for his food). What matters, at this new level, is the control of wills—not things—since the chief fear is of control by other wills, not by the natural forces of hunger and cold, and the chief glory is in prestige.

The pre-psychological materialism of the early Socialists misled them. They felt that they had to explain everything in terms of what could be put between forefinger and thumb. But Marx stirred up his followers by the inflammatory power of his ideas to accept a dialectical philosophy constructed of reversed Hegelianism. To the validity of that philosophy I return for discussion in the last chapter. I do not deny that the chief object for the mass of men in the achievement of democratic power, in an age when protection of life and limb is at last taken for granted, is to guarantee food and security in a job. I do, however, say that this desire for a guarantee of food is not more fundamental than the desire for a guarantee of life itself against aggression, the guarantee of liberty against the power of others, the non-economic need for at least a measure of power for oneself to assert one's own will. That the need for liberty and corporate power of the workers is now chiefly concerned with economic matters does not mean that an explanation in terms of consumable goods can be found for the desire to protect life itself or to uphold our will against our neighbours.

Men desire power to preserve their bodies against enemies, to preserve their freedom of bodily movement, and to preserve their freedom to gratify their tastes, including vanity and the wish for the upper position. They desire power to enjoy the direct exhilaration that comes of victory. To defend our lives, to impress by our prestige, to consort and propagate are not, in common parlance, economic objects: erotic desire is not economic, and not all the objects of power, either the simplest (such as defence of life) or the most subtle (such as Napoleonic mania) are economic. If the acquisitive or economic motive must be controlled in the interest of civilization, so also must this other individualistic, aggressive motive—the power-lust—and it will be no more simple.

The early materialists—not Hobbes, but the successors of Ricardo—were wrong in seeing only a contest for economic goods, and not also for freedom and dominance. I admit that defence of life against cannibalism can (not without paradox) be called economic. I admit that the proprietory sense of the patriarch towards his wives, as adverse owner against all comers, is economic. I admit that the warfare of nations for territory is economic. But neither freedom of movement and behaviour nor all the clash of wills which arises from the assertion of this freedom is economic. The desire to give orders, instead of taking them, is not economic. How we will to live, when we possess, is not economic. The meaning of group pride and attachment is merely befogged by explanation in non-dialectical economic terms. The whole conduct of man may be changed by control of his economic life, of his very diet. But change of physique and conduct cuts no deeper than—not so deep as—the attachment to life and the aggressive urge of vitality.

The human tendency to conflict, dominance, and resistance is not *entirely* explained by discussion—although this discussion may be indispensable—of one of the major matters about which conflict arises. Men do not want prestige chiefly for the sake of a greater accumulation of consumable goods, but a greater accumulation of consumable goods as a testimony and an instrument of their superior prestige, power, will, and vitality.

The cure for this disease of lust of power is not only to be found in better economic distribution, but also in a better communal life. Russian Communism may be able to exorcise the devil of competition from ambitious men; but it will not do it merely and solely by an even distribution of wealth, though this distribution may be an indispensable step towards a united community. We yet wait to see how much Stalin and his party organization will take the edge off rivalry for power. Hitherto the history of the Russian Communist régime has, rather conspicuously, been a history of expulsion of those who, for their own purposes, have ventured wilfully to deviate from the Marx–Lenin–Stalinist line of orthodoxy, and to put their will against that of the dominant group.

The most difficult problem in human political order cannot be fobbed off with half-explanations. The fundamental desire for freedom is so profound that Pavlov calls it a biological instinct. The guarantee, however, of freedom against alien restriction is power. In the present social order it is still true that men have found no surer form of this power to break through restriction than by the domination of their fellow beings. The era of co-operation, of mutual control in society, dawns slowly. Yet here, in this co-operation, lies another and better arrangement of power.

The reality of the struggle for power, as no less fundamental than the struggle for wealth, is obscured by the fact that the economic anarchism of *laissez-faire* has revealed the latter conflict in its nakedness, whereas the former struggle, the more dangerous of the two, has been mitigated since the days of the mediaeval anarchy by the establishment of civil peace. Indeed, throughout the ages the slow growth of custom and of law has set up an accepted order, what Sumner calls "folkways," so that a man feels that his liberty will be respected by others, even although he personally has no direct power over them. He is content with the indirect power which law, with its public sanction, gives to him. The assumption of the inevitability of this sanction (not, let us admit, made by Marx) is misleading. It leaves the quite false impression that the ordinary man is solely concerned with his weekly wage envelope and not with the nature of the political system under which the employer, having law and power behind him, contracts with him for hired labour.

Over vast fields, however, of human activity there is no such custom of co-operation. There is a custom of competition. The issue of which group has most power, which may seem remote to the man with the pick and the dinner-pail, is in fact very real. Most economic issues are, in fact, political and will be politically decided. There is a competition of groups—men of a certain birth or wealth or profession—of which the consequence is a class structure in our society. There is the competition of states in the international anarchy—of Japan with the West, of Germany with France. The best standpoint, however, from which to observe the psychological qualities of man, this mood of aggression and will, is to be found in the study of the individual competition by ambitious men for advancement to a higher class or to personal power and dominance, where they may *give* orders.

The poison of power is at work—the poison which Lord Acton denounced as the enemy of liberty and morality; and which literally may end in madness—and the happiness of ordinary men is sacrificed to the will-to-get-on of those with their eyes fixed on some main chance of success. Nevertheless, the worship of what Aldous Huxley, following William James, names, with his usual mordancy, the bitch goddess success goes on because it corresponds to an instinctive resistance to frustration. It is highly significant that it is the interests of sex and power which alone are usually dissimulated and censored by inhibitions. It is these impulses, not the economic, which, with their *pathologia,* have provided material for the explanation of human nature in the psychologies, respectively, of Freud and of Adler.

To study the workings of the appetite for power, the tensions between wills and the feasible forms of organization with their balance of liberty and authority is to study the very physiology—the functioning of the tendons and muscles—of the body politic.

The need for freedom, however, in the mass of men does not take a direct shape in desire for power to guarantee freedom. There is, indeed, a certain very limited demand that corporate power shall be exercised by their class or nation. But for the large middling mass of human beings ambition is a word of little meaning and generally of ill-favour. Like "getting ideas" it is to be frowned upon. That life can ever be so generous that insecurity does not have to be worried about—that one can "live dangerously" by choice and not by necessity— is for the mass of men a mere dream. The harshness of circumstance is the everyday fact. The desire for freedom takes the inverted, negative shape of fear of insecurity. Of the great divisions of society the division characterized by those sharing this attitude is by far the largest.

An important task of social emancipation is to awaken these men to the possibility of a life of positive affirmation of freedom and of successful ambition—although not necessarily a life of competitive, private ambition. "This losing oneself completely in the banalities of life," wrote Rosa Luxemburg, "is something that I generally cannot understand or endure." It is, however, in fact endured by thousands, partly for economic reasons and partly because they are so utterly under the control of the wills of others. They have lost all hope of effective escape from the drab and even make of small expectations a religion of resignation and virtue, averting the evil eye of a surly fate. The good and worthy people who are for the most part concerned with bread and butter matters are the stabilizers of civilization. Along with vices of lack of hope at least go also the healthy qualities distinctive of simple folk.

Ranked above them, but still in what Plato called "the nutritive class," are the middle classes of small employers, men of business in the narrow sense, middling men preoccupied with the job of amassing just money. Running between the two, seizing their material, competitive advantage whenever they can, are what Mr. Wells names "the smart Alecs," little men on the make, infecting our culture with their cheap commercialism.

The smaller of the great divisions of society—concerned not with guarantees for small liberties but with power— is a ten thousand which, by a restless spirit, drives civilization on for better or worse. Although smaller, the rôle that it plays in the direct contest for power is so important that it merits closer consideration. It contains two ingredients. There are those who in an earlier age would have been foot-loose soldiers, adventurers, nomads. They may have their own caste morality, but it is consciously different from that of the humdrum plain folk of the tribe. It is a military morality of aggression, superiority, and conquest—a morality of Fascists, black and brown. I speak of a caste; but, in many civilizations, it may be open to anyone to join their ranks who has the taste and the temperament.

Here are to be found the men who are capitalists, as it were, of power, never content that mere economic security is secure, replacing fear by the desperate determination to be in first in the race or to strike the first blow. They are interested in the fight for its own sake and in the prestige, not the cash, which can be made out of it. To this mass belong the aristocrats whose hereditary career is politics, the politicians, the generals who are ambitious to lead—barons, warriors. To this also belong the demagogues who begrudge the power of others, and even the financiers who, debarred from other routes to power, choose money organization as their road, not for the object of acquisition, but for the sake of the sense of power which great investments give. Here belong also the emotional revolutionaries, red and white.

There is a second ingredient. This is composed rather of individuals than of classes. It is composed of those who have become self-conscious and who are spurred on by the irritation of their own sensitivity to unhappiness or by the fascination of finding answers about curious things. Their morality is deliberate and intelligent. For that reason these people may be the directors of morals, guardians, thinkers, administrators, priests, both of the red international and of the black.

There are two moralities, corresponding to the two masses of men, those who primarily want security and those who primarily want to satisfy their wish for power. There is a generous morality of the tribe with its "unintellectual" attachments and mutual obligations, its clan loyalties: here the humble have their place as good workers, good citizens, good fellows. What seems important in this milieu is what the plain mass of folk do in their street and town, be it "Magnolia Street" or "the Five Towns," "Main Street," or "Manhattan Transfer," in their local government, the shop, and the chapel, and not in world policy—the fustian facts of "sociology" here matter and not the pomp and circumstance of "history."

There is also the morality of the ambitious, the second group, the temperamental exploiters and their converse, the temperamental rebels, who egoistically seek success, excusing means by ends, and are cloyed by the tedious presence of the unsuccessful. This morality is one which rids itself of their inferior, clinging, clannish attachments; which achieves the reputation for high altruism by its power to confer benefits only after it has acquired that power by ruthlessly avoiding entangling responsibility; which achieves idealism and salvation only as a Brand, ruthless to human sentiment, and by escape into detachment and impersonality.

What is to be the solution of this clash of moralities, the appeasement of this restless desire for power which inspires some men to upset society by their desire to dominate and which moves the mass to disquiet and slow resentment?

Can it be that with some "priestly" or "fully conscious" group, if anywhere, is to be found, as Plato long since saw, the solution of the problem of politics? That seems to be Mr. Wells' answer, in his noble encyclopaedic work on *The Wealth, Work, and Happiness of Mankind.* Is the reconciliation to be found here that can replace the clash between the aggressive spirit of the man of ambition and the moral condemnation of ambition by custom, the clash between the need in civilization for the devil of ambition and the fear of it, the clash between freedom and custom, individualism and group-mindedness, the men of hereditary assertion and the men of environmental moulding? Those of this group may be the problem-solvers. They are capable of being at once comprehending and disinterested, active and socially minded. The difficulty, however, with priests and their like is that, although all wisdom may be on their side, their personality is not of that imaginative mould which sweeps the emotional mass of mankind into following a leader—those who know can't lead and those who can lead so seldom know. Another difficulty lies in the tendency of every kind of priesthood, whether of science, religion, or public service, to become a caste, contemptuous of common folk.

Is, in short, Plato's answer any longer at all relevant to the political issue as it confronts us today? Hitherto the contests of politics have been contests between ambitious men, sometimes of the military type, sometimes of the more detached priestly type, for the control of the reluctant slow-moving masses who, compelled by changing circumstances to unwonted departure from custom, have expected guidance. All politics has been a contest of the few between themselves for the direction of the many.

This remains still true, but there has, in the modern world, been one significant change among these few. To the soldier and upper caste, to the priest, to the financier and merchant adventurer and captain of industry has been added the representative of the workers sprung from the workers but vocal, clamant, and militant. The dissemination of ideas by school and Press—but also by cinema and radio—has changed the old types. While retaining conservatism in manners, even the rural workers are prepared to contemplate great changes in civilization. Especially is this true in all those matters where the hope springs up that security can be guaranteed by ousting the possessors of power, instead of economic insecurity being part of the order of nature. Above all, the modern town worker (so different from the townsman of the market town who remained, in effect, countryman), organized in unions and often without property of his own, ready for change, is stirred by the new ideas to follow leaders who will contest with the possessing classes their control of power.

The history of politics is the history of a battle carried on between the possessing few and another few with a gift for leadership and some singular appetite for liberty. These few may be members themselves, as were Mirabeau, Saint-Simon, Engels, Lasalle, and Lenin, of the possessing class. They yet fight on behalf of the hesitating majority and are in integral unity with them, thanks to a sharing, native or acquired, of interests and (still more) of experience.

The problem, then, of our lasting social peace is that of how to strengthen the power of that minority of which the interest is in fact integral with the rational interest of the whole; how to secure this identification of interest between individual and society; and how realistically to forge such an instrument (perhaps by this very identification) that the disinterested, and not the self-interested, shall in fact exercise power and dissipate the prestige of their opponents.

This statement, however, of the general nature of the political solution is not likely to go without challenge. Too great a stress, it will be felt, is placed upon the function of the minority. It will be asserted that power must lie equally in the hands of all, not be made a disinterested quality of a vigorous minority. An analogy is made between power and money (which can be equalized) and not between power and management. Ever since the days of (by a strange irony) the Cynics and of the Stoics the theory of human equality has always insisted on a hearing. The endeavour to find some psychological technique, thanks to which the desire for personal power may be allayed in those who lead, may be met by the allegation that this is misdirected effort, that leadership can be dispensed with, that the powerful can be deprived of their power merely by repressive legislation and that the anonymity of directive influence presents no difficulties as the attribute of a permanent system of government. No psychological problem is involved once human equality is recognized.

As has been pointed out, the equalitarian and democratic movement of recent centuries has passed through three stages, legal, civil, and economic, of which the second—the civil, electoral, or parliamentarian stage—has just reached its conclusion. The movement for political liberty has rippled to the shore of accomplishment as something universally recognized to be just by the granting of political powers to women in all the more advanced countries of the civilized world save France and Italy. In universal suffrage we have apparently the solution of the problem of power. Rousseau's ideal is realized—or would be realized were economic equality added. No limited group would rule. Rule would rest in the hands of the entire citizen body.

This apparent solution, however, in terms of abstract human equality as the answer to the problem, rests on an ambiguity. Those who talk of democracy far too seldom make it clear whether they mean, by the word, the political system which gives embodiment to the sound principle that there must be no power without accountability or whether they mean that the power of political direction springs from the people in whom sovereignty resides and that ministers and statesmen are merely the passive functionaries of the popular will. It is futile to maintain that this latter position is a mere abstraction held by no persons requiring serious consideration. On the contrary the first half of this statement is embodied in most of the Liberal constitutions of Europe, while the second has the respectable authority of Rousseau and is, throughout America, the customary interpretation of the democratic tradition of Jefferson and of Jackson.

In brief, there are not a few people but a quite powerful section of the electorate which does, in effect, believe in precisely what Sir Norman Angell pilloried as rule from the barber's chair. The plain man, while waiting for his shave, gives his opinion. That opinion is the representative voice of the people. As such it is sovereign, final, and wise. This belief is held, by Russian Communist and by Italian Fascist alike, to be a dangerous Liberal superstition. The same belief in its germ was held to be a superstition by Cromwell. The problem of leadership—and of disinterested leadership—is not so easily and crudely solved. Nevertheless, the belief goes on being held. There is yet no sound argument in favour of placing the effective direction on policy of our most vital interests into the hands of those who are ignorant about the necessary facts upon which alone a sound judgement can be founded.

Politicians should be accountable for the results of their work and, if they fail by their policy to alleviate the grievances of the average man, they can very justly be brought to book. The whole community, alike in industry and in civil government, is the sole judge of ultimate policy, and any particular policy must be made acceptable to this community which suffers by its failure. But this is not at all the same as saying that the political leaders are not the guides but merely the subordinates, not the commisars but the commissionaires, in the army of democracy. They are still common mortals, but common men with a duty to do and a function to perform. A policy agreed upon or indicated, theirs is the moral responsibility to fight for its realization and upon their energy and foresight it depends.

Despite, however, all the fine logical arguments by which this absurdity of government by those who don't know has been exposed, in a literature of which Sir Norman Angell's books and Mr. Lippmann's are good examples, the belief in this inspiration with political wisdom of the plain men, of which the absurdity is frequently excused by a suggestion of mystical reasons too profound for argument, persists and flourishes. The grounds for the strange persistence of this belief are worth examining. Since they are not logical, it may be suspected that they may be psychological, using intellectual arguments to rationalize a concealed impulsive drive. The problem is no new one: the old arguments of Plato in criticizing democracy still demand consideration. We shall discover that, indeed, there is not a single but a twofold problem of power—that the problem of power has a reverse side, and that the emotion behind the theory of equality is intimately connected with this reverse side. We are confronted with a species of Oedipus complex, directed against authority as such. The theory of human equality does not so much solve the problem of the demand for power in the vigorously ambitious few as indicate a new problem of power among the jealously suspicious many.

A PREFACE TO ACTION

There is a political equivalent of the second law of thermodynamics concerning the degeneration of energy. There is a psychological force at work in the human race steadily challenging all eminence, especially when stereotyped as privilege and deprived of immediate justification, and tending to reduce all men to a dead level. That force is the power of envy. It is the reverse of the medal of ambition. It is operative in limited, peasant circles, even in a torpid society: it becomes virulent in one of widened horizons and of great expectations not often enough fulfilled for the individual to his satisfaction.

Here, I suggest, is to be found the explanation, not of the rational argument of democracy that there should be accountability in the exercise of power, but of the pseudo-democratic idea, which Americans call Jacksonian, that any man is competent for any job. The burden of the song of equality, in the mouths of many of its exponents, is that some occult superior ability of the plain man must be honoured. This doctrine flatters human conceit even more widely (if not more profoundly) than the belief that one's own talents are unique—and is obviously a doctrine far easier to hold without incurring jealousy or ridicule. It is, after all, a subtle flattery of their neighbours by those who think themselves the abler.

The democracy of envy—the democracy which perverts the attack on irrational privilege and uncontrolled power into an attack on all eminence, and which muddies the estimation of the high civilized virtues of modesty and respect for human personality by its demand that any "tough" is entitled to his way of life without censure from those who are, ought to be, and should be affirmed to be his superiors—this democracy of envy may appear to indicate the actual road that will be followed to the solution of the problem of power. Envy is the fruit of the desire for power in the man oppressed by fear; and fear is the manifestation in the weak of the appetite for liberty and preservation of life. "Every man looketh that his companion should value him at the same rate he sets upon himselfe." All superior individual powers may be flattened out by the mass power of persons rid of their immediate timidities and yet virulent with a more permanent inferiority complex. Every man of good ability, under such a system, must, under pain of ridicule and of political impotence, call high heaven to witness that he is a very ordinary man, a veritable mere squit of a fellow. This method of securing equality, it may be urged, will "work"—can be made effective, thanks to the superior power of the mass.

It is a first principle of political science that a force does not cease to be such or to affect the dynamics of the social system because this or that moralist may happen to dislike it; it has to be studied, explained, and allowed for, not frowned upon and dismissed as too base for notice. It is the business of the political scientist merely to record, without value judgement, the various possible equilibria in the distribution of power. It is, nevertheless, the business of political philosophy to adjudge motives in the general context of human nature and life.

I cannot imagine any more deadly travesty of democracy as a sound system than this policy of the inferiority complex, this minoritarianism of temperament, this under-doggery for all. It is, not a destruction, but a maintenance of servility. It is the opposite of the bold assertion of the human values of all, of disciplined and reserved self-respect for each, of the tendency of every worthwhile person to seek to find his superiors, from whom he may learn, rather than to be surrounded by inferiors who may solace his own sense of inferiority. It is no possible basis for a young civilization of imagination, of vision, of confidence, of creative power. It is, however, possible to go beyond a philosophy of motives. It is possible to state that this attitude displays contempt for the biological and psychological facts of actual human diversity of talent and, therefore, offers an unsatisfactory basis for any permanent system of social relationships consonant with natural law. Any such system must take into account all the human facts, not base its plan of social convenience on ignoring half of them—the half not least important for human advancement.

A sound polity is a polity of plain men—not one waiting for Messianic leadership by a man on horseback; but it is a society of plain men guided by reason and not a society of men guided by envy, jealousy, and a sense of inferiority. It will be a society in which adequate recognition is given to the fact that we have no present knowledge of what appropriate conditioning, nurture, education, and economic opportunity could do for Smith and Jones. It will be a society expectant to develop whatever power may be detectable in any citizen, without respect of status. Envy, however, has to be counted with as a political force: it must be cured, not ignored. To the discussion of that envy we shall return. What I desire here to emphasize is that it is foolish to undervalue the strength, in moulding the social order, of this force which is the inverse of the intensified appetite for power. Just as the Protestant Reformation was made an effective political force, not by the devoted idealists only, but by the aid of greed, so modern movements must steer a cautious course if they are not, as the price of success, to enter into a compromise with this *unter-mensch* envy—not of privilege, but of any quality of eminence whatsoever which makes the envious feel at a disadvantage. Ambition, nevertheless, will not be exorcised by its sister, envy.

A reasonable belief, however, in what is generally called human equality is not without foundation. It is a belief, indeed, in human potentiality, in a respect for human personality. It, as much as the recognition of distinctive talents, is important for the future of civilization. It is founded on a conviction that, however much they become just weary mules turning the machinery of civilization, yet human beings should be treated as ends and not as means. It is a belief which results in protest, noble and invaluable, against the tendency of administrators to regard human beings as just cattle to be competently shepherded—even by shepherds proud of being of a different race and tongue: the offence of which well-intentioned British administrators in India seem at the moment to be guilty. It is a belief, moreover, consistent with scientific caution.

There is an essential cheapness in the frequent attempt of society, for its momentary convenience, to classify people apart from all particular valuation of them and their abilities or character as individuals. This attempt is vulgar, as the Webbs have excellently said in their *Decay of Capitalist Civilization*. It is also contrary to the interest of an efficient society in which everyone, locomotive driver and banker alike, has pride of profession as well as pride of person and of individual citizenship. It is entirely undesirable that everyone should be considered, not as the craftsman, but as the employee of the vast anonymous—as the good machine. As the spirit of a machine age and of a rationalized civilization becomes more pervasive this risk of sacrificing the "becoming," the potentiality of the spirit, of this or that individual to the expediency and convenience of treating men in the mass is likely to become more insistent, although the need for efficiency and for the dynamic confidence and satisfaction behind most human efficiency will also become more insistent.

Instead of being only the vice of a so-called aristocratic civilization this lumping of men together in anonymous subordination to the works manager or the official may become a democratic tendency. In either case it is to be resisted. The only effective campaign against a Philistinism which refuses to differentiate according to the quality of this individual or that is to insist that, if and so long as men are to be treated in the mass, they shall all be treated as equals with equal and inalienable rights to liberty, Jack Everyman as much as the newest Commissar or Party Secretary.

It may be argued that there is yet such a thing as intellectual pre-eminence and that this is entitled to leadership. It is an argument which has never convinced plain men that it is not guilty of priggery and even more offensive than the pretensions of the stalwart possessors of power. It is, I suppose, for this reason that the half-derisory word "intelligensia" has been coined—for the men of more ideas than character. The argument has, however, a certain theoretical plausibility. We tend to talk, as self-evident, of intellectual pre-eminence, as though intellectual ability were something as specific and assessable as ability to play the flute. Either one has it or has it not. . . .

On the contrary, not only are there a myriad forms of intellectual ability, but those who have high mental gifts in one direction may be quite incompetent in

THE POWER IMPULSE

another. It is, I believe, true that the eminent really are the intrinsically eminent, despite all romantic belief to the effect that every common fellow, could we but explore his personality, would be found, not just another bourgeois, but a mute Milton. There are yet many very dissimilar kinds of eminence. Intellect is not a neatly measurable quality, thanks to which we can sharply distinguish an intellectual aristocracy from the rest. There is a diversity of gifts, but no gift such as to justify its possessors in constituting themselves a segregated governing caste.

It would, of course, be splendid if "superior" human beings were sharply separated off, by some kind of heroic stigmata, from other mortals, just as some would think it splendid and only right if all men in the economic market, as of course, showed their superiority to all women. Unfortunately, it is not so and, hence, some folk desire to establish upper classes by authority. It might be splendid if all superior people were at once intelligent, able, masterly, and beautiful, καλοὶ κἀγαθοί. Unfortunately, it is not so. Much of the indubitably significant work of the world is done by otherwise quite ordinary folk. Manhattan expresses the idea, like Babylon, of incredible human power, but its builders are not such striking people. The same observation is even truer in the realms of science and philosophy than in that of architecture. That is disconcerting; and the wise man will learn to avoid snap class-judgements and to cultivate a rational humility until such time as we have found means to breed this race of all-round supermen. We do not yet know of what human material the race will have need.

The justice, then, of the onslaught upon many false forms of inequality is apparent. These false inequalities, fostering a class insolence and unjustified presumption, are something less than civilized. They nurture crude young men into a contempt for that quality of tragedy and pathetic comedy which is to be found humanizing the life of every country girl and ordinary fellow. That contempt and insolence grows readily, feeds upon itself, and speedily becomes a threat to order, progress, and the rule of reason. It is true that we cannot romantically feel the thug or, for that matter, the charlady who breaks the cat's neck and puts its corpse in the furnace to be persons of equal sensibility with the most delightful of our friends—but then, neither do the millionaire Loebs or Mr. Harry Thaw, or persons of more wealth than morals nearer home, come into that category.

Thanks to this onslaught on false inequality, first in the seventeenth century, equality before the law was established in England; in the eighteenth century a beginning was made in France, with the Revolutionary attack on political privilege, towards equality before the ballot-box; today the fight is concerned with asserting that power in society belongs to those who serve it and not to those who know how to acquire wealth in it.

I repeat the words "that power in society belongs to those who serve it." This implies permanent diversities of power, although it does not imply, I trust, either a moral tyranny or the priggery of government by some self-styled educated class. I do not agree that power should be exclusively absorbed by some party aristocracy, Fascist or Communist; although I do agree that a new meaning and face may well be given to the word "Party," as a freely chosen, active, and homogeneous group. In the heterogeneous society in which we live many diverse persons are entitled to their diverse ways of life and yet may peacefully regard themselves as good citizens. I am, however, prepared to maintain that those with any clear social plan, as well as those capable of disinterested service, are entitled to take the lead in moulding the social order. I am prepared to maintain that men active in public life, active party members, who accept a certain discipline in public life, have a better right to the exercise of political power than apathetic, undesirable, or privately preoccupied citizens.

It may be true, as Lincoln said, that no man is so much better than others as to be entitled to order them about without their consent. It is, however, true that the man who has a clear idea of whither to lead and of how to administer will always be entitled to endeavour to gain that consent. And the minority which has such an idea and plan has a similar right to offer guidance to the majority. This guidance, however, involves a sense of unity, if it is to be valuable, between guides and guided in one community.

As Edmund Burke, who will not be accused of communism, phrased the principle: it is necessary that those who have the lead and direction in public affairs should have "connexion with the interest . . . with the sentiments and opinions of the people." Let us consider the implications of this.

Plato's criticism of democracy is that, with every man believing himself to have a right to an equal opinion at least in the social order, no leadership is tolerated because no authority of social standards—of these rather than of those—is admitted. There is cultural nihilism. The philosophy of Thrasymachus reappears. The "tough" sees no reason, save in the malice of superior power, why his life as a "tough" may not be morally justified;

to himself he is a brave and successful man. The restrictions of religion are regarded with scepticism and are dissolved in the interests, not of reason, but of the liberty of the plain layman. (Incidentally it is thereby made certain that, when society emerges from this anarchy, there will be a reaction beyond religion into the denial of reason, as with American sects, in favour of superstition, occultism, "blood-thinking," and the like.) With destruction of respect for reason as universal arbiter of values and sustainer of authority, the sense for law is lost. Only the custom of the clique is left. In the United States the result, in some areas, is such as almost to remove the primary conditions which are usually accepted as a test of a civilized community. The need for leadership is apparent.

Leadership and complete cultural nihilism, in which opinion is held to be as good as knowledge, are inconsistent. In America (but not only in America), owing to a false theory of democracy, the time seems fast approaching when such cultural nihilism will be predominant and when no one will dare to lift up his voice who does not confess a democratic theory of this dye. All cultural standards will be regarded as an offensive sign of "superiority," and among the more intelligent a radical scepticism will prevail, such as is already indicated in Lincoln Steffens' fascinating *Autobiography*, mitigated by an optimism about some providential good which will come out of this great experimental cauldron—this social experiment far more prepossessed in favour of novelty even than Russia.

Liberty, in a compulsory society such as the modern state, demands freedom to decline to follow any but one's own ideal or opinion and a leadership consistent with that ideal. But it does not demand or require that

THE POWER IMPULSE

there shall be no leadership in cultural, moral, or political standards. Such leadership a progressive civilization and any intensive, worthwhile culture requires. Such leadership must, as Plato said, itself be classless as touching birth and wealth. Only in such a fashion can one get rid of government, in the bad sense, as the arbitrary and irrational rule of men, contrary to their natural good, by some group possessed of power, and substitute the administration of things in accordance with rational principles that intelligent men will respect as for the common good.

Could unhealthy competition be damped down, so that ambition beyond the limits of a vital and not displeasing vanity could assume a restrained, impersonal, and social form, instead of being unbalanced and morbid, the third greatest cause of disquiet in the world would be brought under harness. The world would be less full of little men with jealous eyes and of clever men, Mr. Wells' "smart Alecs," waiting to thrust a shoulder or a foot into every half-open door. Such energy may be good in its odd, sordid way in breaking up an old, unjust, and insolent society such as has itself by reaction produced this envy. It may be quite necessary for the practical campaign against that injustice. But it provides no mood in which to establish a better society. It is suitable for organizing a political campaign against privilege. But stimulation of this competitive impulse is unsuited as an instrument for political victors when they are themselves confronted with the task of moulding a satisfactory social order.

As it is, the secular world—especially the male world,

A PREFACE TO ACTION

but increasingly the entire world—is perfused and saturated in all social reaches above the economically middling and lower (and even here in a petty but not less malicious way) with struggles for place and for prestige; for small bribes and great bribes; with neat calculations of importance and publicity value; with the stupid snobberies of those who accept without criticism the established social hierarchy and the genteel cut-throat contests of those determined to crash their way up to the seats of the mighty; with the pot-of-vipers venom of the disappointed and of those still arriving; with the ingenious schemes of the gunmen bravos of Chicago and Berlin cutting across the rules of the game and arriving at success by crime and corruption; with the determination of the revolutionary to overthrow the thrones of the existing mighty and to trample upon them. Already Mr. Wells' prophecy, in *The Shape of Things to Come*, of the end of our civilization in a period of unrestrained crime and of renewed crime on the high seas, is justified by the report from New York of infernal machines placed in ocean-going liners in order to extract ransom from the shipping companies.

The self-assertiveness of man, which is so near to being the very life of man, the lust for battle and victory, is not to be swept aside or allayed by a few words. Skin for skin, what would a man not give for his skin. "Felicity is a continual progress of desire from one object to another; the attaining of the former being still but the way to the latter . . . so that in the first place I put for a general inclination of all mankind a perpetual and restless desire of power after power that ceases only at death. . . . It is true that certain living creatures, as bees and ants, live sociably one with another: and therefore some man may perhaps desire to know why mankind cannot do the same. To which I answer, first, that men are continually in competition for honour and dignity which these creatures are not, and consequently among men there arises on that ground envy and hatred and finally war; but among these not so. Secondly, among these creatures the common good differs not from the private."

The most eminent of the world's philosophers have seen no solution for this problem, of the egoistic man, save in terms of the belief in immortality. The psychological cure lies in the shift of the focus of ambition. The dispute among them has only been whether the immortality shall be of the individual—who may still remain an egoist in the saving of his soul through righteous works or mere faith—or whether it shall be of the individual in and through the community, actual or ideal. It seems reasonable to suppose that rest from the morbid overvaluation of the individual as distinct and isolated from others is to be found in a recovered and renewed sense of identity with those others. So long as the community remains merely the government or the mechanical state or an agglomerate called society, without any thorough and out-and-out admission of responsibility for the individual as a member, the individual, by ambition and the pursuit of power, must warily fend for himself—no sense of identity can be developed for the excellent reason that identity of interest is not there.

The remedy for the mere sense of insecurity is in the development of the recognition of mutual obligation on the part of society towards its citizens and of citizens towards society. This is possible in a purely utilitarian society in which there is no need to assume any high degree of like-mindedness or common ideals. It is useful to all that the revolutionary unrest should be removed which has its roots in insecurity in the common pursuits of life, insecurity of personal freedom from violence by war or crime, or from starvation or shortage, and in like miseries which a well-ordered society can obviate. The remedy here is the common sense one of social democracy.

The problem of the removal of the fundamental disaffections of envy and of egoistical ambition, with the threats, rivalries, and unhappiness involved, is not so easy of solution. It requires, for its solution, more than merely a utilitarian society in which authority will guarantee the rights of all, so far as is consistent with not disproportionately restricting the liberties of each. It requires a society of common loyalties and values, a non-heterogeneous society, in which this kind of suspicious defensiveness or personal exploitation becomes pointless. It requires the rebuilding of intimate face-to-face groups, moved by principles of trust and honour, and the placing of such groups in positions of effective control.

This has been the principle that has accounted for the success, in the larger society, of the great religious movements (including the "Society of Friends" as well as the "Society of Jesus"), and the aristocracies, military and professional, of the past. It is the secret of success of Communism today in its task of building co-operatively a new civilization. So far as Communism has, in fact, not succeeded, this has largely been due to the inadequacy of this loyal elimination of personal rivalry in the ranks.

The egotism of the group can be controlled by considerations of utility, humanity, and reason, where economic self-interest is not involved, provided that the group itself is not merely the instrument for realizing the latent appetite for glory or phantasies of grandeur of individuals. How group ambition must be controlled is one of the issues with which we shall be confronted in the second part of this book. The basal problem, however, is that of the egoistic assertion of the individual.

This assertiveness will be replaced by an admirable enough desire to do work of distinction when social recognition is assured for every good talent. Morbid assertiveness arises from the sense of isolation and defensiveness—*homo homini lupus*; man to man a wolf. The emotional corrective for the power impulse is to be discovered in the erotic impulse, just as the check on a sensuous eroticism is to be found in an ideal ambition.

The remedy for an assertiveness which can perturb all social life is not to be found by strengthening the negative and deadening emotion of fear, which is the recessive aspect of the impulse towards liberty. It is to be discovered in terms of a community of mutual feeling, held together, if not by direct erotic bonds, then by bonds of some ideal friendship—held together, as like-minded, by some common impulse or purpose or by emotional or mental inter-stimulation due to a common tradition, a common religion or some like mutual congruity. Through such a close community, moreover, an effective power, not neurotic but emotionally stable and at least susceptible to rational control, can be built up and exercised over the great society of heterogeneous humanity. Such a community, homogeneous in ideals, can have the driving-power of a monastic order and the cultural intensity of a Greek city state.

If we are to be saved from over-emphasis upon ambition for wealth, power, and self-advertisement, with their restless competition and perversion of values, we must re-stress, in their direct or sublimated forms, the equally powerful and more generous impulses. It is a psychological problem that must be attacked; and, primarily, a psychological problem of the individual. The neutralizing of group aggression can never be effective merely by stressing individual aggression, but only by passing through, and on beyond, loyalty to family, clan, and tribe to wider and more liberal loyalties. Loyalty to abstract ideals represents the end of this historical cycle.

These more generous impulses require for their play kindly and unsuspicious association with other human beings, not merely as individuals, but in the context of an ideal scheme or of a devoted movement. The demand for such movements is today urgent and written large in contemporary history. Repose and balance in the individual personality having been assured, reason disinterested skill, science, and art can thus be freed from bondage to private ends in order to play their ennobling part, first, in the local community, and then in the civilization of the great society. How to secure that disinterested or religious devotion is an immediate concern. How to prevent it from being perverted into a religion of group aggression is the problem that we have to consider later.

§ v

The Religious Impulse

Repeated attempts have been made to suggest or to discover the origins of the religious impulse from the days of Herbert of Cherbury and of Pascal to those of Freud. Fear of spirits, an instinct of abasement before immense power, the desire for magical control have all been assigned as reasons. One great school has deduced the religious impulse, as the love of gods and men, from a sublimation of the erotic impulse. It becomes a supplement, a compensation and a rival. The religious impulse, it is asserted, starting from a baulking of direct erotic expression and the substitution of ideal and mythical objects for the more concrete beloved one, thrives on the ascetic tendency. If the direct erotic impulse is developed, the indirect religious impulse declines.

Historically it appears to be true that the democratic pursuit of happiness and the religious impulse, with its brooding sense of sin, have tended to vary inversely. If it is true, then it is highly important. It means that the survival of democracy depends upon the intelligent control of the religious impulse to ascetic sacrifice of oneself and others. The passionate preaching of sacrifice, sometimes called "the sublimity of bloodshed" in contemporary Germany, is an interesting confirmation of this point.

The Freudian theory, however, of the exclusively erotic origin of religion is probably too simple. Mere frustrated eroticism alone does not explain (as Freud himself has confessed in his most recent work) all asceticism, which also draws on the embittered springs of the frustrated desire for power.

A PREFACE TO ACTION

It is argued by students of the history of religion that the diffused sexuality of the higher animals and of primitive men, expressed towards the social group, as advance is made in imaginative intelligence and in sense of individuality, becomes directed upon an object more definite than the group, upon a personal symbol, upon the tribe's leader and god. These totem gods, however (gods very different from the Absolute of the metaphysicians, the Lord God Omnipotent of the churchmen—and yet with a pygmy kinship), awaken other sentiments besides affection, whether they be the representatives of the social group and the guardians of its safety or animist personifications of outside nature. They are embodied moralities protecting the tribesmen against death or they are the shapes of unsounded and untrustworthy forces of earth and sky. They are instruments of power. They stand threateningly over the individual, menacing him if he does the forbidden and unlucky things. The worshippers must propitiate and learn the ritual of that ascetic denial which is pleasing to the divine jealousy and which indicates humility before omnipotence, instead of the Babel-sin of pride. The awe of this power is a constituent in the primitive attitude of the god-fearing man.

It certainly does not follow from the description of primitive religion, given by anthropology, that, in the name of happiness or of democracy, all religious systems, as relics of an ancient and cruel magic, should be discarded. Such an account of religion, typical of the age of Paine, is entirely superficial. An immense historical force cannot be dismissed so cavalierly; it has to be explained.

There is an emotion involved which, however nonsensical or grotesque may be some of the objects upon which it expends itself, cannot be eradicated or, without psychological injury, suppressed. Although adulterated, both by superstitious fear and by hope of reward, the sense of exhilarated reverence, aroused whether by the symbols of the community or of natural forces, remains definite. Its development offers a means by which the individual may lose himself in an adoration for that which is greater and more significant than himself. The desire for identification (and for that power which is given by self-fulfilment through identification) with the greater and nobler, of itself provides the motive for submission to a preparatory discipline in life. One needs to enquire of every religion, discipline, and self-sacrifice what specifically the practice of it will do for the good, not of God whom we have not seen, but of our brethren whom we have seen. By making, however, discipline for ideal ends desirable, religion is on the credit side of experience. This desire, moreover, for identification has, psychologically, to be satisfied in some form. The task is to find the form that is least dangerous and yet most profound.

Anthropology, on the other hand, gives no encouragement to the opinion that all religion is self-evidently a good. On the contrary, it is patent that many religions have been very far from anything of the kind. The words of Lucretius concerning the ignoble acts to which this impulse has driven men have been in all too many cases abundantly justified. The new forms religion assumes today are assuredly no exception.

There seems little reason to doubt the permanency and the immense strength of the religious impulse, but,

A PREFACE TO ACTION

in this present age this impulse appears like some great stream which has run into a marsh. Our civilization is full of relics and rites of religion, but, while the forms and the institutions remain, the vital energy and the confident faith have gone. The emotion has become contorted by rival currents of thought and feeling; it does not flow clear.

The traditions become every year less vital and, once intelligible as the garments of a great human satisfaction, they now remain empty clothes, incomprehensible to the critical eye of the mundane understanding. The danger, once obscured by great emotion, becomes patent of founding morality, not on ethical principles established by the sensitiveness of the human mind to developing experience, but (for example) on the moral precepts and tabus accepted at various stages of their evolution by a barbarous, if precocious, Asiatic people. The religious emotion is slowly taking new form. Reason, change of interest, and increased mastery of nature have increasingly rendered men hostile or (which is more significant) indifferent to the old forms. But those who, from sentiment, prejudice, or lack of imagination, are impervious to new influences, decline to admit the change.

If it be argued that the sacred books of the Old Testament are to be put aside, like others of the more edifying sacred books of the East, as not the infallible word of God but merely a fascinating record of moral evolution, it is not clear why the books of the New Testament, which must be set against the Old Testament background and the Old Testament claim to inspiration, should not be considered in the same light.

THE RELIGIOUS IMPULSE

The reason for accepting the miracles of the Old Testament—of Jonah, or of Elijah the Tishbite with fire, or of Moses with the plagues in Egypt—is a strong will to believe. The historicity of certain of these miracles I am neither concerned to affirm or to deny. In the copy of *The Times* under my hand I read that a cripple has become able to walk, thanks to the sudden effect on him of first seeing the majesty of the *Aquitania* in port—which would not be a reason for starting a beatification process for the *Aquitania*. The moral basis itself of this will is removed, if the problem is perceived to be whether the biblical ethic is itself completely satisfactory and if the answer given be negative. The effect upon young minds of inculcating, as moral examples, the character of unheroic heroes—of the deceiver Jacob, the unlovely Joseph, the ferocious Samuel (who, from righteous indignation that massacre was not complete, hewed Agag in pieces), the penitent murderer David, the vindictive Elisha cursing small children—can only be minimized by any educator who supposes that the story can have no significant impression. The normal psychological effect of worshipping a jealous, raging patriarch as Eternal God must be to produce a god-terrified or, as the phrase is, god-fearing people with a morality shot through with furtive terror. A century ago this effect was apparently produced.

The answer vouchsafed to the enquiring Job—if we turn to happier instances of Old Testament moral teaching—amounts to little more than that the atrocities wrought by nature under the directing finger of God in fact happen, that truth describes them, and that the wise man submits to cosmic truth. The logical hiatus between the concepts of power and goodness has never yet been bridged—not even by the genius of Spinoza or

Hegel. It remained unbridged by Job; nor is reason here given why we should worship with reverence what is for us the unjust. We may accept necessity. We do not, however, bow our souls in such a temple any more than a courageous man bows himself before any mundane oppressor, from Assur-bani-pal or Nero to Caesar Borgia or Ivan the Terrible.

Nor can an abrupt distinction be made between the Old and the New Testament by Churches which retain the former as divinely inspired . . . nor, indeed, is the New Covenant God of Calvin so different from the tribal deities of the Old Covenant: "through the eyes on the wrinkled face of the god glares the hatred of the savage." Both are Gods of Hell-Fire—and of human sadism. I write these things with no pleasure. It seems, however, improbable that true religion can prevail until the trappings are seen for what they are and are discarded.

The mild religion of Christ springs from a life of which the drama must command the adoration of the humane. Any ethic, however, which is a revealed, and hence a retrospective, ethic would appear to be a dubious ethic. (I do not forget the declaration concerning the mission of the Holy Spirit to lead on to further truth or Newman's Doctrine of Development—the Church has, however, made little play with them and the Protestant Reformed Churches have turned their back, on principle, on the future and have harked back to the primitive; that is the significance even of the contemporary, fideistic Barthian movement.) Instead of resting upon a rational adjustment to current life, this ethic looks mechanically backwards towards a moral system absolutely established by somebody held to be, in some peculiar and non-human sense, divine—miraculously infallible beyond all criticism of reason. What, after all, matters is not what

Christ, according to the scholars, is supposed to have said but what is the truth.

That this ethic, at least as legitimately interpreted by many people, may be actually maladjusted to contemporary needs the following quotation from a letter in a current journal, selected at random, will indicate: "May I point out," says the writer, on the subject of the Church's duty by the unemployed, "that Jesus Christ never contemplated a world society imbued with his doctrine, or energized by his spirit? Far from it: 'My Kingdom is not of this world.' The Sermon on the Mount, about which people talk so readily, was spoken to disciples. It was *overheard* by the world; that is all. The world itself never meant, never means, to put Christ's basic principles into action, though it may think or pretend to think that it is doing so." No one acquainted with the history of chiliasm will assert that this statement is inconsistent with historical doctrine. It remains questionable whether an ethic which diverts so much energy from indignation against present wrong can be regarded as satisfactory.

Those who have read the miracle-soaked New Testament Apocrypha, which forms a bridge between the canonical books of the New Testament and the rest of this apocryphal literature, will be the less disposed to make any sudden division between the Old Covenant and the New. Anyone who will examine the early Epistle of Barnabas or the second-century Acts of Paul and Thecla will discover how different from the present was the context of belief in that long past age of the Primitive Church. The canonical writings of St. Paul are capable of a construction—which has, in fact, historically been put on them—resulting in the condonation of slavery, the persecution of witchcraft, the depreciation of marriage, and the subordination of women. The condonation, indeed, of these offences would be historically explicable and negligible in literature, but are scarcely so in a sacred and final book of revelation. We are left, then, with the ethics of the parables and the Sermon on the Mount.

Even here the problem of reconciling the humanity with the divinity of Christ, in any other method than that which would allow to every man some measure of divinity, has never been satisfactorily solved for nearly two millennia. It has led to intricate dispute since the days of monophysite and monothelite until its present subsidence in apathy. The miracles of the Church, such as the Virgin Birth and the Ascension (with flesh and bones, as says the Article of the Church of England), are intelligible enough as myths portraying the irrelevance of paternity and ancestry to that divinity in man which is of universal relevance or the connection between actual men in the transient world and ideal types of timeless significance. As statements of brute fact they so far violate every canon of probability as to throw doubt upon the critical judgement or the intellectual and moral integrity of those who accept them. The Bishop of Birmingham (who accepts other miracles) even holds that it is incredible that the divine should dwell, numinous for the worshippers, in the bread and wine of the Christian sacrament: this, however, is philosophically more dubious. All this is not to deny that the Church may have been wise in condemning a modernism · which asserted the insignificance of the historicity of the divine drama of Christ. The practicability of an ideal cannot be affirmed by the use of a fiction. The "beautiful" is weakened when it is not also the "true." But the assertion of the historical basis is not to affirm the historicity of improbable subversions of the natural order of events.

The Christian Church appears to be in a condition of intellectual bankruptcy. It is in danger of so far abandoning the noble scholastic tradition, which was in its day a monument of the logical reason, as to fling itself into movements of crude irrationalism. The issue is Mr. Buchman's mission to the rich young men, or Miss Aimée Semple Macpherson, or such a notice as that displayed in London the other day: "Greater World: Clergyman and Ghostly Dog." We have travelled far since the days of the doctrine of Incarnate Reason.

Even more apparent is the bankruptcy of the practical organization of the Churches. Such an immense organization could not have been built up unless it satisfied some profound psychological drive in human nature. Now, at least for the present, the living impulse seems to have departed from it. Protestantism, unlike Catholicism, is essentially an episode, a protest rather than a system. It has not even gone to the intellectual effort of producing a connected philosophy, save so far as Kant or Schleiermacher has provided one ready-made. The only logical Protestant body, the Society of Friends, carries its protest against the intervention of a priesthood to the correct conclusion of declining to have one and of leaving everything to the enlightened soul, in a state of inner grace.

The priesthood in other Protestant bodies is left in the absurd position of having no specific function. This ministry may "preach the word" and lead in prayer. Both of these functions, however, a layman may perform and the first he should perform, although he may lack rhetoric. The administration of the sacraments among Anglicans, the visitation of the sick, the thousand and one other tasks of a clergyman's life, are none of them so specific in function that the social function of a clergyman can be defined with that precision which is immediately possible in the case of a lawyer or physician.

To theological and philosophical leadership many clergy would offer no pretension—nor, in fact, is it any longer true that the local parson is normally the best educated man in the neighbourhood. Often a conventional education and a legalistic morality have even blunted that keen moral delicacy which would make him a sensitive guide and a patient educator. Too often dogmatically "he knows," blundering in where the wisest physician would fear to tread—an amateur constituting himself actually a danger in semi-mental cases. Like the old-fashioned bolus and black-pill doctor, he administers a predetermined, if vague and general, remedy for all spiritual diseases. If the result is unfortunate, the blame is held to lie with the patient, not with the revealed ethical dogma. The result is a treatment incredibly wooden and unexperimental.

Immense sums are devoted to maintaining this clerical profession. Yearly it is recruited by devoted men. And yet —certain supposedly sacramental and privileged functions arbitrarily reserved to the priesthood apart—there is nothing that is done by its members that could not be done with an elementary training by others. The distinctive function of the profession reduces itself to something painfully like the recitation of ritual by members of a caste—an act which, from the point of view of Protestantism itself, must be condemned as merely magical.

In brief, we must reach the conclusion that the clergy is a body of devoted men expending great energy upon performing no very specific function. That may explain the present failure of clerical education. The priesthood and ministry alike persist because early Protestantism, and especially official Protestantism, regarded any complete breach with the tradition of a clergy, however consistent with their own doctrine, as too revolutionary. As Lippmann says, Luther stood for the right to their Protestantism of folk whom he thought of as remaining good Catholics.

Catholicism, far more logically, insisted that, as the phrase goes, priesthood and sacraments should "come between man and his Maker"—that is, that man attains personal value, by identification with the enduring Reality, which is God, primarily as a true and spiritual member of a significant society, not as a self-sufficient individual enjoying, thanks to arbitrary grace, some inexplicable favouritism.

In England—if I may digress, in the discussion of the breakdown of this connection between psychological need and social organization, to mention the almost humorous idiosyncrasies of one country—we are left with the preposterous situation that the spiritual life of the Anglican Church is controlled by that section of it which is best able to gain the ear and prejudices of Parliament. This is a secular body of men probably half of whom are "decent fellows" enough, but who would not be called by their best friends religiously minded and who, almost certainly, would not hold their present positions had they ventured to drag religious issues into their election addresses. That section of the members of the Protestant Established Church of England (which numbers three and a half million persons energetic enough to enter their names on a roll in a country of forty millions) who are most confident that they have the ear of a body of legislators elected on a purely secular basis not unnaturally endeavour to cover over the absurdity of their position. This they do by persistently pretending that these legislators, many of them avowed agnostics, are unchanged in temperament since the days of Elizabeth, when they would have been fined in the magistrate's court if they had not attended church each Sunday. As Sir A. T. Wilson recently wrote in *The Times*, "the functions of Parliament" (in which an atheist but not an Anglican rector has a right to sit) "are as truly Christian as those of any ecclesiastical establishment."

The cure of souls by skilled men, urged in the Protestant bodies by such writers as Dr. Kirsopp Lake, is an immensely important practical task at the present time. Without debating what we mean by soul or psyche, it may be admitted that this task is no appropriate one for the medical professions as at present trained any more than for the family lawyer of an earlier generation. There is a task waiting for a profession and a profession waiting for a task. There are already waiting the resources and the prestige to make this profession play an eminent part in the practical service of humanity. At present the Protestant clergyman is forced into the unwholesome position of having little else to do concretely except to set a moral example to his flock—that is to say, to be a professional prig. So intolerable a function, with its spiritual pride, is one which many earnest young men very properly decline to assume.

No amount, however, of realistic revision of the education of the clergy to fit them as directors in mental distress can be beneficial, unless it is recognized that their first professional obligation as clergy is to truth and their secondary one only is to apply the medicine of Christianity as it may be shown experimentally to be most efficacious. No medical man today would admit to adhering to the principles of Galen beyond the warranty of clinical experience. Similarly a clergy is required which will be a profession first and a body of Christian dogmatists second. It may be that, with the growth of theological Liberalism, this position will actually develop.

Much of traditional Christianity, with its diffused asceticism and inculcation of god-fear and the terror of vague sin, is almost certainly unhealthy. Fortunately, Christian practice is often much better than traditional Christian principles. Much of the weakness of the Christian Church is due, not to the human part of the system, with its immense wisdom and its roots in the religions of a dozen countries—the Egypt of Isis and the Rome of the pontiffs as well as Babylonia, Hellas, and Judaea—but in the effect upon it of unreasoning reverence for the palladium of a miraculous revelation handed down by a salvation-hunting primitive Church. Catholicism would perhaps be all right were it not for this kind of Christianity.

A priesthood, however, cannot become merely a service of mental hygiene for spiritually sick individuals. In part its task is not only to emphasize the importance, for the soul's health, of correcting the demand for egoistical salvation—"the flight of the alone to the Alone": the Protestant religious individualism—by the sense for the community, but to prescribe the kind of community which man needs for his growth. A priesthood must point to a Church, whether that Church be the nation or the Communist Party or the Plymouth Brethren or the Society of Jesus. Again, much as a physician requires instruments for dealing with the body, so a drama is required as a legitimate form of prescription for inducing in some people harmony of soul. It is an ancient prescription and not necessarily an obsolete one. The trouble, however, with these myths is that they are too often substituted for the truth they should teach.

The fact remains that there is a need, not only for sensual love but also (although the distinction between the two is gravely over-estimated by philosophers) for ideal love and for a symbolic object of ideal love; and not only for human personal love, but for impersonal love. Until that love finds its object and satisfaction there will be no spiritual peace. At present there is not that peace. The priests have not found the way to it any more than the economic road to social health has been found by the capitalists or the political road to the good society by the power-hunters and privileged persons. The real question of today is where we are to discover the impersonal object of devotion which millions, a century or two ago, found in the Christian Church or in the triumph of their sect. God, the object of this love, has always had—except for a few mystics—to have, as invisible, some concrete manifestation. Sometimes—although condemned as anthropomorphic heresy—it has been an imagined figure, whether conventionalized by portrayal or not. Orthodoxly it is the figure of the Incarnate Word. Usually it has been, moreover, a figure in a movement which included the believer also. The Holy Spirit moved in the Communion of Saints.

Today the object of devotion has become, in most cases, the nation—or the state emotionalized as a nation and symbolizing the nation through its concrete organization and pageantry. This change over from ecclesiastical to secular religion is an outstanding historical fact of the age. What M. Benda calls the *trahison des clercs* is almost complete among ecclesiastics and men of letters alike. The Vatican alone offers some systematic resistance. The Church has become an aspect of national life and God a Being to whom attention is directed by the Churches as the final confirmation of the moral values embodied in the nation. As Treitschke wrote, "the Church is today indubitably poorer as a spiritual power than the state, or science or even economic organization." . . . It is ever more generally accepted that it is the state or nation to which a man should look for the fulfilment of his earthly immortality. Herr Hitler, in *Mein Kampf*, declares that civilization will fall "If men forget that they owe their higher existence, not to the ideas of a mad ideologue, but to understanding and ruthless application of age-old natural laws." One is left wondering whether it is to the Second Person of the everlasting and undivided Trinity, which was before the worlds were, that the distinguished lance-corporal is here animadverting.

It may be, however, that a reaction is setting in. The whole world machine creaks and shivers as its directors hesitate down which path it and civilization shall go. The priesthood of the present consists of the national leaders and the leaders of the parties in the new sense, Fascist and Communist. Our need is for a revival of the dispassionate and humanitarian tradition of the clerks—the men of science, learning, and spiritual wisdom.

The religious impulse by its very nature seems to require to satisfy itself by the formation of a brotherhood—a close brotherhood of persons moved by a like spirit. The explanation would seem to be that the religious impulse becomes emphasized in proportion to the intensity of the unsatisfied need for community life. This needed life promises an intimacy which, historically, civil society, with its large and heterogeneous association of human beings and its mechanics of government, does not provide. That has been looked for in the Church, which became emotionally unsuited to an unascetic age. It is now looked for in the emotionally unified nation; it may perhaps be looked for in some other, less parochial, community which we must seek to discover and define.

For modern man his sense of intimate dependence is not upon a nature which he no longer regards as animate, but upon his fellows; in them he finds his intimate satisfaction.

For primitive man the natural world, animate, was penumbral to the human community, all of a pattern with it, quite without sharp distinction. For modern man intellect and emotion may require him to protract his demand for human harmony into a demand for world-harmony. In some cases that means a demand for heavenly fatherhood; in so-called Southern Buddhism religion is able to dispense with the notion of the personality of God. Man's demand for everlasting rest, moreover, may lead to the requirement for an assurance which no limited human community can give, but only an unlimited, everlasting community. The cosmic and eternal element in religion will not be repudiated. It is the Athanasian God, autocrator, the Absolute, the non-human God who is ruler or life-force of the universe, who triumphs. The Incarnation is brought in as a corollary. It cannot stand alone, any more than any merely humanistic religion has been satisfying as a religion. All this is true. It is also, however, true that today a religion, which must offer a cosmic drama and a metaphysic of all reality, yet will find its centre in the craving for satisfaction in the love of the brotherhood, for assurance through love and faith, for enhancement of personality through the discarding of the restless strife of individual assertion.

Self-consciousness has done its work in the development of assertive individuality. No mere external incantation by social authority can banish that spirit of the ego, that lust for individual power, that ambition which we discussed in the last chapter. Only the slow recognition of the paradoxical rhythm of the emotional life can avail. Thanks to this rhythm the spirit of assertion, which seems to be that of life, exaggerated becomes a spirit of destruction and death, whereas the spirit of community, which seems to be the sleep of the individual, is a spirit of racial life and hence of personal life—a spirit necessary to the completion of the instinctive personality. For religion individualism is death—it is the taking charge by what Adler calls the power-impulse and Freud the death-impulse. But "death in the community" is life. This community, however, can be no mere megalopolis and artifact such as a modern, heterogeneous state.

This spirit of devotion to the community, whether Christian, Fascist, or Communist, is the core of the religious spirit, although religion may take many forms which conceal the fundamental nature of the human need which it satisfies. It would, of course, be entirely false to conclude that it is the religious spirit which moulds those communities that historically exist. On the contrary, it is precisely persons devoid of the religious spirit who are able to exploit communities inspired by that fraternal sentiment and to gain power over them. The community is frequently—almost normally— governed by those without a sense for community— politicians of the lesser breed. What, however, is true is that, without this religious spirit, the community breaks apart into a number of warring, self-seeking individuals. It is further true that the only fashion of preventing this egoistic anarchy spreading is the strength, increase, and protection of the religious spirit (in the sense in which I have here explained and used that term). To that task not only priests but statesmen are busily setting themselves today. Which of them are doing it wisely it is our duty to enquire. At least this is clear that twentieth-century politics is becoming a conflict of religions.

The conclusion of our quest into the nature of the instinctive life shows that the erotic desire and the craving for security against hunger and for security against deprivation of liberty in each case demand, for their stable satisfaction, co-operation with others in some aspect of friendly social life. They are specific and precise phases of a demand for loss of consciousness of the needs of self and for satisfaction in identification with otherness and the interests of others, which demand is the essential manifestation of religious desire. Consciously lust of acquisition or of power and eroticism may lead to violent self-assertion; but they are doomed to proceed from dissatisfaction to dissatisfaction and to increase of anarchy if pursued along individualist lines. Only along lines of identification of interest with that of the community—not calculatingly but intuitively—can they reach permanent satisfaction and repose.

This craving for community identification underlies, and is the profoundest form of, the social sense—of the feelings of conscience and duty and of the distaste of running counter to them. We must now face the question whether this craving for identification with the community which is for ever manifesting itself, when socially frustrated, in new religious form—this sublimated desire for a return to the protective mother in the guise of the community—is itself a permanent psychological quality of human nature or is, at least in its form as impulsive craving and not as demand for rational social organization, merely a sign of immaturity and of the childhood of the race. That issue now confronts us.

This, at least, we can say: the community that we desire should be shaped by reason, but it will be built and cemented by emotion. The taming of that emotion by reason is the task of political philosophy. That much the eighteenth century recognized. The recognition, however, of this part that will be played by the irrational is the chief feature that sharply distinguishes modern political thought from that of preceding centuries.

A political structure that is to last must satisfy the lasting requirements of what reason detects as human nature. This the eighteenth century knew. Human nature, however, contains non-rational demands—demands of lust, but also demands of loyalty and religion—demands which may be logically described, but which require sensuous or emotional satisfactions. The twentieth century has recognized this in a fashion unknown to Kant and with a fullness not possessed by the hedonism of Helvetius and Condillac and, still less, by the utilitarianism of Bentham and the Mills.

Our task has been to seek for a rational scheme that includes the full gamut of instinctive and irrational forces. Our task now is to indicate a system that satisfies those permanent demands of human nature that underly the conditioned play of historical and changing forces. This scheme must include the irrational, *but within the rational idea*; and this system must survey historical flux from the level of psychological permanence and natural law.

PART II

§ 1

Is the State the Community?

It is important to insist, in countries where the educational system supplies most kinds of information except that which is relevant to good living, that the scientific inventions and immense mechanical changes, which have made the last century and a half qualitatively distinct from all the preceding ages of human history, do in fact constitute a revolution in the environment of civilization which must be taken into account even in political organization. Consideration of these changes must enter into the judgement of the function and efficiency of political institutions or groupings. During forty millennia the human race was able to place to its credit fire, the plough and wheel, writing, printing, gunpowder, zero and the decimal system, the compass, and a few other major inventions. Developments in hygiene were impossible without the microscope, which depended on the development of the glass industry. Steam power could not be utilized on a large scale without improvements in the quality and scale of iron and steel work. Early locomotives crushed the inadequate steel rails, which were the best the foundries of the day could produce. In the last two centuries these difficulties have been overcome, with their effects on every field of production. Electricity has been harnessed. The miracle of Moses has been performed on the rocks and the whole earth smells with the petrol that gushes out. Absolutely accurate steel lathes, with all that their invention involves, are recent. The invention of the aeroplane is of yesterday.

This age is, as Mr. H. G. Wells has said, that of the

conquest of power. The extension of man's primitive tools, his own hands, and five senses, which has been proceeding with infinite slowness since he emerged from the ape stage, has now rushed forward so far that we are stupefied, each new invention rendering possible for the first time a series of others in geometrical progression. Medicine and man's control over his own body and life have been changed utterly by the discovery of anaesthetics. Perhaps, on full consideration, one of the most revolutionary changes from animal life, if one of the simplest, is the new power to regulate population—and the fact that now high officials of the British Medical Association are declaring that it is our social duty to practise this regulation.

Less is accepted as "given"—a brute fact of nature or consequence of the will of God, to which the only philosophical attitude is stoic resignation. More is thought of as changeable, malleable, controllable. Political and social institutions, even those which have hitherto remained unchallenged, are, at long last, regarded as something which man may modify for his own happiness and not merely as something to be accepted on tradition uncritically, since the memory of man runneth not to the contrary and the custom of the grandfathers is hitherto unbroken in the matter.

It has been the great work of such contemporary writers as H. G. Wells and Professor Charles Beard to insist that no part of human life can be torn away from the context, that the changes in the industrial world must have their repercussion in the social world and that, if politicians were intelligent men of vision, they would direct their minds to considering what the nature might be of the new social adjustments which will be required in the new civilization—in the new civilization, for example, of

IS THE STATE THE COMMUNITY?

mass production and of population stability or of population saturation. I am not here begging the question whether these recent mechanical changes are for the good. It may well be that they themselves urgently require better adjustment and co-ordination with human needs. I am asserting that states built in the Louis Quatorze style, and even the Parliamentary system of Mr. Gladstone, are not appropriate political instruments, unmodified, for dealing with the problems, such as they actually are, of the twentieth century. Civilization, in all its aspects, economic, political, cultural, religious, is of a piece integrally connected. Although this or that custom may represent what is technically called "a cultural lag," this lag cannot remain, without injury to the whole, in any part of civilization that is vital with the present interests of humanity.

In the political institutions, that are the necessary concomitant of any community life, such a "lag" in fact very markedly exists. It exists in the mind of the society that maintains those institutions. This inability mentally to catch up with the implications of contemporary innovations, although men in practice may have become habituated to these innovations themselves—the tendency to think politically in the terms of the nineteenth century and to do business in terms of the twentieth is one of the greatest obstacles to rational government. A generous recognition of the movements of scientific discovery and of industrial improvement, with their immense potentiality for increasing the power and even the happiness of man, should push men towards impatience with yokel provincialism, with tribalism, and with the attitude of those superior persons of leisure, the modern equivalent of the dilettante slave-owner, for whom culture is intimately connected with philology, but only soiled by the oily rags of engineering knowledge. Too seldom does this impatience make itself effective.

There is, fortunately, already a just indignation against the perversion of inventions in chemistry and machinery, with their prospects for human well-being, for the ends of destruction. When Colonel Lindbergh landed, after the first solo transatlantic flight, his machine, it is reported, was inspected with curious eyes by aeronauts with a view to judging . . . how far a machine of this type might be of service as a bomber. The words of Mr. Fairey, of aeroplane fame, were interesting when he welcomed Miss Amy Johnson on her return from Africa. "The cause of aviation never needed moral support so much as at the present time. Military aviation was the scapegoat of disarmament. Civil aviation was to be put under international control. . . . It was not science that had failed them but social science had failed to keep pace with it." In sum, most of our social life is confounded by a political system utilizing institutions entirely incongruous with our contemporary material civilization and out of joint with such a moral system as would be proper as the counterpart of such a civilization.

The revulsion, however, against this sinister stupidity of tribal jealousy, which reaches its peak in the subsidizing of the spying system and in the invention of weapons for the obliteration, in agony, of masses of the civilian population of other folk, leads by an understandable reaction to the making of a gospel out of the mere mechanical interconnection of the various parts of the modern world—to what may be called the internationalism of the telephone and of the Herzian wave, of which the tutelary deities are Edison and Marconi.

It seems little less than blasphemy that national animosities should pervert and befoul the Promethean

IS THE STATE THE COMMUNITY?

gifts of science. Thanks to new invention this entire small globe is being bound together—this globe which Mr. Post, the North American Indian and return gift of America for Columbus, can circumnavigate in eight days. At such a time, when the world is being united into one system of communications and of economic interdependence of the parts, it seems, as Sir Norman Angell has insisted, not merely obscurantist but the sign of a malevolent heart to perpetuate and emphasize political divisions or to set up the seventeenth-century state as a final unit of social organization and a climax of human communal evolution.

Other facts, however, are not so kindly to the internationalists in their disparagement of the old sovereign-state system. Mankind lives in many different societies with markedly different customs, standards of living, and standards of the value of human life. The rules of life in Copenhagen are not those followed in Ashanti. World organization, indeed, is the guarantee of world order. Law and order are high values for humanity. But they are not the only values. In the framework of civil order what affects men most is the stuff of social manners, the customs and standard of living of those among whom they live. An abstract cosmopolitanism, either Liberal or Communist, tends for its own reasons to ignore these differences. It does not, however, immediately affect my opinion of the standards of honesty, of honour, or of public spirit of the people of certain localities or my aversion to their vermin, dinner table, or style of amusements that trains in the modern world move very fast, aeroplanes yet faster, and that all finance is now being centralized on the International Bank at Basle.

Both tribalism and the antipodal position of cosmopolitanism are unsatisfactory. There is a perfectly legitimate feeling possible on behalf of local habit and standards—so long as it is not inspired by the malignant imperialist conceit which would impose these habits on others—against a steam-roller flattening out of humanity by internationalism. We have got to find our way through to an internationalism that does better justice by the notion of the local community. We have, also, got to find our way through to a true and intimate community—what Plato called "a community of pleasures and pains"—such as will alone satisfy our emotional life.

The world is becoming mentally and culturally more similar because the better and truer is driving out the local good and the temporarily true. Increasingly differences become, not as it were matters separating different animal species, but matters of taste and fashion, in which liberty and group autonomy are desirable. The process, however, is remotely far from completion. And the world in which we have to live is one in which it is incomplete. The need is for patience, realism, and a clear perception of the ultimate objectives. Unfortunately, however, according to some exceedingly well-informed judges, the next European war grows nearer and enters the field of immediate practical calculations.

The root of the difficulty experienced by most people, in forming their judgement on the need for international organization, lies in a failure to make an essential distinction. The man of sentiment objects to the interference of foreigners in the domestic affairs of his nation or in the curtailment, by external tribunals and councils, of the free-will and prestige of his sovereign state. The feeling here is the same feeling as that which most men entertain about their own liberty and which foments resentment

IS THE STATE THE COMMUNITY?

against unnecessary extensions of state law as an intrusion on personality. Feeling is, however, here checked by common sense. Unfortunately, the need for international regulation, although perhaps the more apparent of the two when a world war is threatening, is more spasmodic in its manifestations than that for national law. Hence the common-sense demand for this universal reign of law, internationally, demands more imagination and is less persistent than that for law observance at home. The need, however, for this reign of law, instead of international anarchy, is not the less there because it does not daily impinge upon the lay mind.

This need for the formal reign of law is yet a mechanical need, a matter of the external, administrative machinery of government, singularly little concerned with sentiment and spiritual values—any more than is the ordinary court of law. The choice of organization through which law shall be realized supposes the discovery of the proper area for efficiency of government in the "administrative community," which is not psychologically a community at all. And the answer—whether the chosen area be Belfast, Ulster, Ireland, United Kingdom, Empire, or world—must be given not in absolute terms, of some area appropriate for all purposes, but in terms of the specific function under consideration. "The end of government," as Woodrow Wilson said, "is the facilitation of the objects of society." The means for facilitating the world-wide mechanical objects of administration are sharply different from the means for developing the intimate community of common culture.

It is essential to distinguish very sharply between two

fields of government, the negative and the positive, which fields roughly correspond to the mechanical and the cultural. The negative field is the old, well-recognized field of government of the Whig philosophy. It is the hindrance of hindrances. Its object is to release the individual to develop himself, apart from all paternalist interference. It has no excessive claims for its own importance in a better world. As Paine said: "Society is produced by our wants and government by our wickedness." The positive field is sharply different. It is constructive. It is Platonic. It is concerned with the building up and nurture of men, thanks to legislation concerned for their education and well-being, physical and psychological. All social and welfare legislation comes under this heading; all those means of law and custom whereby the distinctive culture and spirit of a nation expresses itself; all policies for maintaining national standards of civilization and living.

The negative field of law and order is the appropriate field of international government, which rests on reason and not on the sentiment of this people or that. Here, if we are not to have chaos, *pace* Senator Borah, the interests of peace must take precedence of those of liberty, since no full liberty is attainable in a world which does not respect law. With time equity may modify the strict letter of treaty law—since often *maximum ius est maxima iniuria*: the extreme of legality is a refinement of injustice. In time the basis of power will be found actually in the will of the majority, instead of in that of certain great nations, armed like the barons of old. Even at present the nominal will of the majority (however influenced by the Great Powers) must, as a matter of due process in international government, be permitted to have sway. We are no more entitled to say in international

IS THE STATE THE COMMUNITY?

affairs than in national legislatures, with M. Clemenceau, "the voice of the majority is the voice of those least interested." The voice of the majority is that of those interested in the general peace as distinct from those partial to this or that particular gain. It is the formal condition of sound law. At present, however, peace and order are made and maintained by the will of the Great Powers. The interests of peace and order, moreover, are substantial, fundamental, and must be given precedence of all other considerations.

The positive field obviously appertains to domestic and local legislation—whether that of the Conference of the British Commonwealth, the Parliament of Britain, or the County Councils of Wales. Here everything depends upon the attitude of the people for whom the regulations are made, their own public opinion, their own notions of their welfare, their sense of kinship and common tradition, and little upon the logical deductions from the principles of peace and order. The law needed here is that appropriate for an intensive community with its own spirit, and not for an extensive society in need of the mechanics of government as a framework for civilized development.

It must yet in frankness be recognized that there is one overlapping field intimately concerned with the problems of order and force and yet intimately concerned with cultural autonomy, domestic spirit, and national personality: it is the field of national prestige and sovereignty.

Let us revert to the analogy of the personal prestige of the individual. This is not today usually thought of as being curtailed by the law. Indubitably, however, there was a time when the extension of the province of the law and of the king's power was felt to be a very serious infringement of the personal prestige of free fighting men of honour. The rule which has come to obtain is that if a citizen's personal egoism and prestige comes in the way of sound law, so much the worse for the prestige. The same rule must obtain as touching the "sacred egotism" of nations—which is a claim for a territorially limited, collective personality to have those privileges which are not accorded to the real personality of the individual. I write privileges and not rights, since there are no rights outside positive law or (according to the interpretation of the word "rights") outside sound morals. There are no indefeasible natural rights—not of physical persons, and certainly not of sovereign persons. The reign of law, and its logic, must be universal against such antinomian claims.

In the Middle Ages it appeared obvious that the prime allegiance of the small men, of the *arrière-ban*, was to the local baronage and not to the ultimate suzerain, whether emperor or national king. The villager's first duty was not to any remote, unsentimental national rulers, but the lord of his manor and to the soil of his county. To the man of Somerset the man of Devon was a foreigner; to the Cornishmen the wars on the Tweed were foreign wars for which they should not be taxed. In sixteenth-century Germany there were three hundred odd principalities, free cities, and minor dominions claiming, under the remote and nominal rule of the emperor, independence and a measure of sovereignty. It was left for the philosophers of that day, in reaction against this chaos, to demonstrate that there could be no such thing as a measure of sovereignty: that sovereignty was absolute

IS THE STATE THE COMMUNITY?

or nothing. The conclusions, however, drawn from this thesis were able to be the most various. In the nineteenth century, for Lee, Virginia came first; Virginia was sovereign; and still in the popular parlance of American State Governors their states are spoken of as sovereign.

To this day the contest rages concerning where sovereignty reposes in the United States constitution. Legists and students of federalism in North America are again today heard uttering the heretical words that there are in the United States greater and lesser sovereignties. League of Nations Mandate Commissions find that, in the matter of mandates, the awkward concept of sovereignty does not apply. The embarrassments of the doctrine of sovereignty, internal and external, as "entire empire" in certain territories, are numerous. But the steady trend of opinion is to relegate absolute state sovereignty, as it has traditionally been understood, to the same limbo as that to which the baron has been consigned whom the mediaeval lawyer, Beaumanoir, claimed was "sovereign in his own barony."

Here is not the place to explain how far the concept of sovereignty may be valid, within certain limits, as a notion of a function of final arbitration—as an essentially judicial function. In the executive sense, with its military analogies, as an authority "absolute, omnipotent, uncontrollable," and so in all countries, the doctrine is based upon abstractions and is practically misleading in the extreme. It is the legal crystallization of the notion of the state as an entity, being (as Bosanquet in a memorable phrase said) "not a factor within an organized moral world." In the words of Mussolini: "Everything to the State, nothing against the State, nothing outside the State." Hence (as Treitschke wrote in his *Politics*) "sacrifice for an alien nation is not only immoral but contradictory to the idea of self-maintenance which is the highest content of the State." It is not perhaps wonderful that Treitschke's work produced such a stir in Britain at the beginning of the War; but the transition from the urbane civic moralisms of Bosanquet to flamboyant jingoism is yet entirely logical. The doctrine of sovereignty is the legal crystallization of the notion of the nation as a super-person with a "group-mind" of its own, distinct from that mere bread-and-butter corporate consciousness which, not only the nation, but a thousand and one associations in the nation and transecting national divisions, possess. Sovereign Leviathan uncaught by a hook is *fera naturae*—a very dangerous animal. Here is the very heart of the trouble of the international anarchy— not in patriotic emotion or in a sense of cultural independence, such as any Welshman or Scotsman or Bavarian or Briton or Catalonian or Sicilian may feel, but in a sentiment made rigid and venomous by lawyers' metaphysic.

The late war and the iron necessities of military action tended to make the conquering nations fall victim to that very German philosophy against which their learned men had protested that the Entente Powers fought. In no small part the genius of the English Pluralists, G. D. H. Cole and Harold J. Laski, was responsible for restating Pluralism in a fashion so incisive as to give cutting force to the attack on the doctrine of the absolute sovereign state, "girt with armed might." This can be stated with the more impartial emphasis since the philosophic conclusions of Laski, with his "conditional anarchy," are by no means identical with the Platonic conclusions of this book. Laski prevented the reaction from the War from being lost in mere befogged disillusionment while rallying to the attack the fatigued followers of Liberal

IS THE STATE THE COMMUNITY?

individualism who had seen the author of *On Compromise*, John Viscount Morley of Blackburn, resign from the Cabinet in 1914 for reasons more pettifogging than splendid. Laski made the attack on the state—the old, absolutist, Austinian notion of the state—concentrated and real. Austin's conception of the community was intolerably mechanical and was ripe for attack.

If it be true—as it is—that the prime function of the state is to keep the peace, then (as Dante showed long ago) a form of state which is incompetent to keep, and which even threatens, the international peace is a bad and incomplete form of state. The organization only inadequately fulfils its function and marks an advance only just so far as state is more than city or tribe. And the lawyers' metaphysic, therefore, which justifies the imperfect organization as perfect is not even good metaphysic. On rigorous logical scrutiny a local or national sovereignty is a contradiction in terms. Only an international authority competent to sustain the universal reign of law can be fully sovereign in any sense in which it is profitable to retain this word.

It is the task of another book than this to enter into the subtle arguments of the jurists—jurists such as Kelsen, who spike the sovereignty-men on the point of the logic of their own arguments. In substance the argument of sovereignty and of the sovereign state as ultimate community, "society" itself, is an argument of war. That is the kernel of the whole matter. The wills of states can no more be supposed to be unalterably moral than the wills of individuals. The interests of states are likely to be asserted even more vigorously and egotistically than the wills of individuals: there is less legitimate field for spontaneous generosity. Their consciences are no more infallible than the consciences of individuals, unless one holds, with Thomas Hobbes, that the moral law should be abrogated when the state has spoken, and assumes that the opinion of the sovereign is the norm of what is moral. No pre-established harmony in the relations between sovereign states, themselves no part of any larger moral whole, must be assumed. It is, then, our attitude towards war which will determine our attitude towards the state as final community, and not conversely.

The statement seems to me well founded and unexaggerated that war is one of the major curses of mankind. Were it not true that many who would endorse this statement would also cheerfully invest money in armaments or patriotically help recruit a battalion of infantry, it might be dismissed as a platitude. Indeed, we have here one of those odd situations where human beings are prepared to entertain opposing opinions and unreconciled contradictions in their mind rather than confront the necessity for rejecting either a civilized ideal or a rooted tradition and loyalty. Most admit that they genuinely abhor war, but abhor still more being thought afraid: as in the fairy story, no one is prepared to declare that the prince with the invisible garments is naked lest he himself be thought an immoral man.

The legitimate affection for one's own place, even although suffused by yokel distrust of the foreigner and by conservative moralism, an affection characteristic of an earlier, rural age, tends to pass over into worship of the national Moloch. It has become a blind devotion and an imperative duty towards the idea, the phantasy, of the group which lives on so many square miles of earth—which devotion and duty to the "national idea"

IS THE STATE THE COMMUNITY?

are superstitiously supposed to be subject neither to conscience, civilized religion, nor natural law. That devotion only marks a step forward in so far as it is an advance beyond devotion to a smaller tribal Moloch. It is not yet a satisfactory and rational religion of social sacrifice.

There is one way of ending private wars. This is not to fight them and to compel others to desist from such arson against civilization. Unlike earthquake and drought, the issue is in human hands, to be wrought out through human organization. But to do this involves the destruction of the whole notion of the state as, not administrative instrument, but final community.

The route away from war is only to be found by smashing through the boundaries of the present sixty-odd sovereign states of the world. Peace will only be ensured by establishing a League or an International which, while not itself a unitary super-state, yet shall not be lily-handed with sovereign "rights," but shall deliberately infringe, in theory and practice, the sovereignty of private states, its component and subject members.

As in the fifteenth century, it was fought out and decided that prime allegiance lay to the national king and not to the local count or baron, so now, with a like clash of duties confronting us, it has to be decided that allegiance primarily lies to the ideal of an international civilization and to its concrete institutions, and only secondarily to Wales or India, France or Germany. The notion—Sir Austen Chamberlain's—of a "free assembly of sovereign states" must be converted into that of a sovereign assembly of free states. That sovereign power, as the realistic French have seen, must be armed as a means to making effective the will of the world federation, embodying the world community, to which allegiance will be due as once the Bavarian acknowledged allegiance due to the Holy Roman Empire, its Diet and administrators, or as modern Catholic archbishops acknowledge it as due to the Vatican with its international and devoted Civil Service. It should be armed unrestrictedly with every weapon known to man. If it is effective, it need never use these arms.

It was Immanuel Kant who said that men would establish a federal state of the world, as the only rational course, were they, not altruistic beings, but even devils, so be that they were intelligent devils. Kant was more right than he knew. The calculating self-interested individualist is readily enough an internationalist. The trouble is with the confused idealist who cannot bring himself to pay the cost which political science rigidly sets as the price of peace and who amiably hopes that, among good men, it may be possible both to eat the cake of national prestige and also to keep it. No great advance of law has been made save at the cost of what some section of people regarded as their personal honour. So the family feud, the private war, the duel have been abolished with their "points of honour": so will be abolished the private war of nations, subject to world organization and the reign of law. Those who foment dissension and secession will be stigmatized as criminal persons and traitors: they will be as much guilty of rebellion as were the Southern States of America.

The requirements of the League are the establishment of direct relations, including taxative relations, between itself and the democracies of the countries members of it—just as in 1918 Wilson appealed to the German people over the head of the Kaiser's Government; the establishment of the majority principle in legislation; and the establishment of provision for punitive measures against

IS THE STATE THE COMMUNITY?

rebellious national sovereignties—measures such as, in 1861, the American Federal Government took against member states endeavouring to secede. I see no reason why it should not guarantee the issue, perhaps from Basle, of a stabilized international currency. The League requires an Alexander Hamilton. Further, there must no longer be permission for states to "take the law into their own hands." In the eye of international law the ultimate ethical justification of action—let us say that of Japan against China—is a secondary matter to be adjudicated at a later stage. The primary matter for any court is that action shall be only by due process of law and that any state adopting self-help and infringing the process of law is a criminal corporation. To abet such an infringement is itself crime.

We require, in brief, the re-establishment, after a modern and federal model, of the two-millennia-old Roman Empire—the Empire that was, in Dante's phrase, "especially good because peculiarly one," competent to give and maintain the *pax Romana*. We need to recover from the nationalist folly of the last century and from the anarchy of the last four centuries with their "balance of power"—itself now unbalanced. Metternich and Alexander of Russia were not all wrong: how far they were wrong we shall see in the next chapter. It is not difficult to see upon the will of what Powers the establishment of that *pax mundi* depends.

The establishment of these things may be remote—these harsh guarantees of peace and law. War is not remote. It is, as Treitschke said, an ever present medicine for mankind diseased—but not as Treitschke meant it. It is a black draught mankind will go on being compelled to swallow till, out of its agony, it learns wisdom. Our choice is whether we will adopt the harsh safeguards before the experience of another war, or only after it. Is the United States of Europe, is Mr. Wells' age of the international transport control, is the road-controlling new Roman Empire to be built—built by the will of the predominant Anglo-Saxon powers and the U.S.S.R. —before another world-war, or after it?

If all the dead of the late war started marching past the Cenotaph at a brisk pace, four abreast, some November day, they would still be marching past a month later. The next war, however, will not be as the last. Major Lefebure, in his excellent *Scientific Disarmament*, has pointed out a few of the possibilities. Disease germs can now be distributed from the air and careful culture can enable the more delicate germs to withstand exposure until their work is done. Dr. Ewald Banse, in Germany, has noted that fact. "Reports have been called for by the League of Nations, 1922, from international bacteriologists of great reputation, and they have established that this method of warfare has great and horrible practical possibilities." A few walnut-bombs of poison gas can flood the streets of any city and no adequate scheme of defence has yet been discovered. The Earl of Halsbury alleges, in a recent article, that "one single bomb filled with modern asphyxiant gas would kill everyone in an area from Regent's Park to the Thames." The gases available are of different varieties, some more suitable for the asphyxiation of civilian populations, others of a less pleasant variety for use at the front. Apart from such mechanical toys as tanks able to leap obstacles, the American Army has, at its plant at Edgewood, facilities for the production of 800 tons of poison gas a day or, in other words, Edgewood is able to produce in two months as much gas as the Germans used throughout the late war. Of one poison gas, diphenyl-chlorarsine, Professor

IS THE STATE THE COMMUNITY?

J. B. S. Haldane says: "Soldiers poisoned by these substances have to be prevented from committing suicide—others went raving mad and tried to burrow into the ground to escape from imaginary pursuers."

A good war, as Nietzsche said, hallows any cause. There is no reason to suppose that any soldier, embarked upon a war for the defence and honour of his country, would turn back when his objective—like Jerusalem to the Crusaders—was in sight, because of a certain lack of humanity in the means. The safety of the national state is by tradition the criterion of morals—just, indeed, as for Machiavelli the interests of an Italian township constituted the criterion of the laws of God Almighty. The use of these means is all a matter of how much time has been permitted to elapse for the emotions of war to warm up. The clumsy *flammenwerfer* of the last war will be outdistanced by more perfect instruments for attaining an objective.

If the immediate moral obligation is to construct a new social framework and to reject the inconsistent claims of older community forms, the question arises how practical effect can be given to this moral imperative. Only a few will argue that the most successful methods of resistance are those of non-violent non-co-operation adapted by Mahatma Gandhi. It might, again, be that all those people who are in a position to do so would merely leave a state which did not provide that peace which is the prime function of the state institution to provide and would emigrate to a state which did provide peace. The Moloch worshippers would be left to carry on their bloody rites by themselves without any undeserved countenance being given to their rational and moral disreputability. There is nothing at all absurd in supposing that an Erasmus, a Voltaire, a Goethe might have pursued this course, however much it might infuriate the bulls of Bashan. It may be argued that it is not necessary to meet mass madness by heroic abnegation, although, before the tradition of human ritual sacrifice is exposed for the nauseous barbarism that it is, this may be necessary in many cases. It is, however, probable that more active and constructive measures than mere abstinence will be required. A good war against war hallows any measures. If to fight is natural to man, he had better die fighting for something that does some permanent good.

The only route across this Hindenburg line of embattled folly, short of the civil war of which Mr. MacCarthy writes, is to have the courage to smash the entire instrument—not the brute weapons of war, but the organization which renders almost inevitable the use and perfection of those weapons: to smash the sovereign national state and to decline pugnaciously to define patriotism in terms of it.

The argument used on behalf of war by distinguished soldiers in the popular Press—that is to say, the representative argument—is that all nature is a field of struggle and in this field man cannot reserve to himself a secluded and peculiar ground. One soldier recently, in the *Daily Herald*, went to the length of conceding that the bees were social animals and that the individuals of the species did not fight among themselves. He pointed the moral that man also, a social animal, fights guided by the instinct of the herd. That hives do not fight between each other is an item omitted in drawing the moral from this lecture on natural history. Man, he continued, is, blindly and instinctively, a fighting animal on behalf of his group, his tribe, his nation. This pugnacity, the foundation of much heroism, is ineradicable. The only modification possible, he urged, was that certain perverted persons may satisfy their pugnacity and individual

IS THE STATE THE COMMUNITY?

aggressiveness by fighting against their nation instead of with it—these people are called conscientious objectors.

There is a large measure of truth in this argument. In beginning a recent article I wrote, "I like war." Immediately all the pacifists, without reading further to enquire what war, took up their pens to write denunciation. It seems to me quite pointless to deny that national war is attractive in its initial stages. Besides the brave music of a distant drum or the nobler sense of duty performed, the tension of a fight is to many men a pleasure so deep that their blood surges and their very intestines respond.

The lives of most men and women under peace-time conditions are intolerably monotonous and most attempts at break-away from this monotony are contrary to convention, immoral, if not criminal. War raises human experience to a new and exhilarating level of experience, while patriotism applauds the new conduct as not only moral but heroic. Even the latent criminal in man wakes up to find himself socially useful and morally justified: the great lead weight of civilization is lifted a little. The heart beats faster: the pulse is quicker. The unsatisfied craving of man, in an artificial civilization and in a heterogeneous society, for community is satisfied. Under the stress the heterogeneous state acquires a common purpose; the unity of the nation manifests itself; all march, act, and sacrifice as one. It is a moral revelation—at first. Unfortunately, the expense of war, not only in mendacity, barbarism, and moral atrocity, but in the aftermath of human misery, is too heavy for the benefit conferred by this moral elation, especially when moral alternatives may be discoverable by minds not wedded to sentimental stereotypes and *idola tribus*.

What matters is that men should fight about something

that matters. To this statement, of course, the religious objector, the passive pacifist, will object. For him a man is not entitled to do evil that good may come, nor is a man entitled to commit manslaughter with aggravation at the expense of a morally innocent individual because his country, or all the kings and governments that have ever lived, tells him to do so. Nor will he admit that a man who serves in the ranks of the armies of a morally guilty nation is a morally guilty man. He will enquire how we may indict a nation; appeal to common sense concerning the individual army ranker's guilt; and ask, with Kant, what impartial judge there has been who may say that this or that nation is guilty or unjust when impartial tribunal there is none?

I admit that this kind of objector may stop war in his own country by jamming the military machine. I consider that this course is a legitimate alternative. It corresponds to the temperament of some people, natural passive resisters. Man may be naturally a fighting animal as he is naturally a sexual animal, but civilization has brought both instincts under considerable rational control: that is what civilization is for. For some people to resist warlike preparations as individuals is more natural than to co-operate to repress private war by organization. Others, however, have another temperament than that of the Friends.

It does not seem to me that human life is absolutely sacred, whether pre-natal or post-natal. The issue seems to me to be one not of taboo, but of the reasoned social good. There is a high moral obligation to the exercise of humanity in conduct; but each act must be put into the perspective of the whole. The present issue is that of destroying the institution of private war between nations. Already the Kellogg Pact has done one thing—the one thing it has done; and that formal and legalistic. It has declared that wherever there is a war there is a guilty party, a criminal. There is no war legitimate for all parties. This is entirely consonant with the old scholastic doctrine of the just war. The present task is to give sanction to that pact by demonstrating with the requisite force that crime does not pay. That sanction is a radically different thing from criminal aggression and immoral force. If attacked, Peace will defend itself.

Both courses, pacifist and sanctionist, appear to me to be concurrent, since the effectiveness of coercive pressure depends upon the prevalence of the moral conviction of the iniquity of national war as a means no longer justifiable by any ends in civilized progress. Quietism, alone, however—which permits the pirate state freely to punish its victim until such time as the quietist spirit comes to pervade the conqueror—is not enough. Avoidable injustice is tolerated. Every man—quietist and activist, not treating their activities as mutually exclusive, but each being complementary—must be mobilized for the single task of rebuilding this international order, this new Roman peace. Such a peace will mark a vast advance in the war of reason to dethrone fear.

War by the nation was justified in building up the nation when the nation—and not the province—was becoming the unit of civilization. War by international authority is still justified, in an historical ethic, now that the cause of civilization is international and the nation itself has sunk into the position of a province. What is not justified is war which perpetuates, for the local interest of this or that individual nation, an anarchy inimical to the interests of the rest.

The reign of law must prevail over the widest area of civilization. And it must be enforced. The policeman does not now murder the thief, whatever the sheriff may once have done by way of rough justice. So, too, the threat of united international action, if foreign secretaries are taught by popular will their obligation not to finesse, will be adequate if its effectiveness is certain. Until it is certain, probably international action will have to go on taking the shape of mass murder against atavistic and recalcitrant groups. How soon foreign secretaries are to be taught this lesson rests not with remote cabinets or governments but with the common elector. Governments receive their mandates to defend the interests of their nationals—as the nation itself persistently understands that interest—from those nationals themselves. Theirs is the responsibility if governments insist that men corporately cannot practice a rational self-abnegation that is laudable individually. It may be that, by now, these nationals are beginning to decide that state prestige maintained, as some absolute matter, against international judgement, frustrating the rational purpose of the state as organ of peace and order and fomenting the chief of human plagues, is a prestige tawdry, detestable, and infamous.

The state is, then, an administrative organization at a certain stage in the development of civil order. It came into being in the fifteenth century, was named by the Italians at the turn of that century, came of age at the Peace of Westphalia, and then acquired its heralds and court philosophers. There was a time when it was not; and there will be a time when it will not be in its present sovereign form. Against the background of the civilization of past centuries the organization has adequately fulfilled

IS THE STATE THE COMMUNITY?

its function. We have now in this age to ask ourselves whether its present mechanism does not crush down smaller areas more intimately corresponding to the regions of genuine common life, while being inadequate in scope to fulfil the more external and universal functions of maintaining peace and rational order in civilization.

In relation, turning outwards, to this larger task the present state is rationally justified so far as its citizens choose to strengthen it, use it, and subordinate it to the purposes of the building up of a system of international order as broad as civilization and to the purposes of the realistic enforcement, by state power in the world federation, of international justice. So far as that end is in fact served I have no objection to military service, large navies, or other displays of power. There is one test: the advance of an effective international order.

In relation, turning inwards, to the genuine community, which is a thing of the soul, not mechanical, states are shells of which the use is to protect but not to crush. Mere administrative areas should be, at one level in that hierarchy of administrations that extends up from rural district to world federation, of like extent with the cultural areas. At this level the administrative area should have charge of all those concerns of government that affect the *moral* and manner of life of a people. At least, the administrative area should not be so drawn as to destroy cultural autonomy. The cultural area need (and should) not be a sovereign area, but no sovereign area should rob, by its powers, the cultural community of its free vigour. The love of power of the individual, be he dynast or common man, becomes suicidal if it sublimates and concentrates its hopes of glory upon the prestige of a state in such a way as, not only to wreck the rational order of the great society, but to crush down the liberty of the true community.

The state, however, is not generally understood to be just the administration, the civil government. The state is, indeed, an organization and instrument of the social will and idea—whether the predominant will of a nation, or of a conquering power, or of a baronage or oligarchic group. Mr. Leonard Woolf, in his excellent book, *After the Deluge*, insists that the state, regarded as the aggregate of the agencies of government, shall be judged, as we judge a sewage farm, in terms of the efficiency with which it performs its function. This is the traditional Whig attitude. This, however, is not entirely adequate in view of one meaning generally attached to the word "state." The state is a concept which lives a Jekyll and Hyde existence, passing from the one rôle to the other in a roseate cloud of philosophic profundity and legal opacity.

In one rôle this state is the superior, it is authority, it is government: as such it speaks. If, however, we enquire what entitles this voice to speak and why the fiat of government should be obeyed, for example, when it declares war, on other than utilitarian grounds or after such examination as we would usually give to the pronouncements of the functionaries who represent popular opinion, the state then assumes another rôle. It becomes the nation, the group with a personality, mind, will, and spirit of its own, the population civilly organized, the inhabitants and their country, inspired by tradition and purpose. The word "state" might quite well be dropped out of the language of politics and political science would not notice the difference, although the theology of politics would be gravely affected. The words "government" and "people" cover the field. The purpose of the

IS THE STATE THE COMMUNITY?

corporate people is, however, more than that of a sewage farm, despite Mr. Woolf.

If, then, we ask whether the state is that community of which we are in search, as the desideratum of social construction, the answer must be "no." The state as government clearly is not the community. As a group of administrators with their area of administration it is, even on the merely external and mechanical side, an incomplete form of social organization.

If states are to be regarded, as the Webbs have demanded, just as areas of administration, then they are satisfactory only in the context and setting of larger areas alone competent to deal with modern trade, transport, hygiene, finance, and law-maintenance requirements and more nearly coterminous with the integral area of modern civilization.

A state, however, in popular speech, is much more emotionally, if it is much less territorially, than such an area—at least, it has recently become so. The Hapsburg Empire of Metternich was an administrative area imposed by the authority of an upper few and held together by an immemorial tradition and by the calculations of political advantage. It reposed upon the utilitarian recognition of the necessity of peaceful government. The modern state, however, attracts sentiment, as well as calculation, to its support by presenting itself as a psychological or spiritual unity.

The state presents itself as a community, with a rational claim as such to autonomy, by identifying itself with the nation. The nation can have a quality of spirit which the state, whether as government or as mass of folk held together by government, justified as a utilitarian necessity owing to human perversity and need for guidance, quite lacks. The heterogeneous state, however, as such—the state, for example, of the Hapsburgs, the Holy Roman Emperors, or of the Roman Emperors, or even of the Kaiser-i-Hind, the last of the Caesardoms—is not a community, any more than Babylon was, for Aristotle, a *polis*. The state is a clear part of the externalities of coercive administration. As the need for coercion may perchance disappear in part, replaced by the authority of voluntary organizations, in part the state, as an organ fulfilling a utilitarian and temporal function, will wither. If it is to the area normally embraced within state frontiers that we are looking for a community, seeking to discover it occupying this same territory exactly or approximately, then it is to the nation that we must look. When we talk about the state we talk about an instrument, not a community—an instrument in need of reshaping in a fashion more consonant with present requirements and the efficient fulfilment of its function.

A community, however, instinctively we demand. It is the desired object of the emotions of sympathy and self-subordination. Upon the discovery of this object depends the advance of our civilization towards economic and political justice; towards the proper satisfaction of the instincts; and towards power of personality, acquired in and through the community. That community we have still to seek.

§ ii

Is the Nation the Community?

Persistently, in the contemporary world, explicitly or tacitly, one is confronted with the claim of the nation to be the final and morally satisfying form of human community. Usually this amounts to the claim that the nation is always right and that, when it is wrong, it is to be treated as right. This opinion is sustained by the support of many eminent philosophers. Its more thorough examination must now be undertaken.

The first objection with which we are confronted, in that study of social relations which is politics, is that there is, in a sense, no such thing as human nature and no such corporate being as humanity towards which men may feel loyalty. As de Maistre said, there are Frenchmen, Englishmen, Germans, but none who are just bare men. As for Man, "if he exists, it is without my knowledge."[1] The answer to de Maistre is that, in the same sense, there are no such persons as Frenchmen, but only individuals. The sense of nationality is, nevertheless, a reality, although nationality itself can scarcely be defined, as Renan discovered, save in terms of the sense of nationality. 'Tis thinking makes it so. Certainly there is the historical experience of a common tradition, but sometimes the sense for it flows merely from the association of individuals or groups, for example, of immigrants, with the stem of such a tradition.

The sense of nationality is natural and healthy as the expression of a certain like-mindedness in a group. It has fruits in co-operation, self-respect, and subtleties of

[1] *Œuvres* (ed. 1815), I, p. 68.

character. The claim of a people to cultural autonomy is part of the proper development of human liberty. The sense of nationality only becomes immoral, let us repeat, when the "we-group," constituting a certain nation, regards itself as subject to no higher moral claims; proclaims the nation no part of any larger moral whole; asserts that the interest of this or that particular group is deserving of a paramount and unquestioned allegiance; declines to offer any justification for its claims in terms of some broader rational purpose; and abrogates the universality of the moral law.

Briefly, the problem of the community as nation assumes the shape: How to destroy, not only the current, Austinian theory of the state, but also the *sacro egoismo*—the sacred egotism—of the nation, without destroying sound civic sense and the emotion of loyalty in the performance of public duty?

Nationalism is the modern counterpart of tribalism; its most customary (but not invariable) characteristic is a belief in the common blood of the whole group. This belief is its characteristic myth.

It is, however, superficial to brush aside this myth as contrary to demonstrable fact and merely superstitious. It issues in the practical accomplishment of a necessary social work, the binding together of the members of large groups. In the East it has probably still a work to accomplish, although, with its threat of revolution and boycott, it will be one which Western administrators and traders must necessarily be inclined to look upon with very mixed feelings. In the West it is already changing form. Whatever may be the situation in France, Italy, and Germany, in the United States and in the British Commonwealth confederation the sentiment of common blood is being replaced by the sentiment of common

IS THE NATION THE COMMUNITY?

tradition and, in the latter case, even by the sentiment of common outlook and purpose. There is, however, underlying even this more attenuated feeling a consciousness of common race and of common culture. That consciousness is, in fact, the basis of much of such public spirit and devotion to the common good as exists. It can be effectively appealed to where self-sacrifice is demanded as a condition of great social reforms.

It is not true that a Canadian has the same feeling of unity with an Abyssinian which he has with an Australian, nor is he prepared to make the sacrifices (perhaps not unlimited in either case) on behalf of the Abyssinian which, in a grave emergency, he would be prepared to make in the case of the Australian. The Liverpool traders dependent on shipping may regard Southampton with jealousy; the Englishman may suspect the economic penetration of the Scot, and the Scottish navvy that of the Irish navvy; the textile manufacturer of Massachussetts may fear the textile manufacturer of Alabama. But this jealousy and fear is not of the same quality as that which inspire the German or American in relation to the Chinese or the English settler in Kenya in relation to his negro co-subject. This feeling, however, is similar to the fierce enmity which once inspired the relations of the seafaring men of Dover towards those of Lowestoft or the citizens of Venice towards those of Genoa, or Spaniards towards English in the days when it was seriously bruited about that the English were sometimes born with tails. The old sentiments of community and of enmity are present, but they operate through new groupings. Our problem is: what new groupings?

Despite Geneva, Locarno, talk of European customs unions, and the contempt with which the idea of nationality is regarded by at least some writers, such as

Tagore, in the East, it certainly cannot be said that the problem of nationality and of national envy is solved and left behind. This problem has burdened Europe since the international revolution of the Jacobins and the international Caesarism of Napoleon dissolved into the popular consciousness of the national state and into loyalty to the eagles of its legions. In some part any answer to the problem of nationality must indeed involve an answer to the more fundamental problem of race which, as it were, projects that of the nation on to a larger screen. Let us, for a moment, consider the racial problem, in order to get perspective, before reverting to the national one. Let us look at the problem writ large.

M. André Gide reports how in the French Congo he saw, "escorted by guards armed with five-thonged whips, a line of fifteen women and two men, tied by the necks with the same rope," hostages for villages which had not sent their quota of porters demanded by the administration as part of the work of industrializing Africa for the benefit of civilization. It may, however, be argued that what is here at work is economic cupidity rather than racial callousness. Although the French Republic does not today (the Capetian monarchy did) subject its white subjects to corvées and press-gangs, at least it treats them all, white and black, strictly impartially when it conscripts them and drills them in European barracks. Colour prejudice shows itself, not here, but when a responsible British military officer can insist that the first thing to understand in Africa is that the African native is not a human being, in the way that

IS THE NATION THE COMMUNITY?

a European is one, but an animal (I quote from a personal conversation).

Part of the explanation of this attitude is probably to be found in the moralism of the English, which stifles that aesthetic sense that enables the Frenchman to appreciate the varieties of human custom and negro gifts in music, art, and imagination and which induces the Englishman or American to regard those who differ from him in moral behaviour as mere spawn of Satan. So far as this is the explanation, the trouble is remediable by education.

Apart from this remedy and for suggestions which take the shape of pointing out the necessity for bringing non-European peoples into co-operation, whether as citizens with citizen rights in predominantly European states or as associated powers in a world-federation, the core of the racial question, including the question of intermarriage, remains one of the problems of politics at present almost entirely unresolved. A useful anthropological and biological literature is being accumulated, not least about Africa, which may some day give a clue. At present, apart from the resolute equalitarian of the Communists—not so resolute, as touching the negro, where Russo-American relations are concerned—and the equally resolute attitude of the South African speaker who recently explained that the black should not be educated since God made the black to serve the white, no firm answer has been given to our queries about what action should be taken to end this impasse of racial relations. Almost one is tempted to suggest that the Workers' Travel Association had better arrange tours of adolescents with a view to group marriage.... Some day it will have to be considered whether the American method of the melting-pot will not only have to be tried between nations, but also between races—let us say between

A PREFACE TO ACTION

Portuguese and Moor, blackamoor and West African negro. A philosophical essay waits to be written on the beneficial functions of the immoral in history.

Despite, however, the obstinate biological kernel a large section of the racial problem is not so difficult of solution. It is surrounded by economic and cultural questions which admit of separate analysis. On the one hand there is the fear of competition from those maintaining a lower standard of living, a fear which is rational and entirely justifiable. The answer lies in the regulation of competition and the raising of backward standards of living. On the other hand, there is a preference, proper if intelligent, for the manners and customs of the people of our own neighbourhood as of old and tried acquaintances. Its intelligent basis is (although less cogent) the same as the preference for the customs of the group of our own deliberate choice. A group, even of a lower civilization, of which the members do not believe in their own common outlook, contribution and purpose can have no disciplinary, no educational, no moral effect upon its members. In so far, however, as the Northern or Southern European rationally believes that his customs are actually more civilized and better than those of the Bantu, it is his duty to preserve them and not to pursue a course of action which reduces the customs of the world to the terms of their least common factor. It is also his duty, with intellectual honesty, to detect the significance of the contributions made by other peoples.

Let us, at this point, revert to the simpler problem we have set ourselves. Intermarriage, the habit of co-operation based on educated comprehension of outlook,

IS THE NATION THE COMMUNITY?

perhaps a common business language such as Britain provides to English and Welsh, moderate the tension and jealousy of nations as blood groups. Mixed races, such as the British and Americans, and mixed peoples, such as those of the British Commonwealth, should especially be able to view these problems coolly. The separable facts remain to be considered of attachment to a common culture and to the common character and *moral* that go with it—the very life of community sentiment—and the economic interests of areas of like standard of living. Let us take the cultural problem here. The economic problem is discussed at a later stage in this book. In part it results from a sense of unity in competition against foreigners, who are not "us," which has been induced in the body of the workers of a country for reasons that are not economic.

The ultimate moral values of man do not rest finally on his reason but on certain direct intuitions which yet, like an ear for music, may be strengthened or weakened by education and environment. The direct pleasure in the approval of our neighbours, the desire—which is somewhat different—to be at one with our own people, is something which can be built up or weakened by a corrosive individualism. If it is destroyed, if we come normally to regard our neighbours as unpleasant people and their good opinion as of negligible importance, save as less inconvenient than their threats, there is no purely rational ground which can be adduced why we should seek their good.

Public spirit reposes on this community sense. It is, indeed, reinforced when we have a deliberate belief that the specific customs of our community are choiceworthy. Mere conscientious performance, however, of public duty has no direction until we have an intuition where duty lies. As a matter of fact, the sentiment which, in fact, does today most readily evoke such willingness to behave in a fashion dictated by altruism and public spirit is precisely the nationalist sentiment.

I here use the word "nationalism" in its least objectionable sense, not as an aggressive chauvinism, but as a strong, patriotic sense of obligation to those of the same nation as oneself. Admittedly the chief difficulty of nationalism is that the milder sentiment tends to pass into the aggressive one. The question is whether the weakening of this sentiment can end in anything but a selfish, anarchic individualism, and the destruction of that community sense which is, precisely, one of the chief foundations of a sound and socialist morality.

It may, of course, be said that what we require is, not a local patriotism of village or nation, but a patriotism of humanity and a sentiment of internationalism. That sentiment is rational but, at present, weak. The question is whether it will be best to treat it as an alternative to nationalism or as a rational extension of nationalism. It is easy to denounce the second course as "hedging" and I do not doubt that most of the worse foes of internationalism are people who are proud to be national patriots. That should not prejudice a decision. Local patriotism is too immense a force and too instinct with tradition for its moral significance to be dismissed lightly.

British citizens occupy an historical position of singular detachment for forming a judgement on this matter. There is the nationalism of the French Canadian habitant and of the Dutch Boer; there is the national patriotism of the Welshman who remembers the hills of Harlech and of the Scotsman who recalls Bannockburn and those who with Wallace bled. It is true that the Scots of the Lothians had racially more in common with the Saxon

IS THE NATION THE COMMUNITY?

foeman than with a Strathclyde Welshman such as Wallace. It is true that an Adams of Massachussetts or the descendants of Randolph of Roanoake or of Taylor of Caroline have more racially in common with the men of Devon and Lincolnshire than with the van Rensselaers of New York or with some modern immigrant—Mr. Rosenzweig of Chicago or Mr. Cortesiani of Schuyler, N.J. (In the next street to me here in London a Mr. Cremonesi, cobbler, proudly writes under his name the word "British.") Instinctively we feel that these are difficulties of anthropological pedantry—the nation feels itself to be one. There are, of course, such things as Scottish and Welsh blood nationalism. The Germans of Minnesota had a blood nationalism which was a source of anxiety to the American Government in 1917. The "nation," in the American sense, is something of an artifact and periodically shows itself as such. The "nation" in the Scottish sense is habituated to co-operation in a wider patriotism yet, periodically, is not beyond showing restiveness.

Let us then assume that when we refer to "nationalism," we do not mean sentiment for the nation in the narrowest and most purist sense which must lead us into endless difficulties. Such pure nationalism or "race-theory" in the British Commonwealth must speedily lead to sedition and treason. The British Commonwealth, almost alone among political units, is necessarily international. Even, however, the contemporary junker or Hitlerian is a Pan-Teuton or an exponent of some larger Nordic unit of common culture. Let us assume that the basal concept of the British Commonwealth is right and that the basis of patriotism is something able to embrace federated nations in what Mr. Wyndham Lewis happily calls an "Anglo-Saxony," which is part Celt and not a little

Dutch and French. Incidentally, such an Anglo-Saxony cannot exclude reference also to its Western Republican half, as distinct from its Eastern Monarchical half, and to the people of New England and of the Old Dominion.

We have now to ask ourselves whether this sentiment of patriotism, thus broadly understood, relates itself to a genuine community and is to be encouraged by those who aspire to build a world marked by a strong sense of public spirit or whether it is to be cursed and anathematized.

One difficulty must immediately be cleared away. Once this patriotism of a broader nationalism, by fusion with state-worship, becomes an imperialist sentiment authorizing coercive rule over people of other nationalities it forfeits claim to moral respect. The stock instance, so far as the British Commonwealth is concerned, is India.

The British Government in India is as foreign as was the Austrian Government in Italy prior to the Italian War of Emancipation. No one will be found to maintain that this Austrian Government, for all its legal claims, was not foreign, however many natives of Italy may have been counted among its officials or supporters. The British Government is more foreign. The imperial rule of the House of Guelph-Windsor in India dates from less than a century ago. The House of Hapsburg held rule, off and on, for four centuries in Italy. The British Raj deposed its predecessor, by violent military action against the Moghul dynasty, which was once suzerain and host of the British. The House of Hapsburg succeeded entirely legitimately and peacefully to the authority of its imperial predecessors. The Austrian rule was a mild rule, and no profound bar of religion or of race divided Austrian officials from Italian subjects. The princely houses of Austria and Italy intermarried. The British has been a mild rule, responsible for many beneficial reforms, but a profound difference of race and religion separates the British civil servant in India from his Indian colleagues. The princely houses of Britain and India do not intermarry.

The British Government, as represented by the British Viceroy and officials, the rule of the Kaiser-i-Hind, however benevolent it may be, has been in racial sentiment and in mental outlook self-consciously different from the surrounding population, and is an entirely alien government. That is what is wrong with it. Such an artificial inorganic relation of governors and governed has been of the essence of *tyrannis*, however benevolent that rule may be to subjects who order themselves lowly and obediently. That is what, by every principle of sound government, it should not be.

I am not enamoured of nationalism, in India or elsewhere, as a basis for demands for indefeasible rights to independence or for absolute political sovereignty. These indefeasible and absolute rights of nations to refuse to admit common obligations seem to me to be the dangerous superstitions of the lawyers of a past age, made yet more dangerous by popular passion and by the ignorant suspicion by each people of its neighbour. As democracy becomes mature it must recognize the need for an internationally organized world. Indian democracy, however, is not mature—it is scarcely existent. Indian nationalism, as it tardily achieves consciousness through the medium of limited articulate groups, is naturally aggressive. That is to be expected. International organization must itself repose upon consent—the consent of stable nations and

A PREFACE TO ACTION

of their politically active representatives. Internationalism presumes a reasonably satisfied nationalism.

It is, of course, fully possible for a people to consent willingly to an alien administrative rule, preferring good government to self-government. So it was that the provincials of Spain and of Dalmatia submitted to Rome. Rome, that great race-mixer which granted to all the right and fact of intermarriage, in return took from Spain and Dalmatia Roman Emperors—which is more than Westminster has yet done from Delhi. It is not, however, possible for a government reposing on the electoral will and public opinion of the populace of one nation to be capable of giving expression to the inner spirit and social aspirations of the people of quite another tradition, or to the spirit of the laws which dwells in the institutions of another country. These administrators of India can instruct their wards for their good. They cannot be the poets and reformers of the land, and they should not be —where there is no common mind or social intermixture—its lawgivers. They had better not be its police.

Economic ties with India can be woven in a friendly spirit of mutual advantage. The sentiment of nationality, however, has its just, if strictly limited, claims—and this not only for India. In so far as the British Commonwealth represents a desirable association in world affairs, it represents something which is invigorated by a common sentiment of kin in which India can have no part. Austria not only violated justice, but weakened itself by turning its eyes towards the Danube, and by endeavours to appropriate Slav territory which it could never assimilate, instead of turning its attention in directions where Austria had natural affinities. So long as Britain fixes its attention on the route to India, and bases its policy on the retention of the government of India in its own hands, it bases its

IS THE NATION THE COMMUNITY?

policy on something artificial and false, contrary to its own racial and cultural principles. A worm is in the staff of its power. This does not, of course, mean that federation of the Commonwealth with India may not be desirable, not only economically, but precisely as a check against excessive white-racialism[1] and as a guarantee that Britain will support rather a "Roman" than a racial or Nordic view of the international order that must be built.

Nationalism, therefore, we understand to be the spirit of conscious community of a people: it should exclude, as a contradiction, all rule of one nation by another— all bad imperialism. That is a contradiction into which a nationalism fanned for economic ends of collective profit-making is led by exploitative governing groups. Nationalism does, however, concentrate the energies of a people upon the interests and prestige of that people as a group. It has affiliation with racialism and must, for example, issue in a condemnation of the particular form of race treason in the Pacific dear to the heart of some English Tories.

Little advance, I suspect, can be made in a discussion of this subject unless certain agreed statements can be made as points of reference. I take it that all, even anarchists, even the Nietzscheans in their own exotic way, are agreed that a strong present sense of public spirit, and a willingness to subordinate the immediate private

[1] The Hindus are, I presume, in part anthropologically "Aryans" in Herr Hitler's sense; but they are (unlike, of course, the Maltese and Andalusians) not what one of their number has called "colourless men."

interest to the true public interest, is good. I take it also that everybody, including even the Fascist Party, admits that a chauvinism which inculcates dislike, suspicion, and refusal to co-operate with other peoples is barbaric and undesirable. The problem is how far a group sense for the village or the nation which goes beyond a merely individual obligation of duty and involves a readiness to co-operate with some group in their acts, both those of which one approves and those of which one disapproves, is a good thing.

The problem appears to be essentially one which has to be solved in evolutionary terms—in terms of the stage in the development of civilization. The patent danger of nationalism is that, for all its glamour, it may perpetuate the curse of private war and, in fact, interferes with the development of international co-operation. Viewed in this light this nineteenth-century philosophy, this immoral gospel of the nation, is one of the gravest practical poisons, and one of the most lethal, of our age. Viewed in another light it provides the practical test of the readiness of individuals for self-sacrifice, provides them with a positive and intimate morality, and is the very foundation of public spirit. It is certainly a precondition of all socialist advance, since a man can scarcely sacrifice himself for his brother whom he has not seen if he has no attachment to his brother whom he has seen.

A rational nationalism would seem to be one in which attachment to those who, by common tradition, speech, and government, are one's own people is fully recognized as one form of community sentiment, but in which the tendency of undisciplined nationalism to oppose the demands of international civilization is specifically checked. The original patriotism, which was that of the *lares*

IS THE NATION THE COMMUNITY?

and *penates*, of the hearth, of one's own blood family, of the local hills and rivers, still remains one of the strongest and most legitimate of feelings; but it is no longer called patriotism. Something nearer the worship of "Roma et divus Augustus" has replaced it. The patriotism of the Macleod extends beyond the Isles to Scotland, to the Commonwealth; the patriotism of the Munich citizen extends beyond Bavaria to the Reich and to the Pan-Teuton tradition. In America the patriotism of Virginia is merged in a far larger attachment. The same is true of Sicilian and perhaps of Catalan. Only in a few instances, such as France, is nationalism almost crystal pure, concentrated on one single area. The spirit of La Vendée and of French provincialism is almost dead; and there is no attachment beyond France, despite MM. Briand and Coudenhove-Kalergi with their dreams of a United States of Europe. (This passage was written before that sudden outbreak of insurgent Breton Autonomism in the autumn of 1932 which, *a fortiori*, confirms my argument.) What that community is which is the nation is often by no means so clear as might be supposed. It is malleable to historical changes and to rational influences.

The question before us is whether it is possible to build up a nationalism that, at once, embraces the sense of cultural unity of a people and yet actively forwards international organization, so that attachment to the nation as a community does not establish a loyalty irrational and immoral. Peculiarly in the case of the Great Powers, which stand for the interests of larger areas than the local community and which have educated their citizens beyond a clannish nationalism, it needs to be asked whether they have a function in a political order yet wider than themselves—whether they are even evolutionary forms towards this wider order or final forms and effective obstacles to a more complete plan.

The imperative need of civilization is international organization, which cannot replace the cultural association provided by the nation, but which, in matters of law and order and of state-function, must override it. That is a rational dictate for our age. The elements of the civilized life must, in their requirements, take precedence of its refinements. The execution of the will of such an international organization must rest upon an authority ultimately backed by will and force. A public opinion which is determined can show its will by support of authority and, at need, by physical support. As George Washington said, "influence is not government." A public opinion which always stops short of personal inconvenience in action against an aggressor is neither determined nor effective. At the present moment, when a genuine international public opinion is in its infancy, such determination rests upon the will of the most powerful states. In so far, then, as the national will of the more powerful states is interested in international organization and in the strengthening of this authority, that national will itself, whether in the British Commonwealth, Sweden, or Russia, is good and should be encouraged.

I should like to see a world in which the command of international authority requires, in order to secure obedience, no exercise of force. Similarly I should like to see a world where no police truncheons were required. The analogy is exact, since a corporate aggressor is a criminal in its corporate capacity, alike in international and in domestic law, and requires to be dealt with by what becomes a police force so soon as an authority is set up extensive enough in its scope to treat disorder as domestic and internal. A military force becomes a police force, not when pistols are substituted for rifles, but when it is sent, by competent authority under law, against an internal disturber. I do not expect to see a world where there is no need to use either force or police. I should like to see a world where public opinion was so set against the private war of nations that no government could live which embarked, with however noble protestations about its honour and sacred cause, upon such a private war. I expect to see that day or that the next generation will.

For the moment, however, I believe that the peace of the world is to be kept by the will and interest of the strongest nations who are determined, if necessary, to keep peace by force. Those nations today are the United States, the British Commonwealth, and the Soviet Republic. I approve of the national strength of these countries being maintained, and I am only anxious to see it used in order to persuade, press, or intimidate other Powers into the maintenance of peace by making them certain of military defeat if they embark upon such adventures. The supreme treachery, however, for the Great Powers is to concentrate (as did the Hapsburgs, unlike the Hohenstauffen) upon building up their own local dominions instead of forging, through the League and by the aid of small nations, an international machinery for maintaining law and equity in the world. The building up of an international order will repose upon the will of men acting through the tried instruments of power. These state instruments are tried and strong because they can rely upon the existing corporate sentiment of nations.

It is, I think, only a proper safeguard against disillusion

to recognize that international authority, at first, must be built by those who can rely upon each other. At present, by and large, only men of one nation or of closely allied traditions have sufficient common sentiment to do this. A united France was built by the cunning and strategic advantages of the House of Capet, resting on the Isle de France; a united Germany was built by the force of Prince Bismarck and the House of Brandenburg-Prussia; a united Italy required the statecraft and force of the House of Piedmont. I see no reason to suppose that the political methods of the past will undergo violent change.

I do not, therefore, myself advocate either British Imperialism or American Imperialism or Italian Fascism. My belief, which is roughly consonant with Mr. Bertrand Russell's, is that less fortunate Powers will find their only hope of checking Anglo-Saxon hegemony (which I expect to see developed) by abandoning their own chauvinism and by emphasizing the notion of a federal and real international organization against that of an organization which is largely make-believe and is effectually dominated by one or two Powers. Here lies the cultural mission of the small nations such as Denmark and Holland, who have no profit to expect—unlike Germany and France—from chauvinism and who have, therefore, never encouraged it. It is not my opinion that the Great Powers, alone, will be able to complete the work of building up a firm international federal state.

I further believe that, slowly, a genuine international spirit will develop, especially among the organized workers who, as a class, are least advantaged, least morally impressed, and least obsessed by the traditions of national prestige. I believe that this spirit will angrily insist that national interests shall be advanced by other

IS THE NATION THE COMMUNITY?

means than war and through international agreement; that the international government shall be directly dependent upon the democracies of the various constituency countries; and that national governments will drop into the position of local administrations. This belief does not seem to me to be unreasonable.

I am not of the opinion, however, that it corresponds to the first stage in the evolution of international authority, during which stage we shall have to go on talking about a sound internationalism resting upon a sound nationalism, without too precisely defining terms or admitting to ourselves that, in certain aspects, the two concepts are lethal enemies.

I have introduced the workers as *deus ex machina* not from romanticism or from some slavish adherence to the economic interpretation of history. I agree that the cause of war and of like actions, inimical to civilization, is the international anarchy and that it is the group-prestige and sovereign punctilios of nations which perpetuate this anarchy. The obstacle to peace is rather the pursuit of power by limited groups of men who occupy the Government and call themselves "the State," than any economic cause whether to be found in the brute facts of natural wealth or in the pursuit of pecuniary gain. Even industrial interests in oil, rubber, gold, and the like are frequently as much concerned with power and rivalry between companies, or in the use of these commercial products for national ends, as in profits and dividends. I do not, of course, deny the influence of dividend-hunting, which sometimes has the issue, odd from a national point of view, that armament firms supply (for example, to the Boers and Turks) weapons ultimately to be used for shooting down one's own co-nationals—if cosmopolitan directors, even when adorned with a K.G., can be said to have co-nationals. Throughout, however, the main cause of war is the corporate pursuit of power by groups working through national sentiment, who do not themselves stand to lose heavily by war, coupled with the desire that one's own nation or "we-group" shall give and not take orders.

The manual workers themselves, let it be admitted, are inclined to reflect upon the advantages in war of assured employment, high wages for those lucky in the lottery, and an end for all of monotony. Other things end also; but human optimism dismisses remoter considerations. These calculations, however, have small ideal appeal and, granted a certain education, the appeal of humanitarianism can be strong among those masses which are themselves just plain Johns and Jills and who have no share in the *esprit de corps* of a class that is a ruling class under the national system. It is not particularly part of their game—this rivalry for power and for new areas of government and trade. In this connection Major Bratt's *That Next War* is worth consultation. The preservation and improvement of standard of living is for the workers a real interest, but other means than war seem to offer themselves as more intelligent ways of attaining that end. The determination of the united workers, with its stress on mass humanitarianism against national leader-following, has, or can easily come to have, the psychological strength required to break up the older system.

The doctrine of the class-war I shall discuss later. I do not wish to imply here either that the economic interest of workers is exclusively international—I hope later to show the very marked extent to which it is precisely national—or that there are not many elements in capitalist society, including international finance and political Liberalism, which are very genuinely internationalist in outlook by interest, taste, and reasoning. I am merely stating what I believe to be a detached interpretation of the historical process: that an international organization can be founded, first, by the preponderant might of two or three great Powers (the Anglo-Saxon nations and Russia) and, subsequently, by the will of plain men, not in the ruling tradition, organized as workers, apathetic to chauvinist nationalism and hostile to imperialism. I do not here say that either phenomenon is good or bad of itself (they are, indeed, contradictory): the end achieved seems to me good which establishes a presupposition in favour of the means. I have even no great confidence that the workers, if successful but badly led, may not themselves in turn become susceptible to national and local animosities; but, by this time, an effective international organization, capable of curbing localism, may have been set up.

The nationalism, then, of the Great Powers is consistent with a rational scheme of society precisely so far as it can and does promote international order. A community spirit which subserves this end is entitled to rational loyalty. An honest man can find in this enlarged national organization, not only a mere mechanism, but a living and reasonable spirit.

All history, however, goes to show that the justifying purpose tends to be suffocated by the immediate sense for the national community, as it is, and for its prestige. A fight will arise between those who see the nation as a community in a mere universal context and those who do not. Apart from that context the nation loses, as community, its rational justification; its worship becomes a tyranny; its organization becomes, for honest men, merely something external and alien. The nation, thus considered, becomes identified with the state. It becomes, like the state administration, something mechanical, something to be viewed from the outside, rather than understood by intuition—but it is worse than the state in this respect, that, instead of being merely utilitarian, it is inspired by an actively false philosophy. If it be said that a national is a man of his nation by birth, whether he likes it nor not, the reply is that by this very sign the nation loses the character of a community which rests on free choice and sentiment. It is pride of birth, and not birth, that makes the nation into a true community.

Against a false nationalism and a perverted community other forces, with more rational purposes, must be called into play. These forces of common interest—forms of economic interest and of religion—will, in their turn, sustain new communities, historically less associated with the state but, in some respects, perhaps better able to satisfy the fundamental needs of human nature than the nation turned coercive and tyrannical. Actually a community consists of, and lives by, those who are members by will and not by intimidation. The nation as mere mass is energized by the nation as community, by those who are adherents of the religion of the nation. The nation as a mechanical organization using the power of the state, which men are to be compelled to worship against their will, is a tyranny.

I see, however, no reason to suppose that the constant historical tendency of an ideal, at first followed by free choice and affection, to become converted into a piece of organization, mechanically imposed by force, is likely to be ended could we rid ourselves of the evil nationalism.

IS THE NATION THE COMMUNITY?

Each community, in turn, is tempted to substitute force for its own true spirit—not only the justifiable force that insists on respect for rights, but the illicit force that compels other men to pay lip-service to one's own religion. That has been the danger of Catholicism, with both Church and state as its instruments; it is the danger of nationalism with the state as its instrument; it is and will be the danger of Communism.

The obligation to make this distinction between the field of morals and the field of law, between the field in which we invite men to live by an ideal and the field in which we compel them to respect the rights of others, is cardinal. It is important that we should observe it at a time when politics are entering upon an enthusiastic and religious phase. Valuable work has been done by MacIver, but the whole philosophy of association and community is a field in which exploration is, as yet, quite inadequate. The exploration has been by men of action.

If we would find the intimate community, such as Hellas had, we must yet look to this field of movements, of religions, of parties, of aristocracies. Among these movements an intelligent nationalism is merely one. To these movements, then, of the present we must turn in our search for the satisfying community.

The true community is not administrative, but psychological; it is not based upon contiguity, but upon like-mindedness. Our psychological enquiry has provided us with criteria for this community; history may provide us with examples. Our study, however, of civilization, of state and nation-state, has shown us what the intensive community is not, although it may have shown us what something complementary in society, the extensive administrative area, should be. We have the bones; we seek the life.

The devoted adherent of a community will be monogamous in his affection. That is the condition of his deeper satisfaction and of his personal force. But history yet offers a plurality of communities to his allegiance. These alternatives we must now consider. The community holds the individual, in his private life, by the emotions. But it is for reason to choose, guided by the criteria offered by the political science of human nature, which communities are most likely to be destined to advance in history the civilization of the world and the freedom of man.

PART III

PART III

§ i

The Religion of Catholicism

The writer of this book, were it not for the result of mere accident, would at the present moment, in all probability, be a Dominican Friar. I believe that technically I am still a postulant of the Third Order. At the same time I take my name from a connection with the strictest sect of the Puritans of Massachussetts. I was brought up in a home where theology was as much a matter of common interest as are in some families stocks and shares. I insert these autobiographical details because this is not a formal treatise, with pretensions to impersonal logic, but a record of opinion and values to which such details are relevant. I approach, therefore, the question of whether the leadership in religion which we require cannot be found in Catholic Christianity without either adverse prejudice or complete inexperience.

If I conclude that Protestant Christianity does not offer a religion adequately distinguished from the various gospels of social reform, of humanitarianism and of Tory nationalism, or from a leaderless individualism, to require especial discussion as a contemporary historic force it is not a conclusion reached out of entire ignorance of that of which I speak. Catholicism, on the other hand, today is a political force sufficiently powerful for an examination of its principles to be required even from a writer who is exclusively concerned with actual political movements in the contemporary world. In Britain and even in America the situation may be so far different from that on the European continent that the Catholic issue is one without meaning in any context of national policy. The fundamental principles of this type of social direction yet remain of unsurpassed interest.

Any conclusions we draw from it may, for example, have bearing upon our attitude towards the very English tradition of Christian Socialism, today represented by persons so eminent as R. H. Tawney and Mr. Lansbury. Certainly such men as Tawney are right in affirming that no religion strong enough to mould personality can be "out of politics"—walled off from the values that determine social conduct. The notion that it is possible to be saved apart from one's community is a sad heresy of men without public sense encouraged by astute secularists. Politics, moreover, is not entirely or chiefly a matter for which moral responsibility can be placed upon the specialists in the arts of electioneering or of bureaucracy. The religious conscience is involved.

The Catholic Church has always very properly insisted upon playing a political rôle; the Methodists have frequently done the same; and by that rôle we can justly judge, and maybe condemn, both bodies. The principles of any religion must be judged by their fruits in conduct and policy and, if the principles are too vague and "washy" for practical application, so much the worse for the religion to be judged. And assuredly, when examining our conclusion that we require a social religion, it would be preposterous not to examine a religious form which has so well stood the test of time.

Catholicism comes with an especial claim to give the world a religion, with a claim which it asserts to be based on divine authority and to be exclusive. It gives us a spiritual and mental aristocracy which yet is a body of poor and devoted men serving ends of human good, usually disinterestedly. It proffers a way of life which it asserts gives the only enduring happiness and, by every psychological test, the claim is justified that it, in fact, can give happiness under circumstances common enough to be fairly regarded as normal. I gather that it is on these pragmatic grounds that writers such as, for example, Mr. Hemingway, and others who do not greatly diverge in character from the mundane average, find satisfaction in it as a religion for civilized men.

It is James FitzJames Stephen who speaks of falling in love with one's religion as one falls in love with a woman without hope of reward. This seems to me to be a sound description of most religious men's attitude. The issue is not one of argument but of faith and its experienced satisfactions. The Church, indeed, offers a reward for faith, but it is not a reward of here and now. It is a reward in satisfied resignation to those things compared with which the individual admits himself to be entirely insignificant. The psychological key to happiness offered by Catholicism is asceticism. It conquers pain by welcoming it. It uses prayer as a means for inducing a sincere mood of resignation, not as a method of changing that which some philosophers call the dialectic movement of the Absolute and simple men call God's will.

There seems to me little ground for doubt that this is a feasible way to a certain happiness and that it brings inner peace, although it is never likely to appeal to those who look for worldly success or who are warmed by any considerable degree of momentary enjoyment of it. Where the heart is there will the treasure be. It is, indeed, not designed to give any particular pleasure to the children of this world but rather to stand as a condemnation of them. It affirms that life's experience cannot and should not be divorced from pain. It points the pleasure-loving to the menace of this pain which, like death, is part of the human lot. For it the pursuit of pleasure is a cheap vulgarity in a world which is inevitably the graveyard of so many of man's desires and which is so full of tears and tragedy.

I am not prepared to dismiss this philosophy lightly. I know nothing which more entirely shakes the soul, and purges it with reverence, than the celebration of the Mass, in which the central significance of pain and sacrifice, not only in human life, but in the essential scheme of things, is venerably affirmed.

In one limited sense of the word "happiness" every religion has been concerned with happiness and the relief of suffering—"ultimate" happiness and peace. But a common characteristic of the great ascetic religions of the world is that they deny any final importance to that happiness which depends upon the physical conditions of human welfare or to those activities primarily concerned with the relief here and now of suffering. We owe this admission to those religions if we are at all to understand their philosophy. The habitual misunderstanding of Catholicism reposes upon the belief that the reduction of human suffering in this world is a self-evident good—which is precisely what for a Catholic or even a Calvinist is not self-evident. It is, however, exactly on these grounds that I find it impossible, while admitting the allurement to the weary and heavy-laden, to accept the traditional religions as giving that emotional leadership which our civilization requires. I do not accept the inherent necessity of the warfare of the spirit against this world and this age.

Objections to the theology of the Catholic Church are

not (it is my impression) matters of primary weight. It is always possible to restate that theology is a fashion to which no reasonable man, not out to dispute, can well object. I well recall the method by which a well-known and distinguished Jesuit Father convinced me—at a time when I stated that, for myself, I actively disliked the notion of individual immortality—that in fact, as a Spinozist, I did accept the orthodox doctrine of immortality as one of timeless eternity. The body after death, he suggested, might be immortal in the sense that it was identified with the everlasting body of the universe. The "miracle of the Mass" as a matter of metaphysical interpretation offers no difficulties, despite the Lord Bishop of Birmingham and such episcopal anthropologists. The extreme antiquity of this doctrine in the primitive Church appears to be adequately substantiated, even in the opinion of Scottish Presbyterian scholars, such as Dr. Pringle Pattison.

Biblical miracles, being affirmed to be facts, are a far greater obstacle to the acceptance of either the Protestant religion or of Catholicism. The doctrine of the Mass, with perhaps some straining, could well be justified to any pantheist. And as a pantheist I am willingly prepared to accept this identification of deity with common things in the bread and wine, food and drink. Certainly in the ethnic mysteries bread and wine were symbols of the fruitful Earth-Mother who moved in all the natural world. The true Christian addition to the drama has been to make the symbols of the half-alien, if half-maternal, earth also into veils which, drawn aside, reveal to those who understand the mystery, the affirmation of the divinity and tragedy of man. I suppose that even some explanation can be found of the biblical miracles so that they could be accepted without gross intellectual dishonesty. Whether it would be worth doing this is a very different matter.

The objection to Catholicism is of another order. It is precisely its ascetic morals and the practical consequences of those morals which is the real rock of offence. It is not the metaphysics of the Council of Nicaea that disturbs me. This seems to express, with an adequate freedom from anthropomorphism, a quite profound, if hypothetical, truth. What disturbs me is that the Catholic Archbishop of Liverpool makes attacks on expenditure in education without quite necessary reservations concerning expenditure (for example, on central schools for the brighter children) which certainly ought to be incurred. Again, because a woman is a devout Catholic she may find that the Church may expect her to undergo three or more caesarean operations. I admit that the Catholic Church is not peculiar in this matter. In a recent book by Dr. Edward Lyttelton conclusions much more amazing are drawn from dogmatic premises. As we know, the Inquisition acted on the same principle, concluding that any amount of human pain was negligible compared with the salvation of souls according to revealed rule of thumb. Humanity, of course, is not reasonable and it is, in fact, likely to go on sacrificing to the peace of mind of the many humane feeling for the few. We are, however, here concerned with whether we shall approve and support this kind of sacrifice. To say that it is better than the bloody Moloch sacrifice preached by Herren Göring, Banse, and others is not to say enough.

I am not prepared to say that we ought not to sacrifice quite sternly the happiness of individuals to rational

THE RELIGION OF CATHOLICISM

considerations of the happiness of the whole—and by the whole I mean not only contemporary society, but, proportionately to its relevance to practical calculations, the happiness of coming generations. Such sacrifice seems to me the very basis of social life and of moral discipline. We are, however, entitled to object if the sacrifice of particular individuals or societies to the happiness of the whole is carried to such a pitch that we are confronted with the paradox of trying to make the whole happy by, in effect, making miserable the parts. By happiness I mean, not only sensuous pleasure, but that which each man, at his individual stage of experience, considers to be requisite for his actual satisfaction in life, certainly not omitting requirements for the rational satisfaction of a well-ordered life and the discipline, as well as the vitality, involved as a condition of achievement. One is entitled to insist that human conduct shall be related to this social happiness in the present or in the probable future of mundane experience, and not to miraculous revelation or to the dictates of a sacred book, as final and above criticism.

I do not see how any impartial man can do other than flatly deny the thesis of the Syllabus of Pius IX, that the dogmas of the Christian religion are not subject to the criticism of reason and philosophy. I am prepared heartily to agree with the statement of Leo XIII that faith and reason cannot be in contradiction; but I utilize this statement to make reason and ultimate intuition the judge of the objects of faith, which objects must be consistent with reason and fundamental intuition. Neither doctrines such as that of the Virgin Birth (apt enough, indeed, as a metaphor and protest against the dynastic type of religion with hereditary priests and prophets) nor the authorization of the infliction of human pain, for no adequately explained end in terms of human good, seem to me to conform to these requirements and I reject them. Not all the wit of M. Maritain or the more solid argumentation of Aquinas can remove from my mind the memory of these elementary difficulties, although I do not say that they cannot be removed and I incline to the opinion that it would be considerably for the good of civilization if they could be removed.

I freely admit that for millennia the domination of nature over man has been such that resignation, and along with it a series of negative, chaste virtues designed to wean men from all interest in this world, has been the part of wisdom. Now, however, man is no longer the slave of Nature and need not be of his own civilization. We have passed into an epoch of the conquest of nature by man and (we hope) of the deliberate ordering by man of his own social organization. At this stage a negative philosophy of asceticism and world flight—because not only neutral to a sound philosophy of disciplined responsible conduct, but often, if stated absolutely, actively inimical to it—is disastrous.

Catholicism, for good or evil, has stood firmly by tradition. It claims leadership and, in view of its massiveness, is an historical force entitled to that claim. In Germany and Austria it has recently exercised that claim in fact. It is a challenge. That leadership, after consideration and some direct experience, I for myself reject. I think it may be for the peace of the world, but it is not for its independence of soul. The Catholic Church is one of the wisest, but also one of the most dangerous, of contemporary institutions. Nor is it here with "the three gifts of the dread spirit" that I am concerned, but precisely with its Christian religiosity. Catholicism is flight.

I believe we should seek something more difficult and more vital. The only heroism is not that of the passive order. One is prepared to admit that pain is of the texture of things—if not of the foreground, yet of the background. The philosophy of the Crucifixion and of the Mass is a recognition of this necessary part—only immaturity or insensible vulgarity would deny it—of a complete philosophy of life. But it is unhealthy when it becomes the whole or a chief part of it.

There is no honesty in a philosophy that assumes man's omnipotence or that puts an empty denial over against the facts of pain and tragedy. There is, however, great point in not supplanting the human will to conquer the world for man by an obstructive and enfeebling confession of human defeat. The philosophy of the Resurrection is too other-worldly to countervail and to make the message of Christus Regnans—the message of the Byzantine crucifixes with their royal Christ—any message of world mastery or of the art of life in this world. In order to render our religious philosophy satisfactory we need a large admixture of pantheism and of activism—I do not, however, propose to discuss this question here.

The Catholic Christian religious tradition stretches back beyond the events that happened "in the fullness of time" in Galilee. The pontiffs take their name from the priests of old Rome. "Star of the Sea" is the appellation of Isis of the Egyptians. The theology of the Church is admixed with the wisdom of Babylonia and the philosophy of Athens and Alexandria. The mark of the Jewish high priesthood and the Jewish ritual can still be clearly detected. Even the Druids contribute to the Yule feast. As Christianity affected a syncretism with its predecessors, so the religion of today need not avoid, so far as I can see, but can appropriate this immemorial and venerable tradition. I am well content to do this provided that it be clearly understood that this tradition will boldly have fresh interpretations—pantheistic, humanistic, non-miraculous, and concerned with the here and now—read into it and that it will be accepted on these terms.

My conclusion is that Catholicism alone will not suffice, although its drama—its Divine Tragedy—may legitimately be appropriated, as part of the grand tradition of civilization, by the heirs of this tradition in order to give body and power to the presentation of a more entire philosophy. They are too remote, these religions of ghost worshippers. We must turn elsewhere for leadership in the actual moulding of the civilization about us. The person of the Christ (or, for that matter, the person of the Buddha) is no object for cheap criticism. An often cheap world departs from these ascetic standards at its risk. But the need is for a rational, clean, athletic world. This is not to be achieved by establishing a tyranny in our mind of a retrospective and other-worldly morality.

Catholicism, then, the oldest of our contemporary living religions, belongs, in its present form, to an order that is passing and has now passed. The age of the Gregories and Innocents will not come back—nor that of Paul or of Jesus—in the fashion of the past.

I do not doubt that Leo will follow Pius and Pius Leo in endless succession on the throne of the Fisherman in future days, when these problems with which we now concern ourself are dead and remote. The age, perhaps, of poverty, dishonour, and mass-slaughter will have been forgotten, along with that of the hunting tribesman. National war-makings will seem an unintelligible folly of the half-civilized. I do not doubt that Sanctus bell, telling of the divinity of man and of matter in ultimate substance, and that Angelus will continue to ring down the valleys in those days to come, since hitherto the mind of man has designed no drama more replete with power to move the mind and heart than that which they announce.

When the world has turned to Communism, and if and when the followers of Marx, by the aid of machines, have satiated this proletarian world with all material satisfactions and have liquidated the classes that represent human inequality, then the circle will be accomplished. Men will return, it seems probable, in some new form to the international and equalitarian religion of sacrifice for eternal values and for the spiritual community that casts out individual ambition for power. But this will not be yet.

Catholicism represents the end of an historic cycle, although its residue is still a living religion today. It is the chief piece of the old Roman-Hellenic world that we still have with us. Its mind was formed—or reformed after the supersession of Judaism, with its Egyptian and Babylonish influences—in the world of the first four centuries of our era. It represents the attainment, by Mediterranean civilization, of the level of devotion to abstract ideals, or to something as unworldly in its ideals as mankind achieves on a mass scale. It compromised with the perennial demands of the individual by giving him immortality, while offering the doctrine of the communion of saints as an article of faith and membership of the living Church as a condition of salvation. The Mediterranean cycle is over and the world cycle has not yet returned to the phase of mass devotion to a nonmundane ideal such as Paul and Augustine, Dante and Aquinas, Loyola and Pascal, Newman and Mercier, spoke of in their very diverse ways.

Nothing that I have met in life has been more entirely satisfying to the heart than Catholicism; I have met nothing so beautiful. But along with Catholic practice —incidentally, perhaps, but still in effect—goes much avoidable cruelty and tortuousness due to the obstinate placing of emphasis on the inhuman and miraculous values of Kingdom-come. (I know the excuses that, did we transfer our treasures to this world, the wolfishness of man would disturb all things and that each man would raven for material gain at the cost of his neighbour.) It may be that some day syncretism will take place—the precedents are beyond number—between our present mind and the Catholic mythos. I do not know. It lies in a distant future when the passion of today's fights has died down. Anyhow, all discussion of the matter in this English island of humorous sects and bulldog "isms," or in the United States, with the firm Protestant prejudice of its dominant section of society, is outside the field of practical reference. For the rest one must, here and now, be content to put aside, as an act of self-denial, the beautiful and to prefer the sterner regimen of the good, in order to build a happier, more reasonable world with the aid of a religious impulse more mundane in pivotal interest and—let us hope against hope—more merciful in practice.

§ ii

The Religion of Toryism

The Catholic social system has for four centuries been broken up. The Lutheran has demanded freedom of conscience to be a Lutheran. The mirror has been shivered in which all the world was seen united in the magic globe of one philosophy. Dante's vision of the need for one empire and church of peace now appears scholastic folly. The secularism of the Renaissance tempted men to interest in the world as it actually was, unharmonized by religious idealism, in all its adventurous diversity. Protestantism freed the way both for the self-assertion of the individual and for the new religion of the state. The feudal nobility became the modern gentry who, while not discarding the prop of a decorous and established religion, brought up their sons in the professional code of a lay ruling class.

In the countries politically children of the French Revolution the middle class of town merchants and country lawyers attacked the nobility, in the name of equality, but assumed, in the name of education, the right to guide and govern the masses. Before the Revolution, and the compromises of 1832 and of Bismarck, the upper class officially decided what was the will of the state to which subjects owed devotion. After this time the middle class had the predominant share in shaping, for citizens, this will, which yet remained still sacred, because that of the nation-state. Dynastic loyalty was replaced by a new constitutionalism. The religion of Conservatism displayed itself as devotion to the tradition of the nation and its accustomed social structure and government, monarchical or republican. In America alone the primary interest was in self-assertion and the popular religion that of liberty rather than of the state. The United States had a Whig dominance, but no significant Toryism after 1776, until the Republican Party supplied a Conservative religion of the established order founded on wealth.

Toryism is a complete and venerable philosophy which, at least in this century, is usually felt to include nationalism as the whole includes the part. It profits by the enthusiasm of nationalists and tempers their raw deficiencies. It is the philosophy of loyalism as well as the cult of the soil. In the mouth of Disraeli it is able to talk the language of innovation but, as it has developed from Hooker and Burke to today, it is a patriotic cult of the slowly developing established order, the ancient oak-trunk—the order of the state. It is, in the European world, very much a living philosophy of political conduct. As such it demands consideration here.

Toryism today is able to capitalize for its own benefit national sentiment; but it is not the only political movement which is able to do this and it is not itself merely another name for nationalism.

Toryism has its own picture of governmental and social structure, and that picture, where it is unpolluted by Whig commercialism and by jealous individualism, is paternalistic. It assumes a recognized and respected upper class which does its duty in its station towards lesser members of the community. Its very symbol and representative is the squire. At its best it offers the religion of *noblesse oblige*.

THE RELIGION OF TORYISM

It can in all seriousness be argued—and I do not think that we should be fair to the Tory argument and (since to some people this may not make any appeal) to the demands of truth unless we recognized it—that the issue before us is whether we are going to favour the claim to rule society of the ascetic, the plain man, the gentleman, or the "tough." By the ascetic I mean a man of a discipline. By the "tough" I mean men—of a kind that frequently makes a remarkable appeal to their psychological complement among women—who bear down opposition by mere vigour of animal brutality. At their highest they are dictators who do not scruple to employ assassination; at their lower and more common level they populate the morally less desirable quarters of Chicago. It is absurd to dismiss these men as negligible. In many an American city they are actually running the Government. They have been heard of nearer Westminster. In fact they—the frustrated would-be capitalists who cut across the rules of the game to attain their ends: sometimes the successful capitalists who have kept the rules of the criminal law—will run society, since they are men avaricious according to their lights for money and power, unless they are stopped by deliberate action. They have got to be ruled, unless all sound human values are to be overturned, as a determined rider rules a horse. It may be said, incidentally, that one of the many sins of our popular philosophies is that, by their praises of individualistic self-expression, they have connived at releasing popular applause for these men, whether of the healthy ostler or of the braggadocio Renaissance type. The reason why they should be ruled has nothing to do with class division—Count Keyserling also should be ruled—or with any original sin or incapacity for self-government in ordinary human nature, but because they represent an early and more animal stage of civilization.

At the opposite extreme it must be confessed that the rule of the saints has never been a success. The rule of the religious saints has historically been the heaviest tyranny, degenerating through hypocrisy into a pinchbeck priggery. The rule of "the intelligensia," the dons, academics, and self-appointed aristocrats would, if possible, be worse. That criticism is not made because I do not believe in an aristocracy of sound judgement— I do. I do not incline to the opinion that a superior *intelligensia* will provide it.

The suit of *de Brett* v. *Bloomsbury* can be taken as settled against Bloomsbury. When Plato spoke of philosopher-kings, we really need not suppose that he meant some Attic Bloomsbury. The impracticability, however, of this kind of leadership points one warning. I have referred to the necessity for the government, by the more advanced, of those who represent the earlier and more animal stage of civilization. In part this antithesis is sound; in part it tends to ignore that man remains an animal, although a cultivated one, and that an aristocracy which opposes an anaemic rationalism to the instincts and emotions is bound to fail.

Unless we can find, then, an unobjectionable ascetic we are left, on our supposition, with the third, the Tory, possibility of "the rule of the gentleman." This possibility will especially appeal to those who regard a quest for the intelligent plain man as futile. God forbid that I should be understood to believe that every Tory voter is a gentleman. Merely I mean that the best type of

Tory would find this supposed need for rule by gentlemen to be central to his position, whether tacit or avowed. The argument is a common-sense one and a strong one. Nor do I suppose that this philosophy is intrinsically bound up either with the rule of wealth—it will not attack wealth, which is a different matter—or with any crude class domination. The rule of the feudal squires predates the Whig stress on the acquisition and defence of commercial wealth and is not at heart friendly to it. And the word "gentleman" may be understood sufficiently broadly—as a basis, for example, for a civil service *moral*—to permit of the provision of an open career, not only to landed wealth, but to all character of an acceptable kind as distinct from an open career merely for the clever talents. Although I personally hold the argument to be vicious, as will appear, it is at least worth stating with attention.

It is true that this Tory loyalism, with its respect for class, broadly understood, and for the standards and morality of a distinctive order, centring on the squire although certainly not limited to him, does not offer that ready road for the promotion of smart ability which the typical Liberal demands. The Tory insists that, if the road is sufficiently open to enable the aspirant to achieve membership of the ruling class, not in his own person, but in that of perhaps a grandchild (always saving cases of egregious ability or highly distinguished service) social justice is satisfied. I am here prepared to agree with him and to admit that, granted a class-divided society, this steady slow advancement has moral significance, even although it stirs the impatience of the *arriviste* and *nouveau riche* mentality. This point is important since almost all individualist thought has (not accidentally but essentially) omitted the significance of the succession of generations and of the morality bound up with performance of a duty to them or even with an ambition for success ploughed for in one generation and harvested in the next.

In order that I may do full justice by the Tory argument and not build up my own contention by ignoring my opponents, I shall make one further willing concession. The Liberal Democrat believes in a classless society without standards. He believes in every man setting his own standard, with this sole reservation that he shall not claim that his standard is any better than his neighbour's—that claim would be contrary to fraternal tolerance; it is what is termed in America, in a most descriptive phrase, "high-hatting" the other person. So far as this is a protest against irrelevant class-divisions and the insolence of wealth, it is a sound element of social democracy. It is, however, an entire misconception of fraternity to suppose that one idea is as good as another, one standard as good as another, and, for example, that the tactic of acquisition with its shrewd values is entitled any day to push its way in on a level, in the ethical kingdom, with the honest performance of service. It is impossible to condemn too frequently or too severely this cultural nihilism. Thus far Tory and Socialist agree against the Liberal Democrats, with their praise of vulgar confusion and their timidity in condemning the base for what it is.

Mere all-round, back-scratching, intolerantly tolerant insistence on equality of good and bad, noble and base, wise and stupid, civilized and barbaric, is a contemptible ideal inspired ultimately by fear and jealousy. I do not for a moment agree that the best society is that in which everybody who is not actually at the moment in the hands of the criminal law is regarded as one of the best of fellows without further enquiry, although I do not

THE RELIGION OF TORYISM

doubt, but affirm, that a tolerant kindliness is an excellent thing in man when the day's work is done. There is no need to differ from the Tory about the need for standards, which are the very evidence of civilization, but about the nature of them.

The Socialist ideal of fraternity is not one of washy indifferentism but of affirming that society must move together, led by those who feel themselves to be members of a true community. The Tory ideal of paternalism is one of a society moving together, the lower classes led by those whom birth, money, or wits have constituted their betters. The Socialist movement is towards the building of a just social order, discoverable by reason and satisfying the human desire for that personal fulfilment which does not yet exist. It has a discipline, if a discipline which emphasizes the co-operative movement towards freedom. The Tory will condone the evils of present society from his desire to remember the good. He emphasizes a tradition including good and bad alike and objects to analysis and emphatic discrimination. He will claim that he is not in any rash hurry—and, after all, tradition and no hurry are on the side of the privileged.

In a very able book Major Walter Elliot has developed a philosophy of Toryism, of which it is urgent to analyse patiently the oddity. That philosophy is yet explained to be not a philosophy, but the protégé of modern biological science and, says Major Elliot, "science repudiates philosophy." One is tempted to comment, "so much the worse." "Toryism is first of all the creed of continuity," which opposes itself to the pride of the intellect and to the pride of the rationalists who trust in mathematical reasoning, with their talk of "each man to count for one," of majorities, and of "one man, one vote." "The rationalists, the mathematicians . . . opposed to the Tory beliefs an arrogance of the intellect, a disbelief in tradition, a conviction that what has once worked is probably outworn, and finally a certain pessimism." (Major Elliot is almost certainly wrong, as a matter of historical fact, about pessimism from Aquinas to Condorcet—but let that pass: perhaps today the rationalist may have reason for pessimism.) "The creeds of rationalism and mathematics," adds Major Elliot, "do not square fully with the facts of life as we observe it." "The very citadel of reason," mathematics and logic, seems to be yielding before the assaults of MM. Bergson and Eddington. The Tory philosophy, we are told, is nationalism, "nostroism," that is, belief in *us*, and a preference for following one's own devices rather than for being rationally governed.

If biology is of the very heart of Toryism it is somewhat hard to see how "following one's own devices," which certainly is not the principle of biological survival, should be (as it probably is) very nearly the distinctive mark of Toryism. I do not, however, desire to engage in a merely verbal and clever criticism of Major Elliot. I do not want to emphasize his own insistence that the Tory Party is the irrational party or his actual endeavours to bind it up with not-quite-first-rate philosophy. He has a case worth examination. His argument is twofold. There is a stress upon instinct which is peculiar to himself as both biologist and Tory. There is a stress upon continuity which is the accepted Tory argument since Burke. The gospel of nationalism buckles together the two arguments.

I confess to a profound distrust of Major Elliot's instinctivist argument. I consider it anarchistic, antinomian, and uncivilized. The antithesis between rationalist philosophy and science is entirely spurious. There is a confusion between a scientific attitude and scientific material.

Whatever biological science may reveal, the permanent instrument of scientific advance is precisely reason. Attempts, as has recently been pointed out in Germany, to discover the characteristics of the ear of a newt and the like by "intuition" mark the broad high road to superstition and charlatanry. It may be that the conduct of men is less intellectual than the eighteenth century and the Benthamites supposed; but the psychological investigation of how to control and direct the instincts, in a rational and non-abusive fashion, is itself a conquest of reason. Major Elliot's argument, far from providing a groundwork for authority, merely unbolts the doors into a bear-garden of emotion in which habit and custom, unsupported by reason, will not long serve him for checks —the alliance, however, of Toryism and scepticism is as old as that very good Tory, David Hume, who took to writing history to save himself from his own philosophy. A slight and conservative modification would have enabled Hume to write: "To be a philosophical sceptic is, in a man of letters, the first and most essential step to being a sound, believing Tory." Major Elliot has not consciously gone thus far; he is not a sceptic, but a Bergsonian, a man of faith alone, an instinctivist, a biologist of the kind that such professional biologists as Professor Hogben find their choice delight in denouncing. For myself I prefer the attitude of St. Thomas to that of D. H. Lawrence: I leave the alternative to Major Elliot.

I am quite prepared to base the premises of reason and of logical argument upon what enquiry may show

A PREFACE TO ACTION

that our substantial instinctive nature really is. Reason and logic do not work, as was once fondly supposed, by supplying infallible conclusions from axiomatic first principles existing *in vacuo*. There is an instinctive and emotional material, moulding values, upon which reason has to work. That is the thesis of the whole first part of this book. But I decline to discard reason as an instrument in favour of the uncertain flicker of private intuition.

There is, further, the well-worn Tory argument of continuity. Authority and custom are hallowed by the notion of venerability and immutability. The difficulty here lies when we try to discover what, of all that is, we are to be told to regard as being what ought to be. Continuity spells non-interference with national sovereign self-sufficiency (which gets a new philosophy to itself as "nostroism"); with deference towards hereditary class; with the rights of wealth.

The "love of the little platoon," as anyone concerned for the development of a sense of community duty will admit, has much to be said for it. But it is not this that is at issue: on this, although not on national sovereignty, Socialist and Tory can agree. What is less acceptable, what is impossible, is that notion of the finality of allegiance to the nation, which is a betrayal of civilization in the twentieth-century world. (I do not say that the nation, its people's economic standards, and its culture have not rights: I believe they have.) Talk of the natural "rights of sovereignty," legal or moral, is precisely as empty as talk "of the natural rights of man." What is unacceptable is not the notion of leadership—of aristocracy, if one will, so long as by that one means the leadership of men of right character and ideas—but the notion of leadership by a class as of right, when this right is based, not on immediate social value, but upon some putative social value due to descent from ancestors who may have been assets to society—or may not.

Such a system of irrational "deference"—to use Bagehot's all too exact word—is debasing. Respect for the king or squire, or physician or engineer, as servant of the community is one thing: respect for the king or squire simply and solely because he occupies the "big house" is another thing, is servile and should be eradicated. The only respect worthy of the name is a respect due to a social code which is one, not of patronage or ungrounded sense of superiority, but of a disciplinary sense of service. It is not due for a moment to a man who does not keep that code.

Finally, what is unacceptable is that perversion of values which comes from giving social prestige to wealth as such. Wealth, nevertheless, because it is power, must necessarily acquire that prestige unless it be very specifically prevented. I freely admit that there is a precapitalist Toryism of old descent which is jealous of wealth and its commercialization of values. Unfortunately, the vulgarity of mere wealth and of its commercial values will not be prevented from showing itself just by stroking the great beast. And the Tory Party, since the end of the last century, when it became the rich man's party, is, I regret to say, prepared to do nothing more.

I recently turned to a speech of a well-known statesman. "The essence of any struggle for healthy liberty has always been and must always be to take from some one man or class of men the right to enjoy power, or wealth, or position, or immunity, which has not been earned by service to his or their fellows." For myself

I am far more interested in the vindication of true values than in any kind of liberty. Were, however, the Tory Party in England prepared to make that statement of Theodore Roosevelt in America its own, and to act upon it, there might be more hope for it. The religious idea of the British Commonwealth espoused by Mr. Lionel Curtis might conceivably provide more hope for it, although I am not sure about that. Actually, however, Toryism requires, when it offers us its religion of "nostroism," that we should look back, not forward, and accept as articles of the creed the moral and practical non-interdependence of civilized nations; the duty of deference to those who are born sons of military or land-enclosing or beef-packing peers; the inviolability of the present social and political power of astute, acquisitive men. It is not good enough.

The older Toryism stood by the morality of *noblesse oblige*. It insisted on the respect due to the squire class although, since Disraeli, it has learned how to make a popular emotional appeal in the name of country and empire. But it was feudal, anti-commercial, non-competitive, and frowned on the lust for acquisition in new men as a vulgarity inconsistent with aristocratic manners (an attitude not always inconsistent, as the works of such historians as Feiling and Namier show, with a good deal of hearty bribery and corruption). Contemporary Toryism, however, is reinforced from quite another quarter—that of the successful business man. Since the turn of the century the party line has been drawn, not between landed Tory and commercial Whig, but between private Capital, whether Conservative,

Unionist, or even Liberal, Simoniac or pure Samuelite, and Socialism.

On the border-line between the older Toryism, with its stress on loyalty to a ruling hierarchy and on the nation as clan, and the new Capitalism of individual success—once Whig, but now Conservative—is a band of those on the fringe of "Society" who accept the standards of Toryism and the methods of *arrivisme*—who spend their time scoring, by the rules, social victories. I shall not further discuss this snob reinforcement of Toryism. It does not contribute a religion, although it may contribute a ritual, and it has not even invariably the merit of good manners: it flutters on the verge of an "apolaustic bounderism."

Of a quite different order are those exponents of Conservatism who are frankly not concerned with the preservation of the feudal hierarchy, but who are concerned very much to affirm the right of ability—and especially of ability demonstrated by acquisition of wealth—to rule. For them Socialism is a philosophy for failures.

It is possible to proceed against these people by the old arguments of Socrates against Thrasymachus and Callicles—that the pursuit of individual success as such is the pursuit of anarchy, unsocial and immoral, without regard to rational, co-operative justice. It is possible to assert that these devil-take-the-hindermost standards set up by those who themselves respect the criminal law may be applied by unscrupulous men who will gamble on their chances of successfully defying the criminal law.

Such arguments against crude success-worship do not, however, do justice to the strength of the case at its best. The game can be played according to standards and the best type of Conservative will insist, in club and business and politics, on those standards. When all has been said about common humanity and about respect for humanity, even in the most miserable and unfortunate, the fact still stands out of striking distinctions of human ability. Give every man a fair chance (but do not forget the right of every able man to give his children a yet better chance) and these distinctions yet stand out.

From week to week, day to day, hour to hour, there is a clash of men of greater ability against men of lesser ability. It is not a contest of which four-fifths of humanity, comfortable, hundrum men, know anything—or wish to know anything—any more than the ordinary horse knows about the conditions of the racecourse. It is a contest in which people who are even slightly stupid, a little dull, unstable in judgement, lacking in understanding of human nature, weak of energy or physical stamina or whatever the defect may be, are defeated. Every man here watches his neighbour to judge him, to see whether he is going to make a mistake, to see whether he is of the calibre that makes good and goes far. Since every advantage will be seized by opponents and every weakness remembered, it is a game which has to be played with taut concentration of attention and which will be played remorselessly.

From the point of view of the new Toryism this game is good; it is the very game of life itself; it is the guarantee of human progress. All else is stagnation, loving-kindness, vegetation, suitable for unambitious, unimportant folk. The first thing is to ask whether a man is important or not—it is well not to waste one's steel or to blunt one's edge on the unimportant. If he is, one admits him to the game for prizes.

This hard-boiled philosophy of success cannot be dismissed lightly. It corresponds closely with the actual conduct of eminent men in the various walks of life. It is not unrelated to genuine critical standards. It requires the high human virtue of sheer courage. Personality cannot be faked indefinitely; and this philosophy of success requires solid gifts of personality, including an impregnable self-assurance. But it actively encourages the lust for power and forces men, under contemporary conditions, into the hell of astute publicity-hunting. They become what we may call by euphemism undesirable characters. Standards of what is decent may be set up, but these standards will have moral bases imported from a quite different and co-operative ethical sphere.

The doctrine contains valuable half-truths. Stupidity, slackness, inefficiency, instability of judgement, dullness of wit admit of no rational justification. The opposite virtues are admirable when they adorn a disinterested personality. A man seized by a true idea is entitled to identify his personality with that idea, whether it be in medical research or political organization, and to overawe others by the power and pertinacity of that personality. Courage, intelligence, experience, and self-control in pursuing a purpose are never of themselves vices.

Leadership, however, is a function for the service of the community. It is not true that the community is simply the matrix from which spring leaders whom it exists to nourish and serve. That which alone is entitled to ultimate service (if readers will have patience with this metaphysic of a truism which is not trite) is the good, the beautiful, and the true. The first of these cannot be attained by the egoistic man and, hence, the last cannot be attained by him and, hence again, assuredly the beautiful cannot be attained by him so that it is impressed on his own life.

Let me state the matter in a different way. We shall return later to the topic of a legitimate egoism. From the point of view, however, of a satisfying community this individualist philosophy is fundamentally egoistic and irreligious. It is rendered sufferable when suffused with the Tory loyalism; but it is of different origin and is fundamentally inconsistent with it. Its sole basis of agreement is to maintain the powerful in power: *beati possidentes*. If the old feudal, essentially Catholic Toryism offered a religion of gentlemen, admirable in its way, but which yet is not enough, the new, capitalist Toryism, which certainly does not lack intelligence, offers a cult of successful individualism which is, at heart, utterly immoral. It makes out the case for the Marxist argument which identifies class, Capitalism, and self-interest. It does not meet the need which we have set out to satisfy. It negates community.

§ iii

The Religion of Fascism

The Liberals succeeded after the rule of the Tory squire, with his privilege of birth, as the Whigs, earlier, succeeded the cavalier. The individualism, however, of the middle class, the individualism of the counting-house and the intelligensia, became sensitive and alarmed when the middle classes were, in turn, challenged in the name of the rights of the citizen masses. Not the general rights of man, but the particular rights of individuals, assumed importance. A self-interested rally began to the standards of nation, constitution, and property. The Tory faith became popular again, and this time among men whose fathers had fought it. Concurrently, the decay of Liberalism began.

The gospel of nationalism has, however, another and more challenging variety beside Toryism. That new faith is Fascism. The old Tory faith is bound up with the remnants of feudal loyalism. For the Fascist the Tory Nationalist, with his officer outlook, club code, and class policy, has no adequate sense for community. On the other hand, the commercial Conservative contingent, that has come to the support of Toryism, never had faith in much beyond money and its promise of progress by money-getting is being resonantly proven wrong in our own generation. Even America, which has no roots in the Catholic tradition and almost none in the feudal tradition, has been swept into the reaction against *laissez-faire*. For the Fascist the financial Tory is merely an individualist, without religion or the ultimate patriotism, defending his gains.

A PREFACE TO ACTION

If, for the Fascist, the Tory is not sufficient of a Socialist, the Marxist is not sufficient of a nationalist. The peculiar demand of the young men since the War, the inevitable demand arising from reaction against the motley character of a megalopolitan civilization, is for an ascetic discipline as preliminary to the reaffirmation of social values. There is no belief that significant human values can be achieved by empty and easy professions of belief in an automatic progress. Evil is real in life, in society, in the universe. There is no belief that the good society will be built by the pre-determined working of economic forces as the older school of Social Democrats, of the Kautskian profession, chose to teach. The good must be fought for. And the evil is so real that the discipline of the fight must be bitter, must transcend private vagary and license, must sift out the new man from the riff-raff, must build a new religion, intolerant in its fierce convictions.

Mr. Wells has coined the phrase, "Liberal Fascism." The new generation, afraid of the sentimentality of progress but generous in its passion for creative work, tries to find in these words a meaning. It demands reason and discipline. It rejects the optimistic Toryism of no change. It demands fanatically a concept of community such as the Tory has never known. But it observes that to build the new civilization one must begin somewhere. Even Stalin, in Russia, is speaking of "Socialism in at least one country." It asks where to begin.

To this demand the German National Socialist offers, in reply, the nation. If great economic change is to be wrought, it must be wrought at such a heat of emotion, and with such pressure, that the will for change can be effective. If the honour of the nation is to be vindicated, the individual must be content to count himself lucky if

THE RELIGION OF FASCISM

he is permitted to sacrifice himself for the Fatherland. In that sacrifice his petty individuality will be caught up in an ennobling idealism. As Herr Feder, one of the original Nazi leaders, writes: "The fragrance of Germany's soil fills with happiness the wanderer treading on native ground with which his blood is one."

The National Socialist movement in Germany is entirely overshadowed and coloured by the humiliations of the Peace of Versailles. The idea of the nation, as a blood unit, assumes a disproportionate place and becomes obnoxious to all those arguments discussed fully in an earlier chapter. Hence the resulting philosophy, in the German variant of Fascism, often obliterates the distinction between Tory Nationalism and National Socialism and substitutes an exposition of German grievances for the theory of what Herr Hitler, in *Mein Kampf*, insists is a world view and a world movement.

However, something of a general philosophy does emerge. Herr Sieburg devotes a brilliant book to the need for passing from the ideal of humanity to that of the nation, welcomes the charge of barbarism, and declares that "the German is bound to his fellow men, not by what constitutes his personality, namely, reason, but by destiny, which makes him a sharer in the boundless realm of Nature." This destiny, however, appears as the destiny of the German people with whom he is united, above all rational argument, by blood. "Blood-reasoning" stands here deliberately contrasted with rational, civilized, and Hellenic values. It is the philosophy of Lawrence, the war objector, and Nietzsche, the good European, at their worst. It has no reply, this religious mania of nationalism, save force, to the equally aggressive and intuitive self-assertion of the individual. It is the rage and shouting of a resentful and unjustly treated nation, that sometimes reduces itself to the level of gibbering folly. It is a glorification of the great Nordic race in alliance with Japan. It is black with the *furor Teutonicus*. It is Gothic.

A more lucid version of the philosophy of the national community (*Volksgemeinschaft*) is to be found in Italy. Typically, the Latin form places stress on the objective state, the Teutonic form upon the subjective nation. Because it is less spiritually subtle—has fewer spiritual pretensions—it is less dangerous. The stress upon national honour is no less in Italian Fascism; but it is connected with a much clearer notion of the inner structure of the society. It is not so clearly a child of foreign policy, nor is it afflicted, as is German National Socialism, by a nostalgia for mediaeval handicrafts. It is less emotional, more Roman. It builds, not a treaty revision, but a new social order on the sacrifice of the individual. It affirms the classic notion of justice, each in his job. It is Mussolini who has declared that the interests of the state take precedence of all particular interests. Fascism is alleged to be a fusion of all interests into the major interest of the nation-state. The fusion is not temporary, but an adamantine union. "Fascism is monolithic."

This Fascist religion of sacrifice confronts the modern world. The rumour of it is heard even in America. Fascism is represented in Britain by Sir Oswald Mosley, a man in intelligence and ability worth about ten of Herr Hitler. He has vision and *panache*. The question is whether the vision is right. Whether Fascism in England can ever grow, as it grew in Germany, from its present insignificant beginnings need not at this point be debated.

THE RELIGION OF FASCISM

Mosleyism offers a very complete exposition in Britain of the universal Fascist tendency and, as such, its principles demand examination.

At least this movement has the merit of demanding sacrifice for the community and a discipline. Its ideals cannot be peremptorily dismissed as vulgar. Briefly, its aim is to couple national patriotism with the scientific spirit and efficient thoroughness of the modern world. It speaks of the supersession of the notion of class by the notion of the community. It divides from Toryism, because the Conservative attitude to vested interest impedes the efficiency of national organization and narrows the basis of the full enjoyment of citizenship, forgetting the primacy of the interest of the nation as an integral whole. It divides from Socialism, with an accusation of democratic inefficiency, and from Communism, which it charges with a corrupt materialism, with a disruptive internationalism, and with a malevolent separation of each national community into proletarian sheep and capitalist goats.

The objects of Sir Oswald Mosley were—and about this I can venture to speak with some assurance—frankly socialistic, whatever they now may have become in the endeavour to secure support. His last book on *Greater Britain* contains very significant references to my lords Rothermere and Beaverbrook which, were I a socialistic National Socialist, I should find disturbing for the prospect of the classless state. Initially Mosley was faced with the problem of how to supply Socialism with that emotional drive which would make it effective in Britain—to supply it with drive at such a pace as appeared to be required in years of economic crisis. Of the emotional dynamos which might be placed behind an administrative mechanism for national reorganization one, the class-war, appeared to be of dubious efficiency, in view of the British tradition, and destructive of social unity. It generated heat by producing the maximum of friction. The alternative appeared to be to utilize nationalist enthusiasm. In a speech, in 1931, before the Fabian Society, Sir Oswald Mosley made a statement on nationalism and internationalism which was unexceptionable in character. National planning and trade control were treated as incidents in the development of international planning and control, so soon as these could be matured, with a view to the general maintenance, along Socialist lines, of a high standard of living and of civilization. Progressively, however, the emphasis has fallen more upon the nation; in the attitude to Indian nationalism there has been a distinct stress on imperialism; in *Greater Britain* constructive internationalism is not conspicuous. Step has definitely been put on to the Fascist slope.

This book is not a treatise on economics and the economic argument of Mosleyism may be sketched in briefly. The standard of living of the workers in this country, although lower than that of the American or Australian artisan in employment, is high compared with that of most countries. Any international Socialist policy which leads to its reduction must be avoided. Further, labour competition with low-standard countries, exploited by a wage-cutting Capitalism, must be shut out. Thanks to scientific invention we live in an epoch of prosperity-economy rather than of poverty-economy. Most common needs (although, thanks to a rash economy, not some essential ones) can be met by home production and need not rely upon international trade. On the other hand, modern mass-production favours low-grade labour against the highly skilled craftsman (other than engineers) and, hence, is disadvantageous to those countries which hitherto have maintained a high standard of living. The remedy lies in trade control until such time as backward countries have achieved a higher standard of demand. The pouring out of capital into backward countries in order precipitately to develop there the profit-making industrial revolution is unsocialistic and unpatriotic. Through investment boards this capital should be directed into the development of home industries for the home market. In this home market there is a direct relation between the rate of wages, the extent of sales, and business profits. Competent national organization can make it possible to guarantee high real wages. Vested capitalist interests, which oppose this reorganization for the benefit of the whole citizen body, must be thrust to one side.

In order to carry through this scheme of national reconstruction serious modifications must be made in the industrial and financial tradition of such a country as Britain, which has been built up by exploiting free trade with a view to the international sale of its own high-grade staple and luxury products and which has become the world's banker. These factors of prosperity belong to the past. How far British traders have been pampered by their past good luck is shown by their off-hand and bad marketing. The new national units choose to manage their own economic affairs; can largely produce for themselves; and can increasingly dispense with Britain. The memory of this past good fortune by glorifying an obsolete tradition is now an active source of weakness.

Britain must become insulated and self-contained so far as possible, precisely in order that there may be a direct relation, under one political system, between production by wage-earners and the market for consumption offered by high-wage-earners. Even in respect to foodstuffs Britain is able to be self-contained much more than she has been hitherto. Granted bulk-purchases and bulk-sales through export corporations, or at least national control, she should be able to import and export such goods as may be desirable under the most advantageous conditions and without affecting her standard of living. Finally, this standard of living could be guaranteed by trade arrangements for mutual aid and non-competition (at least as touching labour rates) between high-standard-of-living countries, among which the most sympathetic assistance might be expected from those which were also high-standard members of the British Commonwealth. That Commonwealth, actually and latently, is one of the three dominant world Powers. It, with the United States and Russia, has oil and is almost entirely self-sufficient.

A wicked policy has been followed of grabbing at quick returns. The consequences are writ large, as Fenner Brockway shows in his noble book, in the devastated areas of Lancashire. Now there is a tendency to turn in despair to a yet more intensified exploitative imperialism and, following such Liberals as Lord Snowden, to seek to develop at breakneck speed—not healthy organization at home—but backward and colonial areas.

"The nigger who had one bicycle is to take two, and he who had none is to take one." This policy is, in fact, one of the dog returning to its vomit. The initial error yielded incidental gains; we are to repeat the error, hope for the gains and cure ourselves by homeopathy. Whether this exploitation of backward areas is for the good of their peoples is an inconvenient question not asked by the exponents of this theory. As was explained, in connection with the Kenya goldfields, at least it is intended that "not a native shall be the poorer for the discovery of gold on his land." Perhaps he may even buy British goods with the money that he gets for it, if British export goods are marketed vigorously enough.

It is this Liberal doctrine, then, of rash individual exploitation which is basically responsible for the scandal of the gold-rush of the Kavirondo, where an Imperial Government that recalled that an English administrator's word should be his bond should have intervened with a drastic hand. England has been the first in the international market. That adventitious advantage has now long entered on the period of decreasing returns. She has been the world's capitalist, the friend of the bankers. She, above all save America, has imposed an "interest-bondage" on the rest of the world. She now discovers that international investment solely for profit returns and consideration for the weal of her own citizens do not go well together.

What, however, is to be done? The abstract internationalism of such writers as Professor Cassel or Dr. Sprague, with their detachment of a "natural" economic system from political and human considerations, with their subordination of actual human needs to economic laws based upon rather slick suppositions about human nature—their subordination of man to Sabbatic ritual in praise of the fiscal system—means hell for the individual who happens to have selected the wrong decade and the wrong country to starve in. Professor Cassel thinks in nothing less than half-centuries and the world scene. It may be that there is nothing better to do than to install a birth-control clinic in every mining village and to issue bottles of cyanide with instructions for human use as a euthanasia. The temptation, however, of the ordinary human being in reaction against this detached Olympianism is to see salvation in an enlarged nationalism, despite all discouragements about emigration facilities. The temptation is to say, with Major Elliot, "Ottawa or nothing." The old, economic exploitation of the world, disguised as internationalism, is now (as in the second phase of the Roman Empire) to give way to a new, closed imperialism.

I do not wish to underestimate the gravity of the situation. In the United States the economic crisis, although severe, has been part of a strain general to the capitalist world, and broadly unconnected with any historical causes peculiar to that country. In Britain the situation is entirely different. The Free Trade period has come to its catastrophic end, leaving us indeed with the solid fruits of Victorian prosperity (much of it a rackrent on the future), but with a population which we cannot support on our home industries; a dependence for our vital necessities on imports and a corresponding need to maintain our exports at about their present 30 per cent of the total; a need to find markets at any cost for our overproduction for export; a fantastic belief that England can retain permanently the advantage which it temporarily had from being the home of the early inventions and of Liberal ideas of industrial development; the illusion of continuing as the privileged workshop of the world; and the wreckage, short of vigorous national reorganization, of our staple industries. If this reorganization can be achieved by a frontal attack upon those who retain a belief in what can be done by production chiefly for the luxury-grade foreign market, rather than for the popular home market; by national protection in alliance with Commonwealth countries; and by appealing to national determination on a new non-party basis (which, in effect, means a new party basis) against vested interests, the case for such an appeal and policy appears to be strong indeed.

The policy of England, the world banker and the seller of dear, high-grade, and luxury-class goods, has been the economic exploitation of the workers of the world while still backward. The exploitation might have continued had not greed of gold and lust of profits led us to sell them machinery also. Doubtless, despite much suffering, the world is the richer for the economic exploitation carried out by ourselves and (less recklessly from a national standpoint) by the Americans. The world has prospered under the economic imperialism of our free investors with their financial liens in every capital. Now the time has come for us, our population, and our workers to pay for these advantages. We forgot our own national health or attended to it only in the intervals of the great Victorian boom. The profits are now falling. Gratitude there is none. And we have the population, reared to a privileged standard on the world average, to feed and clothe.

The workers of the world can only invite us to get off our high-horse and return to the average—which has a different look to Polish or Indian eyes from that which it has to Yorkshire or Michigan. The employers will call the same process a return to a competitive basis of labour costs. The prime national problem of the moment is how to maintain for our workers—that is, for our nation, our society as distinct from our Society—the present above-average standard of living, perhaps by concerted action with the New World, with its population shortage and high wages. The National Socialists at least make an honest attempt at a solution: they call it "insulation."

And they advise us, if we can and so far as we can, to get the Commonwealth to agree to inclusion in that insulation.

For Mosley an internationalism which is not founded on a powerful common sentiment is without substance. Even in his days as a Socialist minister, he looked for this sentiment, not in the feeling and fanaticism of class-unity and class-war, but in the feeling and fanaticism of racial unity, at least as the first support in the task of building a planned world economy. In the same way he looked to national sentiment as the basis for that performance of public duty and for that public devotion which Socialist theory commends. Explicitly, he would have begun the task of social reconstruction by using this sentiment to the full, without denying the international context, just as Stalin, while talking of internationalism, has actually proceeded upon the principle of "Socialism in at least one country."

For myself I can see nothing objectionable in organization of areas of the world for mutual protection of their standard of culture and of living, provided that these regional agreements do not become nationalist impediments to further advance. On the contrary, I applaud them as steps to practical international co-operation away from the financiers' paradise of *laissez-faire*. The answer, however, to the Fascist or Chauvinist who uses this argument to further his thesis will, I think, be—not that, because human beings are irrational, we must appeal to fanatical national emotion—but that, because human beings are irrational, it is much too dangerous to appeal to unqualified national emotion. The risks for civilization in the modern world are too great. Original sin is too much a reality.

Not a few of Sir Oswald Mosley's proposals, either urged by him alone or also urged by the late E. F. Wise and his group, are now being advocated by persons who will certainly not make acknowledgment of any debt from such a source since for them there is no health in it. The whole scheme of export and import boards, and the rejection of Cobdenite Free Trade with its assimilation of the fluidity of labour to the fluidity of money (as if a man could tear himself and his family up over night and leave for the Argentine because wages, based on natural advantages, are for the moment higher there)—all these proposals are beginning to seep into the programme of the official Labour Party or are being advocated now by active members. The same is true of proposals for the reorganization of Parliament upon a more executive model and even the suggestion agitated in some quarters for the retention of power until the work of reconstruction has been carried through. However, that a very practical expression of the war against exploitative Capitalism is the building up of a trade-control barrier between countries which provide a high standard of living for workers and countries where labour costs are cut, and which subsist on a low standard, is something which even yet is anathema to those who may talk of Socialism, and even about class-war, but who are primarily Liberal internationalists. An early change may, nevertheless, be anticipated in this attitude and in the direction of following the Russian model, with its complete trade regulation.

Mosley's scheme, like Hitler's and Mussolini's, with its downright passionate appeal to national patriotism and other motives not so ideal, proposes to bludgeon out of existence all party dissension, that is, all opposition to its own views. The active Communist threat and the rottenness of Parliamentary Liberalism gave Mussolini his chance in Italy. The War, the Peace, and the economic depression, accentuated after the collapse of the American dream of prosperity-for-all by machinery, the poltroonery of the Social Democrats, the growth of the Communist movement, made Hitler. In Italy there was no established national nobility to "go Mussolini one better." In Germany the selfish divisions among the Junkers and the mistaken belief of the Nationalists that they could use Herr Hitler for their own purposes have placed power in his hands. In England the ruling class has not, hitherto, been seriously unsettled by Mosley; it can play the game better. Nevertheless, Sir Oswald Mosley may secure a degree of workers' support that Lords Lloyd and Trenchard could never command. Further, whatever its prospect of success as a matter of tactics (and this probably depends, not upon the opinion of this politician or that, but upon the international economic situation), the claim of a movement seeking to achieve the Socialist or even Communist commonwealth, by vigorous discipline and action, through reliance upon national patriotism, offers a challenge which demands reply.

The National Socialist idea is valid of substituting, for the notion of irresponsible international exploitation for profit, the notion of building up a planned home economy designed to maintain in decency and dignity the body of the citizens of the country. It is not necessarily unsound in seeking to achieve this end by executive means so long as positive liberty is in fact increased—liberty to live a less impoverished life: the liberty in which the common man is immediately interested—although there is grave peril of undue contempt by headstrong or infallible persons for the shrewd judgement and practical common sense of ordinary folk when left to themselves. Confidence, nevertheless, in this Fascist pursuit of corporate liberty is not increased by Il Duce's talk about the goddess of Liberty being dead and her body already putrescent.

Talk of "scientific government," like talk of "rationalization" and of that "national planning" which followed upon the criticism of rationalization in its relation to technological unemployment, is often a use of big words to conjure with, meaning little. In the opinion of one of the senior supporters of Messrs. MacDonald and Thomas, it is a sure sign that there is "mental woolliness about." If, of course, we mean that any scholar or minister's assistant secretary, sitting in his study, can work out a blue print for the detailed organization of the industrial life of a country at a time unspecified, then the notion is unqualified nonsense. It is, further, true that bad planning is a great evil. If, however, we mean that the Soviet Gosplan, for good or ill, does not exist, is absurd, and, if it exists, ought not to be considered, then it is we who are talking nonsense. We are further talking dangerous nonsense if an indolent, amateur plain-man common sense leads us to treat with contempt the notion of the substitution of exact knowledge in directing the utilization of the community's resources for the opinion of unorganized private individuals and for the chances and hazards of their unconnected activities. Political rationalization (to use the word in vogue before "planning," "technocracy," and the rest) involves the discarding of those institutions which obstruct the efficiency of any organization for its recognized ends and the introduction of agencies which effectively further those ends. All this, especially in view of human fondness for habit as a substitute for thought, is very necessary.

Accountability should cease with power to control in a modern integrated economy, national and even international, it is disastrous to allow a few men (I am thinking of great bankers and industrialists) to act in a fashion which may literally affect millions without a check being imposed, based upon a recognition of the function of these few, its limits, and the overruling demands of the campaign for social justice and against unmerited poverty. In so far as Fascism or National Socialism, within however narrow limits, recognizes this idea of an economy based, not on the calculus of chance among myriads of competing units, but upon deliberate human design so far as is warranted by gross human need, National Socialism has a strong case.

I do not agree with the Hon. Mr. Denman that Sir Oswald Mosley has displayed "a peculiarly talented incapacity for ruling Englishmen." But I do agree that the operatic methods and Rudolph Valentino eyes of Signor Mussolini are inappropriate to this sober clime. We cannot here say, as has Signor Mussolini, "the people are like little children . . . they have not asked for liberty." English workers are probably not fanatical about precisely the liberties that interested John Hampden. But the proportion of born masochists and natural doormats in this country is never likely to give scope for the boot-wipings of a Mussolini. Clearly the British movement is chiefly interesting to the extent to which it shows the power of adapting itself to home conditions and of stressing the notion of the dominant personality in a fashion that will stir British imagination.

The answer to Fascist doctrine has already been given by implication in this book. International organization rests, not upon a sentiment, but upon a rational and administrative necessity. It is not likely to be advanced, or approximated to, by novel applications of the tribal principle or of state voodoo worship—but rather retarded. National areas emphatically have their place in the hierarchy of communities of common sentiment. But the deliberate integration, by stimulating an exclusive and staccato chauvinist sentiment, of regions of the earth, racial or linguistic, into mutually exclusive communal areas, is not likely of itself to advance international organization (save, perhaps, by giving to some one group overwhelming power). It perpetuates the influence of a false principle of local feeling in matters ultimately concerning reasonable civilization, law, and of order. The aggressive nationalist is still far too common for gratuitous encouragement to be given to him. The appeal to patriotism must be a most sober appeal sharply and specifically distinguished from chauvinist heroics and he-man-in-a-cocked-hat stuff. Similarly, at home, the appeal to national community sentiment needs careful handling if it is not to introduce a dangerous irrelevancy which will be exploited by the privileged and particularist groups, as a matter of tactics, while it narrows and demeans the ultimate cause of human well-being and dignity.

Nationalism has its legitimate place, but it is merely that of one circle of human sympathy and attachment.

A PREFACE TO ACTION

Far from hallowing a campaign for the vindication of human dignity, its best hope is that it may be hallowed by it and that national sentiment may be made the instrument—but certainly not the master and judge—of the ideal. It is, of course, perfectly possible deliberately to utilize—as Mosley and Stalin and other intelligent men have sought to utilize—national sentiment as an agent for stirring the mass of folk to pursue ends more elevating than those of private selfishness—but also more important than those of national prestige. It is Stalin who, in a significant passage in his report to the XVIth Congress of the Communist Party, says: "The development of culture, national in form, socialist in content, during the period of the dictatorship of the proletariat, as a prelude to their fusion in a single, universal culture (both in form and content) expressing itself in one language, such as will arrive when men's habits are permeated by Socialism—that is the Leninist dialectic on the subject of national culture." That is perhaps as happy a statement as any that can be placed to Stalin's credit.

Perhaps the best characteristic of the Englishman is that he has been prepared to do his job, the world over, as a man and, therefore, to claim the right to do it as an Englishman. The German has worked, wherever he was, first as a German for Germany, and only secondarily as a man, for which reason the rest of the world has been on guard lest he extend the field of his parochial patriotism.[1]

There is probably no man who is not a better administrator, a better fighter, a better citizen because he feels that, in his own person, he sustains and is responsible

---

[1] I permit this to stand; conversation leads me to think that many Germans would admit it to be broadly true. I hasten to add that I do not think that there is a species "Englishman," more moral than a species "German."

THE RELIGION OF FASCISM

for the high honour of his people. That is good. But the trouble with the utilization of this sentiment for ulterior ends is that the weapon becomes too powerful for him who uses it. National pride is one good sentiment (like self-pride) among many good sentiments in a world of balanced values. But national glory is not an indispensable mark of a good society, and those, like M. Clemenceau, who have substituted this new religion of Glory for the old religion of God are not only infidels but dangers to civilization. And the Socialist who compromises with national "nostroism" (to keep Major Elliot's term) to gain his political ends, himself finishes by being a nationalist who has compromised true values.

Fascism and National Socialism are, it can be argued, compromised, and that twice over. Fascism and National Socialism are now established political systems expressing a spirit from which any individual Fascist leader can with difficulty free himself. It is childish to judge great world movements as one would judge the morality of individuals. There are yet ideals of civilization by which we judge and assess all other and lesser ideals.

By their own admission Fascism and National Socialism are compromised with a nationalism which belongs to a system that has had its day. That reform must begin in a specific administrative area is no reason for excluding consideration of the ends of satisfactory reform, which must lead out beyond this area. All attempts to pursue this national ideal to its conclusions can only be fraught with danger of catastrophe in the modern world—and, not least, in the British Commonwealth, which is already saddled with the results of Irish and Indian nationalism.

The result of that unrestrained and impious worship of the nation spells the Balkanization of the world. It does not put before nations an obligation masterfully to build, as the monument of their highest pride, an international order. Mosley will have to denounce chauvinism very hard and carry the Fascist pragmatism about means into a field where it has hitherto never been carried before he can rid himself of this taint of a national idolatry that logically would disrupt the Commonwealth. This narrow enthusiasm of less than imperial—of national—resentment against civilization is natural with countries who have been left behind, either by isolation, natural poverty, or the misfortune of war, in the race for power. The typical Fascist theory of Japan, Italy, and Germany expresses the resentment of the unprivileged nations, the Cinderellas of history. The nations that militarily have no hope against the imperial Powers voice the reasonable demand for international equity. For the Powers, however, of the second order in national strength the criminal route of private war still for obvious reasons has its attractions.

Herr Hitler has explained to us at length the tactic of nursing the strength of Germany by talk of peace, both abroad and even to his brown battalions. I see no reason to doubt the strict sincerity of the talk of "peace with honour." But national honour will only be consistent with international justice and sovereignty when that sovereignty is armed with unchallengeable power. Signor Mussolini, his emergency being less pressing, has been more frank. "War," said Treitschke, "is a medicine to mankind diseased." "Man," says Spengler, the ex-schoolmaster, "is a human carnivore." Signor Mussolini, at least, will not be accused of preaching the faith of Attila from the swivel-chair of a sedentary occupation. "War," he says, "alone brings up to its highest tension all human energy and puts the stamp of nobility upon the people who have the courage to meet it." That statement is only partly true: the word "alone" is false. "Thus," he continues, "a doctrine which is founded upon this harmful postulate of peace is hostile to Fascism." That the postulate of peace is harmful is false.

The establishment of peace was precisely the ground of pride of Signor Mussolini's own Roman forebears. And that establishment of peace, not the bandit return to international anarchy, demands the highest tension in all human energy. Sir Oswald Mosley may honestly insist that his object is the maintenance of the *Pax Britannica*. His continental associates in Fascism appear to have no such object. His own best chance of success will come if the people of this Commonwealth are angered beyond endurance by fire-eating militancy in countries where democracy has collapsed.

Further, because Fascism is tied to a traditional and obsolescent social order in its relation to the state, it tends to share—however much it protests to the contrary—the privileged class and capitalist traditions of that system. The most important issue for German National Socialism will be whether Herr Hitler and Dr. Goebbels are strong enough to force through their party programme against the opposition of the owners of great private wealth who now co-operate with Herr Hitler and have in the past financed him.

If the situation changes to violence, due to intolerable economic conditions, then it does not seem to me important, probable or desirable to salvage national sovereignty, with its irrationalities, or the power of private wealth as the great principles upon which base to construct a new social order. If we have to go through the Red Sea, let it not be in order to make a detour back to Egypt. Fascism offers, as against a peaceful constitutional régime, violence tempered by nationalism and, as against a violent, innovating revolution, the antiquated principle of the sovereign national state as the great hope. I am unconvinced, despite unfeigned respect for the ability of my late leader, that this new scheme is intelligent in the beginning or durable in the effect. I am unable, indeed, to share the happy instantaneity of Liberal ridicule, which seems to me reminiscent of that laughter of fools which is as the crackling of thorns under pots. I am prepared even to agree that the Liberal Greys and Simons, by their shifts and indecisions, may be more prolific causes of war than the nationalist parades and mass-meetings of Sir Oswald. But, while I am aware that this Fascism will frighten the more timid into Toryism and the more desperate into Communism, I do not feel sure that here we have the new aristocracy of the reign of reason.

To this twofold argument, that Fascism is wholly nationalist and semi-capitalist, a twofold reply will be made. A political leader must be supposed to mean what he says. Mosley has explicitly written, in *Greater Britain*: "Some will see in any such conception a menace to world peace. They assume that a highly organized Empire must be jingoistic and must pursue a policy of old-fashioned and aggressive imperialism. . . . In fact, a British Empire powerfully organized as an economic entity would be a factor on the side of world peace and stability." He repudiates chauvinism. He also denounces the capitalist social system in which the ownership of the means of production is organized for private profit, while he demands the encouragement and reward of socially useful private initiative. He summarizes his position in the phrase: "Our problem is to reconcile the revolutionary changes of science with our system of government, and to harmonize individual initiative with the wider interests of the nation." This summary is sufficiently instinct with a rational and classical spirit. With its stress upon science and order it looks to Greece and Rome for its ideas, and is quite devoid of the Teutonic frenzy.

The principles, as distinct from the methods, of Sir Oswald have scarcely changed since his Socialist days. The opposition to him centres upon the belief that the characteristics of Fascism abroad cannot be avoided in Fascism at home. The smell of the concentration camp surrounds him. He cannot rid himself of the suspicion of meditating those infringements of personal liberty to be seen in Hitler's Germany, which are obnoxious to every Englishman brought up in an ancient and proud political tradition. Englishmen will not go back upon Hampden. The English obstinacy remains. And even if Oswald Mosley repudiates—as he does repudiate—assimilation of his politics to those of Hitler and Göring, the assimilation to Mussolini is of his own choosing.

Englishmen, who threw off the venerable yoke of the Vatican, are not likely to accept political instruction, after centuries of leading Europe politically, from an Italian ex-journalist any more than from a Viennese painter. England has accepted, and is proud of, a Cromwell, but it will not accept some Italianate dictator. Mosley's task, if he would succeed, is to detach himself from these men and to discover, as Cromwell discovered, how to reconcile an iron discipline in fighting a dying system with a passionate belief in substantial liberty and in what Roger Williams, of Rhode Island, called "soul freedom."

At present Mosley is as negligible as Mussolini and

Hitler were. Certain factors may rapidly change that situation. The demand for discipline and renaissance is widespread. At present it is ineffective from lack of sense of direction. The demand of the workers for economic security is always present. Any grave loss in foreign trade or increase of economic stress (due, for example, to a striking collapse of the Roosevelt administration) or, again, any proximate threat of foreign war will precipitate a revolt against moderate and constitutional control. It will, in the present condition of discontent, provoke "activism" and a resort to dictatorial remedies.

This revolt against constitutionalism tends to spread. As each country succumbs, the remaining countries find it more difficult, if they are to maintain their international position, to keep to the liberal and tolerant democratic tradition. Any failure of a moderate Government to fulfil its promises or, in England, any attempt of a conservative group to entrench itself by modifying the parliamentary constitution in its own favour, so as to impede democratic change, will have the same "activist" result. Especially would this be the case were the governing classes and their supporters unable, in these days when their own economic security is threatened, to maintain a certain margin of security for the worker.

The first consequence of the growth of an activist move will be a secession, among the more enthusiastic political workers, from Socialism to Communism on the ground that the so-called more "realistic" Communist analysis has been proved to be right. The failure of reform will be urged as an argument for the need of revolution. The "governing class," it will be urged, has never yet made concessions voluntarily unless it did so from its own superabundance. All hope for compromise, it will be said, has been removed. All common ground for agreement on constitutional fundamentals, on which could rest common resistance to dictatorship, is absent. Justified, in their own eyes, by sincerity and by an intelligent appreciation of realities, the Socialist secessionaries will go to their tents, hoping to win the country to their view within a time, on their own supposition, exceedingly short, and will improvise a technique of organization to meet the impending disruption of constitutionalism. When charged with handling the weapons of dictatorship and violence, this group will reply, in the words of a great revolutionary: "As well say that the axe in the hands of the heroic leader in the cause of freedom has any likeness to that used by the common executioner in the service of a tyrant" (Robespierre).

The second consequence, in Anglo-Saxon countries, arising by reaction from the first, will be a formidable increase of Fascism. Then will come the hour in Britain for so able a man as Sir Oswald Mosley—or for anyone who, in that day, understands the temperament of the country still better. In the United States, owing to its vast size, lack of cohesive opinion, and cultivation of the myth of political individualism, a personal dictatorship is less probable. The American is not easily moved to respect for any political leadership. Labour riots among the immigrant population, developing into race riots and a flood of chauvinist nationalism, such as the United States, unlike Europe, has never hitherto seen, is the sequence that has to be reckoned with in American affairs.

The factors that make for Fascism are contingent. Human nature is permanent, within historical time, but its social expression is not permanent. Human history remains open to be shaped by the will of determined men. For the Anglo-Saxon peoples there is no predetermined course from democracy to dictatorship that must be followed, just as the Roman Republic passed from the tribunate of the Gracchi to the dictatorship of Sulla and to Caesarism. That is mere Spenglerian occultism and irrational charlatanry.

There are yet strong, specific, and rationally discoverable factors making today for Fascist domination, in Britain and America as elsewhere, especially the hopes for a wider life aroused by democracy itself; the tension of economic crisis and of political resentment, among some nations, to the Peace Treaties, with the ensuing repercussions in the policy of other nations; the demand for discipline, in reaction against a standardless condition where the old morality is broken and a new one not found; impatience with democracy, parliamentarianism, and constitutionalism; and the feelings of pride of nation and pride of personal glory as a basis for discipline and values. Fascism has also made a contribution to the politics of the future by stressing, as the Tories failed to stress, the significance of biology in politics—but has, straightway, perverted its discovery to the service of racial theories that few, if any, biologists of reputation can countenance. These theories are as worthless, and more dangerous, than the heraldic lore of the Tories. Nor can all the fury even of General Göring make what is scientifically false to be scientifically true.

Whether this Fascist tendency can be met will depend upon whether, in time, it can be opposed by an equal determination, expressing itself in a discipline no less stringent and based upon a sense of values even more emphatic—instead of by the poltroonery that has sometimes characterized Social Democrats. The task of any opposing movement is to stress the sense of personal liberty existent in all and seeking expression in all fields, political, social, and economic, and to weld this demand of common men for substantial liberty against oppression and injustice, political or economic, into an instrument of power. Its task is to interpret the Anglo-Saxon tradition of liberty in terms of the twentieth century and to set up both a new Socialism and a new Independency.

Fascism, whether as practised at Rome or Potsdam, like the Communism of the Kremlin is, for Anglo-Saxons, an importation foreign in spirit to their own proud and ancient political tradition. The Anglo-Saxon peoples have hitherto given, and not received, their political beliefs: they have been essentially political peoples. Conservatism, Liberalism, the Socialism of Owen and of Morris have been native growths. The Whiggery that is the basis of all American political thought is the pure tradition of Milton and Locke, elaborated by Jefferson and Lincoln. It is more purely English than England's own party theories. It is the task of these peoples again to provide the world with a political ideal that can include liberty along with order, and pragmatism in its view of the state along with idealism in public spirit.

Mosley, on the other hand, has yet to convince his public that his system is English. Fascism has a great advantage in its individualistic appeal to the principle of leadership and in the deep desire of the mass of people to be decisively and personally led by a hero to a new life in a promised land. Through participation in the movement they acquire a personal sense of power. Leadership, however, is purchasable at a smaller cost than that of stamping down all ideals and initiative other than those of the true faith, the new Islam. If, on the other hand, politics is turned into something less than a religion with a discipline in which Englishmen are invited to follow a demi-god, then the dictator merely becomes the supreme demagogue appealing to the gallery. The gift that Cromwell and Lincoln both possessed so supremely, of insisting upon authority in oneself while respecting individuality in others, does not come easily by the way of the Fascists. The call of "England, Arise" and "Awake, America" will not necessarily be sounded on these bugles. The Anglo-Saxon peoples do not like doctrinaire systems and steel orthodoxies.

§ iv

The Religion of Communism

The principles and practice of Benevolent Despotism, with its alleged superiority to particularist interests, were able to sustain themselves in Europe for two centuries. To their exponents they appeared self-evidently reasonable and conducive to efficient government. The principles and practice of Fascism are also unlikely to prove a mere flash in the pan. The seeds of decay in Fascism will, however, grow rapidly if it is so mismanaged as to offer, in response to the claims of personality, only the dictatorship of one man and his lieutenants, the rights, not of men, but of a man; if it confounds its novel biological doctrine of the claims of good stock with a mere barbaric tribalism which ignores the rôle of mixed races; if, despite talk of a classless society and (N.S.D.A.P. Programme, § ii) of "the abolition of incomes unearned by work," it merely places in power the new privileged group of party men besides the old privileged group of inherited wealth; and if its peculiar method of arousing community spirit makes plain that its policy will issue, first, in a sadistic chauvinism and, then, in actual war, destructive of the white races and of the Western tradition.

It is not impossible that this decay, under Fascism as under the Roman Adoptionist Emperors, may take the form of a gradual loss among the masses of all broad civic interests, when the religious enthusiasm of the Fascist dawn is dissipated. It is more probable that the result, certainly after a war of the modern type and even before it, will be a revolt of the masses, taking shape in a proletarian, equalitarian, and international organization and coming to a climax as a Communist rising, similar to that against the last of the old despotisms, the Tsardom.

Such an organization would require for success a discipline and sacrifice fanatical in fervour. Communism today in Russia is a religion. The ikons of Marx and the Communist Fathers have taken the place of the pictures of Christ and the saints. It is the fact that it has achieved this fervent activism that makes Russian Communism an infinitely more powerful force than German Socialism, with its respectable rationalism, materialist philosophy, and doctrine of economic determinism. Communism offers itself as a world religion of social justice.

It is as such that it is formidable. Many responsible thinkers are apparently of the opinion that either reforms must take place, for example, in Britain, of a fundamental nature or Communism must come. "Certainly," writes H. J. Laski, "to counter its seduction means the alteration of the present social order by concessions larger in scope and profundity than any ruling class has so far been willing to make by voluntary act." In the view of Mr. Wells, if "Liberal Fascism" is not possible, then Communism is the inevitable alternative.

The refusal, however, of ancient privilege to yield power is not a law of nature; and the victory of Communism is certainly not the inevitable immediate alternative to the old Capitalism or even to Social Democratic reform. In the pendulum swing of history it is more likely that Fascism will be the consequence of a failure of Socialism and that Communism will be, not the immediate, but the second step in this dialectic: the move after Fascism and against it. The ultimate coming of the Communist epoch, moreover, supposes the failure of other social systems to yield any adequate satisfaction for

THE RELIGION OF COMMUNISM

human needs: that they fail as national systems. The reason that moves in history will, therefore, destroy them. It also supposes that upon some more intelligent scheme of satisfactions Communism can build a structure of determination and faith more powerful than any of its opponents.

To discuss Communism as a religion, and to demand that it shall be discussed as one religion of the future, still appears to conventional people surprisingly strange. The words "Communist materialism" obscure from their consideration the extent of selfless Communist devotion, the idealism and heroism of the Communist martyrs and confessors, such as Dimitroff, and causes them to forget that, if the Nazis have also in Wessel, Schlageter, and Quex their martyrs, they too have their full share of worldly covetousness.

Communism, moreover, is precluded for many people from consideration as a guiding principle in life by their belief that it is associated in practice with exceedingly undesirable persons. That belief has the justification that Russian revolutionaries, including Lenin, have specifically spoken of the utility to the movement of the criminal elements in effecting violent change. And violent change is the specific remedy (as touching means and methods) of the Communists. Certainly an apostate from the Communist faith is often more objectionable in their eyes than a criminal. Fascism and insurgent nationalism have at various times been tarred with the same brush of criminality. Such associations, and reports of mob excesses, tend to rule the movement out for decent people who, as war-time experience showed, were certainly not lily-livered when there was a call to action which commanded their moral assent.

During the War period I recall that bayonet practice was taught on the parade ground by charging straw sacks marked with red blotches indicating vital points in the human body. The significance of the kidneys as such a vital point was explained. The bayonet was thrust home in this practice to the accompaniment of the guttural sound "Ugh," which was held to be a suitable expression of released energy. The bayonet instruction was so far as possible carried out in actual warfare. I shall not elaborate upon other conditions and events of warfare of a more irregular nature. It is enough to point out that this technique at least is approved—Clausewitz will state it in more dignified and impersonal terms—as necessary action against human beings, individually doubtless good fellows enough, in the name of the ideal of national autonomy or of national honour.

In considering any movement which is to achieve human change against resistance—whether it be insurgent nationalism with its assassinations or the movement of the early Christians whom Tacitus described as springing from "the lowest dregs" of the people or Communism or Fascism—I ask myself two questions: "Does it, at its best, offer prospect of a happier condition of humanity than the present?" and "Does it, at its worst, fall below that level of infliction of human pain which the present national system, with its inevitable wars, its bayonet exercises, aeroplane bombers, and *flammenwerfers*, stands for and requires?" It is clear that, if the late war (as part and parcel of the present political system) sets the standard of atrocity beneath which we are not entitled to fall without sinning against civilization, we are allowed no little latitude.

Any humane man would desire to avoid shooting either a Welshman of Glamorgan or an Indian of Bombay, either a Norman of Normandy or a Norman of *Debrett's Peerage*. I am not, however, prepared to admit that, if it has to be done for the social good, the one act is inherently more honourable than the other. I am not prepared to admit that it is good and honourable, *dulce et decus*, to push a bayonet into the kidneys of a German to the accompaniment of the sound "Ugh," and that it is dishonourable and detestable to discuss or practice means, granted that they are less resultant in human pain, for the organization of society so as to insure an increase in human happiness.

Before forcible revolution can be morally approved its ends must be desirable; its means must be unavoidable by any alternative; and its success must be practicable. I admit, moreover, that revolution is a shooting issue—as is war. That, however, seems to me no final deterrent. The English constitution rests on a forcible revolution; so does the American; so does that of almost every European state. The ideals of Mazzini, Garibaldi, and Cavour do not lack attraction nor those of Washington . . . nor those of Cromwell. It is nonsense to exclude forcible revolution from the field of political consideration. It is equally foolish and irresponsible to welcome it when avoidable.

What decent men are concerned about is whether any less disgusting way of maintaining order in this world can be discovered than that of war, as a by-product of the present international anarchy among states, or of organizing the world than by revolution as a remedy for the present internal anarchy of economic conditions.

The international anarchy is today an admitted evil: the only defence, I suppose, is that no better organization (not, it would have to be held, even that of the Roman Empire) has been—or can be—devised. The economic anarchy is something which varies in intensity from country to country. Its consequences are written in the faces of those who from day to day do not know where their employment or their food is to come from. Like the villains of old, they know not on the day what their work shall be on the morrow. This individualist anarchism was doubtless at its worst under the decaying autocracy of the Tsars, when the crude commercial exploitation of the new Capitalism was, with unusual brutality, feeding on the old patriarchal and rural society. It is worse in Kentucky—where they produce unwanted soft coal and, it is reported, remedy their labour troubles by importing criminal characters to be sworn in as deputy sheriffs—than it is in Britain.

The serious question is whether the economic situation in Central Europe, in Britain, and throughout the industrialized world must not become far worse alike for the employer (who will have to sacrifice his last two thousand sterling) and for the employee (who will sacrifice his last two shillings) before it becomes better. Or will the present system of economic distribution stand and remain tolerable under the strain? The Communist answer is "No."

There is a large measure of agreement that the present economic order might be salvaged, if not as an efficient system yet as a temporarily tolerable one which can be revised and improved at leisure, provided that certain steps are taken. These steps involve international action directed towards financial stability, a large measure of disarmament, abolition of war debts and reparations, and some form of international control of trade.

Some people believe that crash can be avoided if these steps are taken. Some people believe that they will not be taken and that crash is unavoidable. The Conservative does not relish this policy, but he desires to retain the present economic system. The Communist does not desire that these steps shall be taken because they are contrary to his religion which he fears to contaminate by compromising with Capitalism to keep it on its feet. Others again are uncommitted to a creed. These desire a radical change of the technique of distribution. Realistically, therefore, they desire the adoption of any means which will give a peaceful time, although one not without menace for industrial die-hards, in which to work at the tempo required to effect a permanent remedy for the economic trouble and not merely at the spasmodic dictate of popular passion. The trouble, however, with those without a creed or fanaticism is that in troubled years they are so frequently without conviction or effectiveness.

I do not share the mystical optimism of some Marxists that, thanks to a benevolent historical determinism playing the rôle of *le bon Dieu*, out of the cruel clash of economic forces in chaos must inevitably come some day cosmos and human good. The determinism of history will have discords in store even after the Marxist revolution: that of which alone we have present certainty is human nature. Nor do I know why I should labour for the common good unless in that human nature lies the intuition of social obligation and justice. I do not share the demonology of those Marxists who hold it of faith that humane persons of themselves naturally good are sharply, clearly, and irrevocably divided into classes, some of which play in history the old part played by the devil, now discredited. I am of the opinion that the desirable liquidation of classes, resting on privilege or on interests unrelated to social function and utility, can be accomplished without so much theological dogma. I believe in religion, but not in an over-loaded, a superstitious religion.

The Russian Communist is entirely willing to encourage sporadic revolt, even when foredoomed to failure, as part of a general plan of maturing world revolution. At least for the Trotskyite wing Communism is only safe if it has been achieved in every country. Its achievement must be a violent process. This seems to be a piece of political mysticism unwarranted by the facts and even inconsistent with Marxism, which asserts that different political consequences will flow from different economic and historical situations. No one can reflect on the half-Asiatic Russia of the Tsar, with its flogging of peasants, its secret police, its "bloody Sundays," its Rasputins, its pogroms, without realizing that the political situation, with its incitement to revolution—that the political tradition—is startling in its difference from the situation and tradition in either Britain or America. This insistence, however, on the inevitability of universal revolution is not only cause but (fully as much) consequence of the position of Communism, not only as distinguished from Socialism by its revolutionary tactic, but as a religion of predestination which has to think in uncompromising and absolute terms, even if the practical conseqence be to build Fascist rule.

THE RELIGION OF COMMUNISM

As a matter of worldly sanity I reject for the European Occident, for Britain and America, the course of revolution, *rebus sic stantibus*, as the practicable means to a more just social system. I cannot prophesy, of course, what may be the case a decade or less hence if international conference fails and moderatism—Socialism, in brief—has been found inadequately masterful to rule the situation. I cannot prophesy what may happen if Socialism yields no such organized, disciplined, and self-sacrificing body of men of creative imagination as Communism claims to offer. I can only say that it is the error of the Communists, including John Strachey, as it was the error of Oswald Mosley, to overestimate the revolutionary nature of the present situation, at least in Britain. In America the adequate comment is the size of the Socialist vote when there were eleven million unemployed: the "liberty" mythology of individualism is still the object of blind faith interspersed by cynical disbelief in all corporate action. This cold-blooded judgement on the defect of Communist means, however, is nearly entirely irrelevant to a question of salvation by faith—by a rival faith to that of "rugged individualism."

It has been the argument of this book that a religion is what this world today demands. I am not now discussing whether it ought to require it: this depends upon whether the religion is advocated as a substitute for reason or as an emotional matrix which gives it body. I am stating my belief that the mass demand exists. That, however, certainly does not mean that any religion will serve. And before we enthusiastically accept a religion of blood it will be well to recall again the resentment of the last century against the abuses of religion and the ancient warning of Lucretius concerning the great evils to which religion may persuade men.

The only question, however, when we come to the matter of a religion, is not of means, but whether the ends sought are such as our moral conscience can approve, and such, indeed, as make on our conscience an imperative demand for a new way of life. Let us then examine, not the Communist means and tactic, which may well be wrong, but the Communist faith.

The cardinal objection to Russian Communism as a universal plan is that, if its tactics are unnecessary, apart from the background of the Tsarist autocracy, its aims are questionable in themselves. By its aims I mean its immediate aims as expressed and visible in Russia today. I am not competent to criticize paper aims which are contradicted daily by actual behaviour.

I admit that, when the transitional period of revolution is over and all non-proletarian classes liquidated; when the class-hatred and class-consciousness of the proletarians in turn are liquidated; and when the plan of a classless society is realized and operative, a condition of affairs very admirable and remote from the present may supervene. I do not know. Communism, so far as its ultimate principles are concerned, stresses—this cannot be said too clearly—the principle of liberty, although it is not so clear that it stresses ability, genius, and personality. It stresses liberty, to the point of anarchism, by its doctrine of "the withering away" of the state. It stresses internationalism to the point of seeking to obliterate race consciousness and race privilege. And it stresses out, beyond class warfare, the reign of peace.

THE RELIGION OF COMMUNISM

What I see in Russia and have to judge is a dictatorship, founded (let us admit) upon popular support, declining to treat the enemies of the régime as individuals or to allow them, or even supporters of the régime, free expression of opinion. I agree with the Communist ideal as I agree with fraternity; but I like Communism or death no better than I like fraternity or death. The cardinal sin which vitiates Russian Communism is that it attempts to realize ideals by force—which is contrary to the inherent nature of ideals. That may be a harsh necessity of tactics—it was found to be so during the English Revolution and the American Revolution—but the tendency to welcome these tactics colours the ideal itself, with its low respect for individual choice.

I am no bigoted exponent of an anarchist freedom of speech or morals. A society is entitled to protect public order. A Socialist society is entitled to protect by law and coercion the economic rights of the plain man. A society, where one is reasonably free to come or go, is further entitled to insist that individuals shall not live in it in a fashion which conflicts with the settled ideals, manner of life, and good pleasure of the body (and mind) of that society. A voluntary society is fully entitled to set up what an outsider may regard as a tyranny in morals provided that the society is in effect fully voluntary and that the society as a whole does not interfere with outsiders. I see little objectionable and much admirable in the discipline which the Society of Jesus exercises over its members. I admire the spirit of the General of the Society who declared "Either let it be so or let it not be." But I do not find unobjectionable the operation of the Holy Inquisition, save perhaps so far as it may have been a legal substitute for mob violence—either the Holy Inquisition of Toulouse, or of Spain, or of Moscow, or of the Palazzo Venezia and the Fascist Grand Council.

Russian Communism establishes a moral and political despotism which is not desirable elsewhere, even were its tactics feasible. It is Asiatic in temper, without adequate respect for personal values. The Catholic Church has been accused of the same fault, but it is difficult to disagree with the statement of Pius XI, in *Quadragesimo Anno*, that Communism endeavours to accomplish by coercion what is only desirable by choice. I do not here refer to changes tending to the more equitable distribution of property, which fall within the province of state legislation—as the very existence of graduated taxation implies. I do, however, refer to a system where men are compelled to live in a certain way of life, as on collective farms, under a pressure which in fact readily becomes coercive, or to work at a given pace, not as a matter of choice in response to incentives, whether of the public good or emulation or piece payment, but by discipline which can and does become a coercive discipline.

A happy and worthwhile society is one happy and worthwhile for the constituent individuals and not one in which a new model of happiness and worthwhileness is imposed on adult beings without choice, even if those adults be a minority in a community of which the majority tacitly and passively accepts the ideal. In order to fight poverty by law and organization, as in time of war, a large measure of individual liberty may have compulsorily to be sacrificed. But in the building up of a new society it is not desirable that "the possession of the greatest possible amount of temporal goods should be esteemed so highly that man's higher goods, not excepting liberty, must be subordinated and even sacrificed to the exigencies of efficient production," or that free choice should be subordinated to some infallible knowledge concerning what is the form of the good society.

The essence of Russian Communism is moral discipline—more than mere negative warfare against political opponents—enforced apart from voluntary submission to its principles. As such, and for the fundamental reasons in political philosophy which I have already given, I object to it.

Communism is monolithic. It seems to me entirely contrary to the spirit of the Communist movement in action to nationalize it and to divide between Russian Communism, German Communism, English Communism, and the rest. I freely admit that each Communist contingent, like each section of the Christian Church, will have its specific characteristics. But the notion of a multiple Communism is the heresy against which Trotsky fought and which Stalin, whatever his attitude otherwise to Trotskyism, has never admitted. I therefore confess to viewing with some initial suspicion John Middleton Murry's endeavour to drive a wedge between "Russian Communism" and a non-violent "English Communism." I admit here and now that I shall attempt to make such a distinction myself, with this difference, that I shall leave to the Communist Party in Russia, Britain, and elsewhere the unchallenged right to the doctrine of Communism by violent revolution without dilution. I shall endeavour to establish over against this a social principle which will be Communist only in the sense that any thorough application of Socialism—that, for example, Plato's application of Socialism—is Communist.

Mr. Middleton Murry prefers to talk of class-war, but

to make a distinction and to explain that he condemns and abominates class hate. The Bolsheviks are not so choice, and I confess that this distinction, although not unreal, appears to be calculated, first, utterly to confuse and, finally, much to irritate the plain man. For myself, while I think I can persuade ordinary folk to agree to the common-sense proposition that there are in society marked divergences between the interests of persons of different economic status or even of different occupation, I believe that either we should accept bloody Communism (which is what Trotsky and Stalin mean) or we should state most plainly what we mean when we use the *cliché*, "class-war." What is our attitude to "stasis"?

There is a war of interests, profound in the tradition of society, between those who believe that a man has a right to do what he will with his own and those who believe that economic power is only legitimate when exercised as a social function. There is a natural initial prejudice against Socialism on the part of members of the classes that hold private economic power. But potential Socialists are to be found wherever there are reasonable and humane men, who are prepared to accept a discipline for the sake of a cause. The divergence of interests, so far as men permit themselves to live and think in terms of pecuniary classes rather than functions, is a fact, but it is a fact which civilized men are prepared to condemn and for it to substitute the notion of a functional society. To preach class interest is not the route to remove the feeling of a class society—always some new group, even if it be that of administrators or that of talent itself, will require liquidation in the minds of the envious. The proper route is the straight one of attacking the power of irresponsible wealth and privilege as such.

For the rest Mr. Murry puts before us a new religion

of Christ. This is something perceptibly different from the statement of Stalin of the policy of Bolshevik Communism. The dictatorship of the proletariat, says Stalin, must be a state that embodies a new kind of democracy for the proletariat and the dispossessed. . . . "The dictatorship of the proletariat is the rule of the proletariat over the bourgeoisie, a rule unrestricted by law, based upon force, enjoying the sympathy and the support of the labouring and exploited masses" (Lenin).

If the Bolsheviks go too far, by substituting force for liberty, Middleton Murry, and those for whom he speaks, seem to me not to go far enough. The constructive side is absent as the appreciation of it is absent in Mr. Maxton's book on Lenin. James Maxton is too much of a Rousseauist. The disciplined organization of the Communism of the Communist Party and of the Communist Popes is absent. This omission gives me no especial pleasure or confidence. A crusading group is entitled to impose its own discipline —a strict discipline—upon its members. It is good that this should be so—although the group is not entitled to impose that discipline upon others, save as an expedient of warfare. Plato imposed a discipline on his governors. The Catholic Church has imposed its discipline on its priesthood. The Russian Communist Party has imposed an exhaustive discipline on party members. It has assumed the principle that he who is not for it is against it. Mr. Middleton Murry's proposals are altogether too esoteric and provide, not a fighting faith, but a delicate sentiment.

Murry proposes to us Communism as a means by which we may be saved—as a means of complete self-abnegation, including economic and cultural abnegation. I shall not review the arguments by which he shows that established religions no longer fulfil this need—in substance they have already been discussed in an earlier chapter. "Social life," very truly wrote Marx, "is essentially practical. All the mysteries which divert pure theory into mysticism find their rational resolution in human activity and in the understanding of this activity." Middleton Murry's complaint against orthodox religion is not the old, superficial one that it is institutionalized and comfortable (a complaint largely untrue), but that it is preoccupied with salvation in an immortality which is a prolongation of individual life as a reward— an individual reward which makes disinterestedness a heresy—and that it has its eyes set away from the understanding of human activity.

To the former objection I attach little importance: it is only effective against popular theology and against the folk whose theology is popular myths—years on years singing in the Golden City.... The second objection is real. Instead of this other-worldly interest Middleton Murry presents us with a religion of intense and very practical present sacrifice—not a comforting talk of it, but a little taste of actual starvation. He presents us with a religion of disinterestedness as touching personal success and of intense sympathetic interest in the human activity of the present and its understanding. His whole position is summarized in his statement that "the essential purpose of the Marxian doctrine of historical materialism is to put an end, once for all, to the waste of the ethical passion of disinterestedness."

I do not propose to discuss here whether Murry's statement is exegetically correct—so far as Marx was an Hegelian I think it can well be argued that (despite all talk of class interest, economic motive, and the like) it is correct. I do not, in this chapter, propose to discuss whether an historical materialism, which declares that it offers an explanation, not only of the contours of politics and industry, but of morals, must lead to an American civilization whose Fate is the Machine. I shall not ask whether Mr. Murry's intrepretation of Marxism is at all possible—let alone acceptable to Engels, Bebel, and Bukharin—according to which it is consistent to separate spirit from morals and to leave spirit flying free and contemplating historic determinism. Such a thesis, consistent with Hegel, is yet the overturning of historical materialism as understood by Lenin, with his doctrine, in the *Materialism and Empirio-Criticism*, of the entire priority, as origin of all, of matter. These issues seem to me mint, anise, and cummin. The point is that we are offered here a religion of veritable sacrifice, consecrated to human good, and the only relevant question is, not about the niceties of the dogma, but about whether, *prima facie*, it is a religion of intelligent sacrifice.

It is, I believe, possible to outline the developing religion of Communism with a firmer hand than Murry uses. The stage of unyielding doctrine and of the revolutionary determination of the will gives way to a stage when a more democratic and lest rationalistic appeal is made to popular emotion. The Communist myth, already extant, will develop. The contrast will be made even more absolute, because religious, between the satanic principle of Capitalism and Proletarianism. The story of the last great fight of Capitalism, in the guise of Fascism, and its predestined fall in the day of the Communist Advent with power will become a matter of faith. This is the religious drama of Communism. It will also be of faith that, until the Advent, the condition of the proletariat must become worse. The Saviour is no longer a person, son of man, but the People itself—the People which hitherto has been humbled and ground down under its oppressors. In terms of this myth the proletariat will acquire a mystic significance with qualities of its own—a significance of immense practical value in satisfying the emotions of adherents. The proletariat is the peaceful, motherly, and equal proletariat of the whole world, existing in a mystic unity, resting equally for sustenance and shaping on the common world-matter and only differentiated by material circumstances. Peculiarly, it is chosen from among the oppressed peoples; and one peculiar people, oppressed of all nations, especially binds it together.[1] When the proletariat, after destroying its enemies with might, enters into its republic, competition and individual strife, which destroy the mystical body of the community, will be no more. Peace and mercy will reign. Each man will have an equal share of those material goods, the basis of all health of the body and good of the mind, whose disproportionate distribution was the original sin of the men of egoism and wealth who brought discord into the world.

This mythos is not superficial. It will bear comparison with the tribal or state "Group-mind" mythos of Fascism; and even with the mythos of Catholicism. It has consequences as touching wealth, nationality, and the egoism of the individual, of immense practical significance. Its acceptance, with dogma, miracles, and revelations complete, will yet necessarily be inimical to the free reason. It may be the least of evils, necessary until the day when mankind is able to treat myth as but dramatic truth and when fanatical propaganda is no longer a necessity of social action. This mythos yet remains a compromise with superstition, wilfully confusing opinion

---

[1] One of the greatest triumphs of English political talent will be if Britain shows itself able to absorb, without friction, this people, the most intelligent and talented in the world, with whom the Almighty still seems to have the habit of keeping His covenant.

with knowledge, however powerful may be its appeal by speaking of the resurrection of the downtrodden and of the new life. The rational residuum is the love of humaneness and the hatred of injustice.

Middleton Murry's plea for a Communist religion is an eloquent one. It is yet an incomplete one. It proposes to sacrifice the wealth, the egoistic happiness, the cultural standards, the personal leadership of the individual to—the elimination of poverty in a classless civilization. That sacrifice is no doubt justified. The end is, yet, not explored so far as to reveal a grandeur which justifies the complete and religious subordination of the individual. The American Middle West in the years of prosperity had (clumsily, no doubt, but in effect) eliminated poverty in a classless civilization. We cannot make the American Middle West the object of religious veneration.

Certainly there can be a religion of democracy—it is Rousseauism—and there can be a religion of human sympathy which is crucified by the miseries of human impoverishment and degradation and by the vulgarities of *snobisme*. We can agree that a religion which, prating of spirituality, declines to look in the face this degradation of spirit, due to the battering of human beings by foul conditions which sacrifice and determination can remove, is a religion of the well-fed, of scribes, hypocrites, parasites, ripe for damnation. The chief defect, however, of the faith declared by Middleton Murry is still that it tells us too little of the society which is to replace the old one—that for which we sacrifice the old culture. Mr. Emile Burns is not much more clear, except when he adds that "in the sphere of capitalist 'order,' political government, there will be complete anarchy"—presumably until new would-be capitalists are born. For all its "historical materialism" this Jerusalem is still as vague as the old Jerusalem laid up in heaven. If Communism does not satisfy (beyond the discipline it gives for the purpose of an immediate revolutionary programme) the craving of the individual for values beyond material goods, values that stir affection and give the exhilaration of life more abundant, then the wheel will turn again and a religion will arise that does give these things.

The type of society sought is, I take it, on the one hand, one of clear-cut leadership for the elimination of poverty and other plagues of humanity and for the establishment of the standards of the good existence for all morally capable of it or educable to it. On the other hand, it is one in which there is not a moral tyranny—in which, however sure some people may be that God has infallibly given to them the correct view of moral discipline, they will yet permit other societies to coexist with them which have other philosophies and ideas. That principle is the very *magna carta* of liberty.

There is one Communism which I will endorse almost without reserve. It is the Communism of Plato. I do it because Plato's state was always so small that it was open for anyone who disliked it to quit it. Nor can a society that rests upon reason be more static than reason itself. In stating, however, this agreement I am making two quite essential suppositions—that Plato's scheme does not involve a class society, and that it does not involve a slave society. Also, I am not sure that human ability is as static and highly functionalized as Plato supposes, or that human reason is as perfect an instrument or, in practice, as kindly to true liberty and development.

Professor Laski speaks of "a Platonic society of firmly

ordered ranks and classes, impenetrable and, because impenetrable, implacable in its relationships." He is here referring to the English system of an hereditary governing class. Professor Laski, however, knows very well that the social order demanded by Plato is one of non-hereditary leadership save so far as eugenics may yield some superior human stock. In stating, however, my adherence to Platonic Communism, with its constructive emphasis, I admit that, in so far as Plato assigns to his leaders functions that separate them from the sentiments of the mass of the community or divide them from that community in any other fashion than that in which the Russian Communist Party is actually distinguished from the mass of Russian workers, the difference is a change for the worse. The fault of an hereditary governing class is that it is insensitive to the attitude of mind of those whom it governs. That is not the fault of any sound Communist scheme.

I see no reason for being apologetic about a social plan which was Plato's. Since his day that plan has always been known as Communism and (did this leave on the reader the correct impression) I would be content with the title. It is more than a plan, as Plato himself saw: it is based on a religious feeling for the community. Such disciplined organization can satisfy the religious sense which is today in need of satisfaction of this his monastic type.

A Communist society, nevertheless, becomes a moral tyranny unless it remains voluntary. Those transitional means which may be adopted to realize the new order of this society against opposition must not be such as to neglect this principle. No one pretends that the legislative enactments which give realization to a democratic society and to the protection of the rights of plain men, as society has come to understand these rights, could or should be executed voluntarily. They are imposed upon dissidents by the will of those who hold power in the state, as is all law. The maxim, however, here holds that authority must not encroach upon individual liberty except where there is clear social gain. The encroachment must be minimal.

The principles which should govern a Socialist government are here no exception to the general rule which applies to all governments. Obstruction to public control should be beaten down by those means which the law constitutionally places in the hands of the government of the day, but public control certainly does not and should not involve the compulsory imposition of the morality of a close brotherhood. Indeed, one of the chief tasks of the Socialist of the future will be to secure the freedom of the individual to criticize and oppose governmental agencies and the danger of state Capitalism. A five-pound note may not be much power against a great employer, but there is this much justification in private property that a five-pound note is just that much freedom against, not only employers, but also the state or any governing group or party. That freedom is worth preserving: no party, however excellent, is infallibly inspired. But in a voluntary society or movement the question of this preservation of freedom does not arise.

What is required is a new Platonism, a new monasticism, a new Puritanism, a like-minded group, that can be trusted to give liberty to others, to those heterogeneous to itself, because it believes itself in the liberty to follow the increasing truth. Its task is to permeate with its ideas the human mass. It is itself held together by ideas. Its duty is propaganda, that is to say, to marry truth with will. From the ferment will result a movement. Within the limits that we have learned are set by human nature and its political science, the nature of the organization of this movement depends upon the time and the place.

It may be that the Communism of Moscovy will be the only effective organization. It may be that the people will refuse, here or there, to follow anything but the eagle of Fascism. After the liberty of *laissez-faire* has exhausted its interest men may turn, in the dialectic of history, to the excessive valuation of authority. Or it may be that, in Anglo-Saxon lands, a new road, branching away from the orthodoxies of these faiths, will be found to give men a religion of the community, a tension of discipline, and a vigour of personal hope, so that they feel that this is a glorious and exacting time for men to live in—this time when history, like the sphinx, sets men problems with the penalty, if their human reason do not answer, that they will be devoured. History is not predetermined in content to fit the prophecies of any faith,[1] the way of the future for Britain and America still is contingent, dependent on human will and on the intelligent understanding of the true permanencies, those of human nature—dependent upon our intelligent use of the teachings of political science concerning the everlasting balancing and barter of liberty against security.

This new road we shall discover by attacking fearlessly what we know to be wrong in the old roads, the irrational privilege of Conservatism, the standardless civilization of Liberal Democracy, the disrespect for all faiths save their own of Fascism and Communism, the passionate hatred that both stir up. Throughout human history, since the days of the primitive forest, fear has been the great enemy, impregnating with evil the soul of man. Neither Fascism

[1] A full discussion of this issue will be found in *Science and Method of Politics*, pt. ii, §2.

nor Muscovite Communism, with their terrors, are guiltless of increasing and multiplying this panic fear. The nature of the new way will become clearer when we have considered the kind of mind required in those who would hew it out. It may be, however, that it will remain unhewn and that the destined course of history will logically move on, from Conservatism and Social Democracy, through the black to the red dictatorship, alike in Britain, America, and throughout the world.

§ v

The Conclusion of It All

The dominating consideration in politics is the practical. Scheme after scheme, which it might be admirable to discuss, must be put on one side as of no political relevance and of no significance in any preface to action. It does not follow that nothing is to be regarded as practical save what the butcher and the banker and the baker think to be common sense. To the Fascist Communism, and to the Communist Fascism, and to the Liberal both will not work well; but indubitably the discussion of them is the discussion of practical politics. They are on the chess-board as it is today laid out. They have behind them those gross emotional forces which are among the conditions of practical success.

Let us, however, for the moment turn away from the noise of conflicting claims and the din of polemic argument. Let us forget that a politician is a man concerned not only with truth but with support, not only with the academic best, but with what can enlist power, popular power, on its side. Let us ask ourselves, not what is practicable, but what is rational. After all, even the gross emotional forces in rational beings are not irresponsive to the finger of reason tilting the balance of judgement this way or that, when emotion counterpoises emotion. Before we pass into action, let us, in the last pages of this preface, ask ourselves what kind of life, what set of values, an intelligent person would desire.

In the mills and the factories, in the mines and the holds of ships men toil. They have little leisure to indulge in daydreams and to ask, if life offered them all its goods at a free choice, which they would choose, and what desire. Such dreams are matters for college dons; to indulge in them the luxury of a leisure class and a characteristic of its civilization with its Greek, its slave-holding, traditions.

Let us, however, suppose that all the work of achieving an equitable society is accomplished—to each man his three acres and a cow or his share in the collective farm; to every family its own house or part in the communal kitchen, and its share of leisure. For what then would, and for what should, these people ask?

The reason why we may condemn the leisure ideals of a limited group is just because, by a rational judgement, we hold that those who live so peculiar a life have not the experience to reach judgements and ideals broad and deep enough to satisfy a fully developed human being. The experience is anaemic and the ideals are precious and etiolated. Let us, then, suppose the more obvious material needs of the many satisfied and the limitations and distortions of culture by a privileged group—distortions due to its isolated privilege—removed.

There are, at the present time, two outstanding ideals of civilization in the world, the one expressed, however imperfectly, by Russia (and, in a very different way, by the land of Abraham Lincoln, America—but that is matter for a book by itself), and the other by France. The first has all the disadvantages of immaturity and crudity; the other has all the advantages of completeness and perfection. The first, if it does not achieve, yet points to a democratic and classless culture; the other preserves in some fashion the grand tradition of the Classical

THE CONCLUSION OF IT ALL

Renaissance, of Catholicism, and of Hellas. Are we going to set before us, as our pattern, something detectably similar to the first plan of life; or are we to hark back, as the alternative, to a yet more rigid insistence upon the second as alone holding the civilized values of which we stand in such need? Are we going to create new values or to restore ancient values?

If we are going to criticize every piece of literature, or book of history written in the grand full-dress style, by asking of what meaning it is to human needs or to scientific truth or to artistic comprehension; if we are going to drive every aesthete and scholar forth to study his world and the human relevance of his subject; if we are going to inspect every ivory tower with an inquisitive eye to discover from just what elephant tusks it has been made—then it may well seem that the rise of the democratic-proletarian culture is the coming of the new barbarism. That is the consequence of following the first of our two courses. All these things, however, speaking in general, are just what we are going to do. Our alternative is a complacent tradition which derives, on one part, from the ascetic ideals of the clergy and, on the other, from the slave-holders' outlook of the Greeks. Diluted with much water it becomes the bourgeois ideal, respectable and self-conscious of superiority. Undiluted, it is the ideal of the mass of the educated European intelligensia. That is not good enough. There may be much that is admirable in this tradition but, to live, it is necessary to fight, and most of that which is worth fighting against is to be found bound up with this tradition. Even Platonism cannot be copied: it must be restated.

I have already quoted the argument of Trotsky, in *Literature and Revolution*, which Edmund Wilson has so admirably reinforced in his literary criticism. The beautiful souls who are so interested in studying the niceties of their own emotions and in cultivating the gardens of their souls, growing the narcissus, ultimately perish from the fragility of their own preciousness. Too often they eviscerate themselves to study the anatomy of their own sentiments. That is the curse of post-War Western Civilization, with its fastidious indecisiveness and sceptical negativity. In a striking passage Trotsky comments on one of the most polished of the Russian middle-class literary groups, men whom he characterizes as "self-possessed Europeans." "Why does their poetry never flower? Because they are not the creators of life, they do not participate in the creation of its sentiments and moods, they are only tardy skimmers, left-overs of a culture created by the blood of others. They are imitators, educated and even exquisite; they are imitators of sound, well read and even gifted; but nothing more." They have climbed a private stair to Heaven, forgetting—and it is the great fault of all subjectivism—that the isolated individual is but an incomplete fragment, a philosophical falsity, when pretended to be a whole, and that reality is not to be found in locked cupboards or up private stairs. It is to be found, if not out in the world, then in the subtleties and intensities of significant and communicable human experience.

It is as valuable to look without, in order to understand and be mental master of one's world, as to look within. Vigour of personality, and the basis for personal values, lies in this looking out and over—not in being, like Peer Gynt, sufficient for oneself. Personality is such mastery. It is neither self-centredness nor is it taking one's value from the herd opinion.

Further, those who look within will find what is valu-

THE CONCLUSION OF IT ALL

able, not in so far as they discover what is an idiosyncrasy to themselves, untypical and maimed, but so far as they discover what is communicable and of common human interest. I take it that the interest of Proust lies precisely in the fact that he made such human discoveries. He, however, who is interested in nothing common to others —who is not interested in communicating such truth as he may have detected or such perception of beauty to others—is, so far, completely without interest, he and his beautiful soul together, to others. Ultimately, uprooted from experience, he will cease to be of any rational value even to himself—such a road of egoistic obstinacy and arrogance ends in madness or is exhilarated by some kind of sadism.

I have forced the argument to extremes to demonstrate the point. Here in this narcissism we have the very core of the philosophy of a class-divided society, since only the few have time or opportunity to withdraw themselves from common affairs. There are, however, aspects of the outlook which I am advocating that are more open to reasonable criticism than its objection to pretentious self-satisfaction. In the mouths of its exponents this interest in the world of non-ego, the outside world, mental and physical, becomes an interest primarily in the material world, in the world of immediately useful affairs, in industry and machinery, in business and activity, the whole characterized by an often idiotic optimism about what "machinery" or "science" can do. This is more true of the American than of the Russian element of democratic culture, but emphatically it is true of the Russian also, with its admiration of St. Khord (Henry Ford) and with its lyrical praise of Chicago, "city built on a screw."

Put aside such crudities of an emancipated Asiatic

A PREFACE TO ACTION

peasantry and turn again to see how it is noticeable even in Trotsky's considered writing. "The passion for mechanical improvement, as in America," writes Trotsky, "will accompany the first page of every new Socialist society. The passive enjoyment of nature will disappear from art." . . . "In the final analysis, this servile preoccupation with oneself, this apotheosis of the ordinary facts of one's personal and spiritual routine, become so unbearable in our age when mass and speed are really making a new world."

It can, however, be argued that it is not true that mass and speed are really making a new world. They are factors which are changing the conditions under which we live; they alter our conduct. Our minds may accept or reject these factors, seek to emphasize or to diminish their influence. They no more necessarily "make" our world, the world that we are willing to accept as non-alien and our world, than a bull "makes" a china-shop. It depends upon whether we consider that it is good, and will accept it as integral to our lives—this increased part played by mass and speed. And some hold it utterly bad, all this and its activist complement in human life and in stress of the notion of flux and time. If their conduct is modified it is unwillingly modified, and they will repel these new forces if they can. They stand, in this context, in reaction against the young, new world. Are they right? Or is there reason behind what such a writer as Joseph Wood Krutch points out as a religion of mass, speed, and power?

Three very different groups are interested in the warfare against what is called "a machine civilization."

THE CONCLUSION OF IT ALL

The first is democratic enough. It is a new Rousseauite group which demands a simple life, and objects (as did Lawrence in *Nettles*) to the violation by machinery of virgin nature. It is easy to say that all this, intellectually, does not amount to much. It is true that the function of machinery is to aid man in the material means of civilization and that the function of civilization is not to crush natural human instincts, but to give them a tutored, harmonious and social form of expression. The trouble is, as Freud has most rightly insisted, that civilization and machinery too often do nothing of the kind when the one is imposed, in its standards and manners, by a limited class and the other is used for the purposes, primarily, of the private profit and pleasure of a few. (Near me as I write a house is being built—a house of fifty rooms—for the pleasure of a small family to be occupied by themselves and those whose function is their convenience. That sets a standard of consumption. I do not know, however, that they sleep ill of night from a sense of sin.) The fear, nevertheless, of machinery socially controlled, so long as there is an adequate sense of human values to refuse to turn any man into a cog or to destroy beauty—even the outlook of a cottage—just to make profits, is a mistaken fear.

"The machine," writes Trotsky, "is not in opposition to the earth. The machine is the instrument of modern man in every field of life. The present-day city is transient. But it will not be dissolved back again into the old village. On the contrary the village will rise in fundamentals to the plane of the city." In all this Trotsky seems to me entirely right. The level of peasant civilization has been intellectually passed and must be permanently left behind. The cry against machinery has been deafening the sky for sometime now, but it is an obscurantist and reactionary cry. It is dictated by habits that engender dislike of the engineer's technocrat world of order and plan. It is, at heart, a cry on behalf of spontaneous impulse against any highly developed and articulated civilization with its complex web of obligations. For it the machine and the wheel are but symbols of this bondage of man to an order in society, not least a socialist order.

It is noteworthy that Freud has come to admit two striving elements in human nature, the constructive or sympathetic and the sadistic or destructive—not only the creative, erotic principle, which he has always stressed, but also the aggressive power-lust of Adler. The censorship exercised by civilization has been built up as a necessary check upon the destructive tendency. "I take up," writes Freud, "the standpoint that the tendency to aggression is an innate, independent, instinctual disposition in man, and I come back now to the statement that it constitutes the most powerful obstacle to culture." It is indeed possible to adopt, with Freud, the position that one regards "without taking umbrage those critics who aver that when one surveys the aims of civilization and the means it employs, one is bound to conclude that the whole thing is not worth the effort, and that in the end it will only produce a state of things which no individual will be able to bear." The permanency of civilization's Devil—of Original Sin—is here, as it was certainly not in the eighteenth century, fairly admitted and the only question left open is whether the Devil may not win.

The danger of a peaceful, machine-using, democratic reasonable world is that its reasonableness may become intolerable. Reason is a jealous and tyrannous mistress who reduces all human beings to mathematical units

THE CONCLUSION OF IT ALL

and applies a law of the average, called morals. A reasonable, cerebral control, acknowledged too implicitly and whole-heartedly, ends by so weakening our own impulses to the shadow of their former selves that, not only is the Satan of aggression and destruction put in chains, but the vital joy of life departs and we are cursed by a restless psychological distress, a growing misery. It is this which Aldous Huxley has endeavoured to avert by building up, over against the throne of reason, his praise of an illogical world. There are irresoluble surds in the universe of reason. The argument, however, is not well taken: it rests upon a misconception of reason of which the function is to provide a release for instinct, precisely universally and for all, but to provide release along the channels of an order dictated by certain standards of precedence in values. That precedence we have here endeavoured to examine.

some urge the argument against machines and "Americanization" in the name of unfettered instinct and against artificiality (was there no artificiality before machines?), others do so, more suspiciously, in the name of a less materialistic, more "spiritual," civilization. The reply of the Eastern scholar, Dr. Hu Shih, is final. Which is more spiritual, a civilization that has machines for its tools and enough freedom from material cares to release men to interest themselves in other things, or a civilization which uses men as animals of burden to draw the rickshaws?

Only a leisured class that regards itself as alone of significance to civilization or a class that identifies spiritual health with physical pain can find satisfaction in the dignity and repose which is sustained by a servile civilization of labour by human tools, mere animate instruments.

The third objection comes from those, not at all democratic, who desire to hold fast by ancient values. Mr. Aldous Huxley, who is a polytheist, denies that there are absolute values or any obligation to be rationally consistent about the values that we have. Mr. Huxley went to America, where he should have found an individualistic civilization sceptical of all absolutes and precisely in accordance with his taste—where the banal man claims his right as a citizen to be banal and to assert that his "-ism" is as good as Mr. Huxley's or any other fellow's. Unfortunately for his logic (which, however, Mr. Huxley on principle doesn't claim) Mr. Huxley was sadly shocked by what he saw. He returned, crying aloud for the maintenance of the ancient values and lamenting over a civilization where, for the first time in history, Babbitts by the million not only were necessary, but claimed to be significant—important, successful people with a right to an opinion of their own.

Others, however, on the American continent itself have come out in favour of eternal values, endorsing the case for these values by their eminent support. These are sober people who have no use at all for the gay irrationalism and engaging polytheism of Mr. Huxley—strict moral monists who know, and know that they know. The present representatives of this infallibility are the people who oddly call themselves Humanists, not because they are either Unitarians (one sect of which church also calls itself by this name) or resemble Erasmus or Goethe—quite the contrary: they are neo-scholastics —but for some reason at present obscure. For them Beacon Hill, Boston, is a new Parnassus, if a Puritan one. Their chief fault is that, as one of their associate friends, Mr. T. S. Eliot, has explained, they have read a little philosophy but not enough.[1]

The thesis of the Beacon Hill Humanists (important men in Massachussetts)—over against such people as Walter Lippmann with his trust in modern science, over against Joseph Wood Krutch with his Byronic pessimism and proclamation that modern science has so far progressed that it can declare the completeness of man's bankruptcy of purpose[2]—is that, in human history, there is a grand tradition which holds to certain received values, recognized and announced by the classical sages.

In Britain Mr. T. S. Eliot, affrighted by the excesses of his own countrymen in adventuring with a noble

---

[1] T. S. Eliot, *Selected Essays*, p. 434; *Humanism and America*, edited by N. Foerster, chapter by T. S. Eliot, "Religion without Humanism": "I found no discipline in humanism; only a little intellectual discipline from a little study of philosophy."

[2] This statement is based on Mr. Krutch's earlier work and on an article, "What I Believe." In *Experience and Art* (1932) Mr. Krutch's position becomes far more similar to that taken in this book. "Order, symmetry, logic are part of ourselves, but we are, with good reason, less sure that they are a part of anything non-human, and the aesthetic experience is the result of anything which, even for a moment, convinces us that they are" (p. 151).... "Some unified aim, some hierarchy of values, some sense that something is supremely worth while, must impose itself upon us with a self-justifying inevitability" (p. 219). Mr. Krutch appears to be in the position of an *âme damnée* who earnestly desires "a passionate and implicit faith," who feels that the modern world may be moving to this, but who himself feels no instinctive response to what he suspects it will produce as its objects of piety—aeroplanes, fast cars, giant machines, bullfights, and such things as yield an animal sensation of power.

experiment, has discovered anew for Englishmen the virtues of their own prejudices and clasps to himself Jacobites and Caroline divines. It would be mistaken to under-estimate Mr. Eliot. He sometimes amazes by the portentousness with which he can explain the simple, on such occasions being more like the London *Times* than *The Times* itself. At other moments he will quote, within the space of a page or two, notes from the Sanskrit, the Latin, French, German, and Italian—which is what is usually called pretentious. These are but Mr. Eliot's *divertissements*. Essentially he is championing what he believes to be the cause of dignity against what he believes to be the cause of vulgarity. That matters. Collingwood, in his *Speculum Mentis*, deplores the shivering by individualism of a connected philosophy of life and society. Eliot is rightly trying to re-establish it against a self-pitying and empty scepticism. Mr. Eliot is asking, and we have to answer before we close this book, whether there are such things as permanent values?

Mr. Eliot's demolition of Professor Irving Babbitt and his followers, who seek (more heavily, but more consistently, than Mr. Huxley) to build a Catholic platform of permanent values out of Protestant planks of individualism, is a demolition deadly and thorough. Mr. Eliot has a distinguished mind and the wit to perceive that a religion which is to be significant, in terms of reason and of human discipline, must be a religion scholastic in coherency and organized, not a religion of private opinion alone. The danger of Mr. Eliot is that he is not content to purchase the appropriate human discipline, and those values which reason assumes, in the field of experiment and experience, but will be content with nothing short of a hypodermic injection of infallibility direct from transcendental sources. In practice that means making cowardice a respectable virtue.

This work, however, of re-insisting upon permanent values has been done by a writer of no little insight and of more philosophic knowledge, if of far more sympathy with American democratic and experimental optimism, than Mr. Eliot. In a brief article entitled "In Dispraise of Life and Experience," Professor Morris Cohen—who has been through the waves of that activism of which he speaks, instead, with the British idealists, of denouncing it like Canutes as it rises on their shore—restates the case for Parmenidean Stability against that Heraclitan flux in which "whirlwind is King." Here, if anywhere, is the line of answer to the pragmatists and experimentalists, the Deweys and Charles Austin Beards, and to all those who, through praise of a democratic culture, lead the way across to a Socialist culture.

The argument of Morris Cohen is, in effect, the thesis of Spinoza. The great American experiment in the pride of human power is approved—as the Russian planning might be approved—but only so long as it is guided by the permanent values which can be reduced to consistency by reason. That manifestation of human mass power which is the beauty of Manhattan is neither good nor bad of itself (beautiful it may be, "like Aztec pyramids of human sacrifice," as H. N. Brailsford once said). Whether it is, in effect, good or bad, as power, depends on the purpose of the men who built it and the behaviour of the men who use it. Mere big talk about experience gives us no criterion by which to prefer poetic inspiration to homicidal mania, to catlike cruelty, or to other errors of the human carnivore.

Any misguided young person can talk about "life"—in a popular American magazine I see, in effect, this theme put forth (fascinatingly enough for a detached psychologist) in an article entitled "Delinquent Girl." Often, indeed, this is coupled with a stress, and a quite reasonable stress, upon positive values which most respectable folk lack, such as animal courage. But the justification here is not "life" (if indeed experience of robbery, abortion, and sudden death are "life"), but courage.

Talk of "life" is part of a typically American attempt to avoid having men of trained judgement judge experience and to let experience, the event—which means the democratic opinion of what succeeds—judge men. This talk is, however, not by any means only American: we find it, in more pretentious fashion, in the utterances of such a European member of the "energist" school as Señor Ortega y Gasset. "The modern theme," he writes, "comprises the subjection of reason to vitality, its localization within the biological scheme, and its surrender to spontaneity . . . the one expedient that has never been essayed is that of living intentionally under the guidance of life"—and so forth. One feels that "A Delinquent Girl" has a case.

The American has (even Mr. Ford, in his own way, has) a great belief in future history—and in the materialist interpretation of history at that—as against philosophy with its talk of permanent values, because he is at once an experimental optimist and a hardened intellectual sceptic. This belief is not without its justification. Too much philosophy is narrow systematizing on valuational foundations of mere prejudice—Kant on suicide and Hegel on the family are instances. It inspires no con-

THE CONCLUSION OF IT ALL

fidence when we read, in the writings of such philosophers of the chair as Husserl and Mr. G. E. Moore, statements which seem to indicate that these grave gentlemen believe that "only George is in step."

"Now as ever," writes Husserl, "I hold every form of current philosophical realism to be in principle absurd, as no less every idealism to which in its own arguments that realism stands contrasted" . . . "our previous reflections have been, as all that are to follow should be, free from every relation of dependence on a "science" so contentious and contemptible as is philosophy." "It will follow," says Mr. Moore, "that, unless new reasons never urged hitherto can be found, all the most important philosophical doctrines have as little claim to assent as the most superstitious belief of the lowest savages. . . ." "When, therefore, Berkeley supposed," etc., "he supposed what was false; and when Kant supposed," etc., "he supposed what was equally false." These are eminent men in their own domain. If this is done in the green tree, what shall be done in the dry when lesser and even microscopic scholars in the groves of Academe quarrel about the original authorship of one-half of a new idea as though it were the patent of the first army tank?

The common-sense judgement yet remains that some experiences are more valuable than others. It is the task of reason to sort out and reject those seemingly valuable experiences which are consistent with other, more fundamentally valuable ones. The best part of wisdom consists in knowing with what experiences we can afford to dispense.

Sound values, indeed, are not something inserted by logic from without and disconnected from the experiences of the individual, which experiences themselves are moulded and coloured by the common impulses and feelings of human nature. The whole argument of this book rests upon the supposition that a rational order embodies natural law and gives, not an inhuman, logical scheme based in axiomatic first principles or absolute revelation, but upon the harmonization of the permanent impulses of human nature which themselves shape and determine any tolerable norm elaborated by reason. The great Spinoza's assumption that man's vital appetites and passions are to be studied rather than censured is most sound.

It is the task of reason—of the reason of those adjudged by common folk to be peculiarly gifted with this quality —to make this world a world of a planned and ordered civilization, releasing vital human impulse so far as is consistent with that order among these impulses themselves and so far as is consistent with external facts. Here, by extending at once our knowledge and our powers, lies the auxiliary work of science. The subjectivist, the quietist, turn aside from the development of this rational work—this hard, disciplined work with its rude objective tests—to examine their own delicate spiritual interiors. Thereby they reject the gift to us from the Father of Lights of a reason which is not, nor can be, private to this man or that, and of experience which is social and cosmic, not private and solipsistic. The specific fault of the subjectivist and the cultivator of esoteric excellences is, not that they seek values and attach importance to them, but that they seek them, apart from reason and catholicity, in the wrong directions. Boasting themselves of an intelligence superior to the vulgar, these choice and select spirits adopt a position which, whether they will it or not, has philosophical implications that carry them further than they suppose —philosophical implications which an objectivist such as

THE CONCLUSION OF IT ALL

Hegel, a far greater philosopher than they will ever be, spent his life in combating and condemning.

The great tradition in philosophy is not on the side of the soul-gardeners. The French self-centred bourgeois interpretation is not an adequate interpretation. The grand tradition is not even, with Professor Alexander, the learned and eminent author of *Space, Time, and Deity*, on the side of those who set up flickering, horizon gods of value—values now detected glimmering on our view, now lost to sight, now not yet found. Mr. Wyndham Lewis has perceived this, although his method of restoring true values is reminiscent of those who would take the kingdom of heaven by violence, so that Mr. Wyndham Lewis, with undoubtedly right good will, hits under the jaw frequently, and with tremendous gusto, that which in fact he could defend.

The great tradition is a thoroughly rationalist and a thoroughly objective, supra-private tradition. Its stress is not a stress on the individual and on his idiosyncrasies. It traces from Plato, with his supreme appeal to reason and mathematical science. With Hegel, however, unlike Plato, Thomas, and Spinoza, it admits the notion of time and evolution. In its last significant revision, by Croce, it admits the importance of the ephemeral, of the here and now. Here the human—*ces passions éphémères*—is given its full weight as of equal reality with the less mutable among experiences and concepts that may be vehicles of meaning. "Appearance" has true value—a conclusion which, by reinstalling in importance vivid perception and imagination, as against "the fact," has revolutionary consequences for practical education. The mutable is seen to be as truly the symbol of significant truth as supposedly unshakeable formulae of the tautological and $2 \times 2 = 4$ order. It also can yield by its fleeting pathos values, in this very ephemerality, of eternal and typical beauty: change also is eternal and true.[1]

As thus humanistically revised, this great tradition forms the solid basis for a democratic culture, as broad as all humanity. It is antagonistic to all attempts to set up little private universes, based on the personal intuition of the superiority of me or of thee, such as must always (as Plato found to be true of Callicles) be the attempt of a leisured, limited, and select class. The Greeks were not preservers—tidy French bourgeois holding tight to the life-line of security—but creators and adventurers, to be imitated most by being imitated least. Only in their rationality are the Greek and French cultures at one.

A rational judgement allows play to the human impulses of here and now, with their value for power and vitality; indicates to them artistic, balanced, and civilized expression; certainly does not permit them to be crushed by mechanism and by the utilitarianism of the middle distance—by the "practical-results-and-damn-the-human-consequences men"—or by the presumptuous dogmatism of theological absolute values or of some infallible long view of Vatican or Kremlin. But it remains a rational judgement. Here is the rock of salvation against the personal passion of powerful men and the private presumptions to superiority of arrogant ones. Here, with its roots not only in the Hegelian rationalist, Marx, but in Plato, is the basis of any sound socialist philosophy.

Ultimately we must be sceptics about the power of the

[1] In this connection it is of interest to recall the words of Professor Whitehead: "The foundation of all understanding of sociological theory—that is to say, of all understanding of human life—is that no static maintenance of perfection is possible. . . . This doctrine requires justification. It is implicitly denied in the learned tradition derived from ancient thought" (*Adventures of Ideas*, p. 354).

THE CONCLUSION OF IT ALL

human reason to establish values that transcend logic and to establish these values with such assurance that the subjective obligation of private judgement is abrogated. There is no reason whatsoever for departure from the sceptical principles of Plato's Seventh Epistle. If we accept an "infallible revelation," if we accept the standards and discipline of a group, it is yet *our* judgement that accepts it. It is precisely for this reason that no standard or ideal can be more absolute than the reasoning and judgement of the group that freely accepts it, or should be imposed by force, as absolute and unchangeable, upon an alien group. Scepticism can logically destroy any one set of values claiming universal validity, but by the same process it can also destroy any other set of such values. We are compelled to fall back upon the observation that increased education and experience leads to approximation in our valuational judgements—as there is approximation in judgements upon music among masters in music—and that groups are entitled to set up, for practical purposes of living, standards which may provisionally be treated as absolute by those who voluntarily and by exercise of judgement so choose to accept them. As increasingly we recognize the importance of mental homogeneity, moral training and of what can be effected by social co-operation and social units in civilization, more and more we shall appreciate the common rôle to be played by these voluntary homogeneous groups. Practical scepticism may be basic to the tolerance appropriate in secular, democratic, heterogeneous society; but it is not basic to the voluntary, homogeneous group with its civilizing mission, and its corporate spirit of community.

If, of course, all values were equal; if, that is, there were no valuational standard by which we might judge one value against another; and there were no hope that human reason and judgement, by training and choice, might reach true values, then indeed one set of ideals might as well be accepted as another. There would be no outrage involved in this nihilism; and the anarchist who turns advocate of force is not only logical, but wise.

The sceptic must, however, consistently be sceptic even of scepticism, as a theory for behaviour, and must find a way out of his deadlock of thought, in action. Throughout this book it is assumed that ideals are merely the ideals of groups which are yet in quest of more complete truth and are guided by our increasing knowledge of natural law and of the norms of human nature. These groups are under an obligation to expose their ideals and discipline for the examination and acceptance of men, of like instincts, in this human society full of diverse and competing ideals, while imposing their discipline with authority on those who accept their premises. Judgements of value are not external, but flow out from the character of human nature; standards of behaviour may, however, properly be imposed upon those who confess to acceptance of these judgements of value.

If it were true that Socialism is merely the economic interest of the majority and that all talk about social justice is clap-trap, then anyone fortunate enough to possess more material goods than his fellows and a correspondingly more advantageous manner of living would be well advised to fight for it.

Once, however, we admit the validity of, and the need for, permanent critical standards, we are faced with the most powerful perhaps of all the enemies of the democratic community (despite all his compromises)—Aristotle. Does not the admission of the need for values spell the permanent need for a leisure class? That we have no right to impose a leisure class on people who wish to live democratically—that we must tolerate and allow citizen rights to those who object to a leisure class—follows from what we have already said. A free secular and utilitarian society must allow for all kinds of men. It is, however, permissible to ask whether, if men already accept by habit or can be induced to accept by education the prestige of a leisure class, this situation ought not to be perpetuated, since a leisure class will better appreciate the choice goods of civilization and will maintain sound values.

European (as distinct from New World) culture, not only derives from, but still is, as we have said, borne up by and presupposes two great streams of tradition—of dogmatic values inculcated from childhood and by all our educational agencies. The leisure-class ideal accords with that lay tradition of culture which traces back to the ideals of slave-holding Hellas and which receives in Aristotle classic expression. Also, however, it happily accords, thanks to a singularly fortunate dispensation in history, with that other Churchly tradition which has so often challenged the Hellenic. The ascetic tradition does not preach that leisure should be spent on secular pursuits; but it does praise the religious life of resignation and contemplation. It deprecates as impious a busy taking thought for the morrow, and any Marxist concentration of attention on the affairs and improvement of this world. It diverts attention from concentration on human happiness and, while praising the life of toil for those engaged upon it, it regards this toil as disconnected from the ultimate rewards of life.

Over against this is to be set the contrary supposition that there is an essential and integral connection between our work and the character of our values. The world is the field of our labours and in this world we realize our hopes. Here, if at all, is the power and the glory. It is that objective web of affairs and ideas which we call current experience that determines the lines of our thoughts; and our best thoughts are directed, in return, to the effective understanding and intelligent modification of it. The man, therefore, who is living a life out of touch with this *grand monde* of common experience and action is living a negative and sterile life. It is not the case, as Aristotle taught, that the ideal is to pass from the Adam's curse of labour to the life of leisured detachment and to the narcissistic contemplation in a mutual admiration group of the garden of the soul. That is false. The ideal is to pass to ever broader and more significant fields of control—first empirical and then by deliberate thought—of this glowing world of life which is ours. There is here no dichotomy, either in the practice of life or in the psychology of the self, between the life of industry and toil and the sharply contrasted life of leisure and civilization.

The essential, and essentially philistine, supposition of the leisure tradition is that life is divided into two areas, that of work—much of which must be slavish and interfere with the independence of a free man—and that of leisure, which is of an entirely different and superior character. This deep-seated tradition gives justification to the tendency to conspicuous consumption. It is clear that those who have to work for their living cannot afford this leisure and, therefore, although the wealthy may, in this century, be too kindly to stigmatize them with Aristotle as servile, they have themselves the satisfaction of being marked out as belonging to a superior class.

THE CONCLUSION OF IT ALL

The great philosopher provides an intellectually respectable excuse for what yet in practice works out (and I here blame the "middle-class" far more than the "upper-class") as the insufferable vulgarity of a class-ordered society. It is vulgar because of its steady perversion of values by the hangers-on of the rich and powerful. The Aristotelian justification is placed on the ground that the utilitarian work of the world has to be done, soiling and cramping although it may be; that the mass of men throughout history (hangers-on included) always have been slaves, with the servile and snobbish minds of slaves; that a leisured few may be made into polished and civilized men; and that it is unreasonable to suppose that these conditions will change.

This argument may be commended to those, bishops and others, who fear the results of a condition of too much leisure, such as may succeed this present year of grace, and that this leisure and lipstick may lead to betting, wars, and worse offences. (Or does leisure only have this evil effect if extended to the vulgar?) The problem of leisure (which hitherto has only been faced by a few writers such as Lewis Mumford) is certainly a chief problem of this century—but of the last third of it. . . .

We have here, with Aristotle, the argument that any civilization which is not a leisure civilization is one not worthy of the name. Only the leisured have time to understand the art of life. The rest are the manure which prodigal nature uses to grow its roses. Spendthrifts, speculators, and loud fellows are vulgar. But there are and there ought to be upper-classes (which means leisured classes) and anything to the contrary is unnatural. These people are civilization, and are the rational justification for the very existence of the rest who have no complete purpose in themselves.

By now, however, the fallacy of this aristocratic argument has become apparent. There is no need, with Mr. Clive Bell, to go off and find our hope and religion in some movement apart, far from the madding crowd, even if we do not robustly assert that the herd exists only to serve this movement (should I say "status"?) and this Society of their betters. It is not easy for the herd that fought in the trenches to agree with Mr. Humbert Wolfe that the object of the War was to preserve an England in which Arnold Bennett might live or that "the best propaganda a great writer could accomplish for England was to prove that England still possessed such writers." Truth, indeed, may be more precious than victory, but truth is little concerned with such vessels of honour and is perhaps less eclectic in her habitations. All this seclusion, eclecticism and creaming off of the best is founded upon a radically false, limiting, and disintegrating philosophy of life. The only sound course —and here the disciple, Aristotle, lost his way—is that of Plato: it is to insist that any aristocracy is such, not by seclusion, but by organic unity and functional coordination with a broad social whole—with a world of common, vulgar men and women and their needs. A leader is not of another species from the led or he cannot lead. Comprehension of the broader world, sympathetic understanding of common humanity and of vitality, is a sign of being a truly reasonable being, who understands the normal and common as well as the abnormal and rare, who is the master and not the victim of his critical powers.

A culture, it is true, which, for the benefit of the whole,

THE CONCLUSION OF IT ALL

might require this sacrifice of some, of a few—either at a given time or in the sequence of the generations—may be a good and noble culture. And (this I think important as a possible bridge with the old religion) a high civilization may have to admit that there is always something higher than itself, always the need, hence, for sacrifice, always a yearning and a rage of incompleteness in the individual. Mere success, ignorant alike of lyric feeling and tragic pain, is a quality of the half-civilized. There is also a burden of misery on humanity which must first be recognized by the successful if it must then be thrown off by the joint action of all. Moreover, Communism, for example, does not (nor can) remove human tragedy —for example, the tragedy of the death of the young. This tragedy abides. All that a true sense of community can do is to make life less like a living death and to give to those who wait for death the consciousness of service faithfully rendered in a continuing workshop that does not grow silent and in a fraternity that does not dissolve.

I do not at present lean to the opinion that the myth of Christus crucifixus regnans, the myth of those crucifixes which show the Lord, as type of humanity, in sacrifice and glory, can profitably be banished from the drama of our new human world, this divine drama of hope in human history. This is a quite critical issue; but this myth still seems to me substantially more profound than that of the great tactician Lenin enbalmed there in Moscow in his alcohol. I may be wrong. I know the other case—all that Christianity has *not* done. I know the grave danger that the human pathos will only be recognized by the successful to indulge their tears and titillate self-pity, and that evil and folly will not be fought. I know that the burden may be recognized by the wretched only to be succumbed to by men enervated by a philosophy of resignation. It may be that the salient fact of history is that after millennia of servitude and starvation the human race at last has a chance for all of adequacy of goods—and that all morals can well wait reshaping as we see the consequences of that anti-ascetic fact. Perhaps, however, human kindliness and unostentatious sacrifice will still have their place as good.

I should be interested to know the judgement a hundred years today after a century of the one religion and just two millennia of the other—whether, after two millennia, it will still be "Vicisti, Galilaee," or whether the friendship of the comfortable will have killed the Nazarene and the petty aristocrat, Ulianov, will have replaced the carpenter. Bluntly, I doubt it. Let, however, the comfortable be careful. It may be that they will kill their master, but the spirit will still live that cried "woe unto you that are rich for you have received your consolation; woe unto you that are full." However powerful and great a civilization man builds, with health and good for all, there will never be a time when those who are full, who have forgotten humility, poetry, and understanding of sorrow, will be preferable, as human beings, to those who seek a more difficult perfection.

It may well be that some measure of sacrifice is intrinsic in the very nature of civilization. This statement, however, is all the heavens different from saying that most men should remain animated tools for the realization of the civilized tastes of an elect few.

It is important to remark the limits of the legitimacy of the claims of taste. The present renewed interest in form, exact scholarship, absolute values is suspicious and appears like an action of self-defence upon the part of leisured men.

This cult is adult, mature, and is one of the few non-religious interests (by which I mean non-social, non-communicative) which, at least in a life of adequate means and of repose, is demonstrably satisfactory. What is ultimately important in the world, because it is ultimately beautiful, is a well-shaped tree. Art, indeed, is a language of communication, but the language has so far its own intrinsic laws and elegancies that attention can be concentrated upon this skill to the extent of indifference to all communication. To that extent, however, and because the beautiful is something essentially significant, universalizable and to be communicated, we have here, in this solitary pleasure, a perversion.

Likewise the speculative, non-utilitarian interest in science or philosophy may reach the point where it scarcely seems important to communicate the results of the speculation. There is a discipline and desert of solitude wherein men, instead of thrusting their services busily upon society, can learn in humility and introspection their own true value, the significance of their own personalities, and how such gifts as they may have may be used with art and civilized skill. This discipline of solitude, however, is different from a self-indulgent detachment.

This spiritual onanism in speculation is utterly vicious, in part because it ignores the human sources and interests behind these rational problems or artistic valuations—fails to recognize that, as Professor Levy says, the interests on which science itself concentrates at a given time are part of this or that social system—but chiefly because it denies the truth of these very speculations and valuations by declaring its indifference to their communication and perpetuation.

The art is made subordinate to the man as an ephemeral individual, and that which sets out to be "pure" and detached from human interest reveals itself as especially human and mere skilful gratification of the individual solitary. The technique of "pure art" has just as much value, and just as little, as long sight. It would, of course, be monstrous if all the short-sighted men conspired to kill all the long-sighted ones. In so far, however, as art has further value than this it is in terms of human significance, it is "impure" (if that be the opposite of "pure"), and it is—as Plato, once for all, said—subject to the judgement, certainly not of ephemeral and expedient moral criteria, but of the cultivated ethical judgement of those whom even ordinary men can adjudge to be *maestri*.

Such is the answer to all Proustian and "beyond-Proust" preoccupations when they lose touch with universality of interest or with interest in being universalized. An exacting world of values is not any lout's world. But that is no ground for allocating it to a Bloomsbury elect. It would be good for any lout, as for any green carnation ne'er-do-well, if it could be his world—just because that lies in the nature of values: to understand and identify oneself with the subtler of them is to be more entirely a human being.

Ultimately politics resolves itself into a question of power; fortunately, however, most men (that is to say, those who usually hold power) can occasionally be induced to accept certain things as high values. I may

THE CONCLUSION OF IT ALL

be wildly optimistic, but so at least it seems to me. When I reflect upon the best English tradition in politics or upon the work of outstanding members of the Supreme Court in America, it does not seem to me that I am entirely wrong. Among these values I place control by reason and its consequent dictates of order, restraint, and rational humility; as well as the claims of vitality, liberty, and courage. Along with these I also place the sense for beauty and for human dignity in oneself and in others, with its concomitants of justice and mercy and indignation for righteousness. It is because some men can be induced to hold to these values that, in any sound community, the control of education in its fullest significance becomes a matter of prime importance.

The mind of man, however, requires, not only a philosophy of values, but a religion embracing and incarnating it. And this religion finds expression in the discovery of its appropriate community. Those, like Mr. Walter Lippmann, who would have us, as mature men, remember only the stark intellectual facts of Chance and Necessity—which of themselves yield only further facts, not values—simplify too much. They forget that it is the mature man who loves, although he loves, not as a child seeking protection from hardship and discipline, but as a man choosing, selecting, in tension, giving the response of a disciplined and subtle mind, conscious of art-mastery and style, loving, not childishly, but with creative passion, himself a full individual.

What I understand by the appropriate community will, by now, be clear to the reader. It must fit within a rational framework which, at our present stage of civilization, is the framework of a world organization. That community will not be the framework, but it may direct it; the international mechanism, unless it is to fall apart, will require the international mind guided by those reasons that issue in internationalism. Unlike Plato's state, it can no longer be dedicated only to local gods. Every man must be guided to his religion by his own experience and temperament, but this does not rid him of the prior obligation in conscience to be reasonable. So far as I can judge the religion of Fascism and much Toryism accord very ill with this rational framework. But I must leave Fascists and Tories to make their own defence.

Further, the appropriate community must be homogeneous, like-minded, at its most intimate a group of friends, actively stimulant each of each and harmonious each with each. Its core is a face-to-face group. So narrow a society, however, cannot in isolation convey— just as the self-contained household-of-two cannot convey —the full and catholic significance of thought, the entire life-stream of those true ideas whereby we attain immortality, to the seeking individual. It would not be possible even if this group were a clique of all contemporary brilliance and genius. No connection or mediation would be established between the intensive group of friends and the extensive field of world organization which is its polar complement.

The middle term is to be found in ideal movements which seek to justify themselves rationally, in terms of their historic rôle in relation to human society as a whole, and which yet are the vehicle through which small groups of co-workers, inspired by common ideas and with faith in persuasion, are able to work out these ideas effectively in practical life. In their freedom is the assurance of liberty. In this co-operation is the satisfaction of the religious need. In these movements are to be found the proper objects of contemporary religion. They are

THE CONCLUSION OF IT ALL

satisfactory so far as they satisfy the tests of reason, in fact inspire impersonal devotion to an ideal and enable the human being to experience the emotion of satisfied love for his fellows which, of all pleasures, is the one most contributory to the removal of human unhappiness.

Even in a healthy society of friends we yet retain an individuality and a tension. Still more is this true, the more heterogeneous is the society. A promiscuous readiness to forget oneself is not an admirable quality. No quality, on the contrary, is more admirable and more important in the man than "shape."

> Supposing I say: dogs are my neighbours
> I will love dogs as myself!
> Then gradually I approximate to the dogs,
> Wrangle and wag and slaver, and get the mentality of a dog!
> . . . .
>
> How can that be my neighbour
> Which I shrink from!

Tension is essential to any fully conscious, dignified, and illuminating experience. Even among those who are like-minded, like-mindedness will not consist in mere reduplication of thoughts, but in mutual stimulation. It is essential to imaginative creation. No talk of Communism or collectivist life must blind our eyes to the importance of this tension—nor should it, unless we construe Communism or collectivist life in some perverse and vegetative sense.

Consciousness of community is not to be achieved cheaply. To achieve it yet remains a social need and a human need. Otherwise a community that does not come from the spirit within but from the mechanical needs of the world without—a counterfeit community—will be set up. And in it we are persons wearing masks to protect our faces. No few of us, I suppose, find ourselves rather like children in an oddly hostile world where men seem to be preoccupied with adding to their wealth or with ferret-eyed ambitions of power or with using their acquaintance for their own social advancement in *réclame*. So it has always been. In each of us we can detect that side of ourselves which also is capable of doing these things or which is on guard against it in others.

The person, the *persona*, very effectually becomes a mask and the true self, with passage of years, recedes deeper and more remote, incapable of expression. With time these *personae*, these masks, eat into our faces so that we have no face or shape or spirit of our own, but only a sense of utter otherness and of all that matters most in us having been made rigid, suffocated, and destroyed. Even a sense of humour reminds one that, in a busy world, those with *le cœur sensible* will be most welcome if they transact their business and go about their business. The qualities of admiration, of vividness of perception, and of truth in expression—all interlinked—become tempered to the hue of the surrounding utilities and prudencies. The capacity for savouring life departs—is deliberately rejected as immature—and calculation takes its place. The great power game wins. The desire for generosity still lasts, but we decide in bitterness that most friendship is also deception and, too often, a shame like exhibiting oneself nude. This loss of intimacy and of sense of community in the modern world is an evil from which we must struggle to free ourselves.

THE CONCLUSION OF IT ALL

This desirable generosity and "outgoingness" is yet something different—and the difference is important—from a promiscuous loving-kindness and from a colourless moral duty of benevolence. It is exacting in what it requires before it will give itself. It corresponds with a vitality and assurance on the part of him who can afford to be generous. There is (as has been earlier argued) an assertive principle in man—a principle of liberty which, in exaggeration, may become a criminal or diabolical principle—which must be accommodated, unless society is to become insufferably "good" and dull. Along with it goes the imaginative demand for assertion and leadership in others—the demand for heroes, commissars, dictators, and such which is a kind of masochistic complement, existing in all healthy men, but liable to pathological exaggeration in paroxysms of deference and in the habits of lackeydom.

The need is clamant, in our heterogeneous and stick-dry social life, for a more intimate form of society, in which a spirit of co-operation can be assumed in the work of satisfying material and tangible needs and cultural and intangible ones. We are eating the bitter herbs of individualism and of negativism. The flower of personality and vitality and of corporate imaginative effort is not to be found on that root. The young future lies with the political religions.

What we need are unpretentious men who will qualify themselves for responsibility by the acceptance of a disciplined manner of life in a movement intellectually and morally worthy of their allegiance and faith. To those whose temperament insistently demands that even a Preface of this kind shall end in some conclusion, specific, concrete, of immediate and local application—to me it seems more important that we should end with an attitude of mind which discovers in experience something worthwhile as a basis of faith and confidence—I would recapitulate what was said in the last chapter.

In the United States it is impossible to suggest what shape this movement should assume until it is clear whether President Roosevelt's experiment will be success or failure. In the latter event, the probable consequence is industrial rioting, followed by race rioting, and a temporary reversion to the autocracy of the industrial magnates, with a wave of intense nationalism or Anglo-Saxonism in its wake. Under these circumstances the casual collaboration of individual men of brilliance, such as at present act as the President's advisers; the informal discussion of technocracy; or a merely negative and carping "progressivism," will be entirely inadequate to control the situation. A Socialist Party consisting largely of recent immigrants will be equally incompetent.

However violent the conditions that may immediately ensue upon the breakdown of the Presidential policy of pragmatism in programme, unsupported by a doctrine or a political religion giving fervour and discipline, America is a country which can afford to take time in finding its solutions. It possesses in abundance that individualism that can rescue it from any urgent danger of a doctrinaire fanaticism in politics. Its immediate need is a Fabian organization of intelligent technocrats to permeate with their ideas those who will take the lead in the country for the next generation. This organization must tame the American romantic individualist, and especially that worst of individualists, the American progressive, to the Socialist notion of discipline for a

THE CONCLUSION OF IT ALL

corporate purpose and to the logical implications of plan, national and international.

It is useful to state the principles for which the required movement in Britain should stand, although their elaboration is not a matter for this book. They are:

(a) The need for opposing systems of government where those in power are not removable by the will of the people declared at regular intervals.

(b) The need for a planned economy, with production for use not profit, so far as this is required in the interests of an efficient campaign against poverty; and the need for stimulation of international trade, subject to the over-riding requirements of this campaign.

(c) The value of personal liberty and of the right of association; the need to make this liberty real by equalizing measures in the economic sphere, and to guarantee it against superior economic might wielded for private ends; the need to satisfy the demand of the citizen for a decent and dignified life in return for social service; and the rejection of any system of government which refuses to men the right to frame their own ideals and to live in accordance with them so far as is consistent with respect for the equal rights of others.

(d) The recognition of the need for the encouragement of personal initiative and the proportionate reward of degrees of social service; and the repudiation of any social system which allocates economic, political, or social power, or inculcates a servile deference, in disregard alike of the personal independence of the citizen and the extent of service rendered to society.

(e) The need for a revision of the educational system with a view to inculcating into the coming generation the sense of citizenship in the community as their community and of their duty to it; and that the efficiency and prosperity of the community is their concern and their creative task, as equal citizens.

(*f*) The need for establishing, maintaining, and developing an international order and federal organization, as the instrument of peace, law, and equity, in which confederacy the final rights of sovereignty must inhere; and the recognition that certain nations today, as the present repositories of power, have a duty and destiny to use that power for the building up of such an international order.

(*g*) The recognition of the need for a spirit of discipline and sacrifice, beginning at home, as the condition of the building of a new, more just, and freer social order in this country and in the world, and a recognition of the need of binding up this sense of discipline for a cause with the sense of this freedom to be achieved.

I do not admit for a moment that the failure or success of such a movement is contingent on the failure or success of the very different and more violent methods adopted by Russia or by Italy. I do not think that we need ape the methods of Georgian seminarists such as Stalin any more than of Austrian house-decorators such as Adolf Hitler. What is required is a distinctively English policy.

Englishmen, who desire neither Fascism nor Bolshevism nor a timid lethargy, are capable of making their own contribution to the establishment of a world policy of peace and justice. Britain is fully able to establish an economy as equitable and as vigorous as Russia, and one immeasurably more efficient, if she can once be stirred by a new vision to a new determination.

If we so live, as members and active adherents, in such a movement, perhaps we shall understand what is meant by friendship, enjoy in action fulfilment of life and in the contemplation of such certainties as we have discovered find peace, before each rows forth on the great journey,

"Pulling the long oars of a life-time's courage."

THE CONCLUSION OF IT ALL

The year is finished, 1932—a year since this book began. The mounted police are clearing Trafalgar Square of the wrecks of a nation's economic misfortune. A great popular "daily" puts out its placard: "215,000 Test Match Scores Competition." One wonders whether any beam to the valley's end can be thrown by the uncertain human lights of reason and judgement.

Yet another year—1933. . . . Christmas, of the *anno santo*, the nineteenth centenary. In two hours from now, thanks to the miracles of modern science, the bell-peal will be coming through the ether from the Church of the Nativity. The cloud of war that was, six years ago when I first wrote, but as the size of a man's hand—that three years ago, in the first year of the depression, was but a small cloud—in this year of the German Revolution now covers menacingly the horizon. Marshal Foch prophesied war in 1935. If it comes, the hope for reason and moderation is small. The march of history through Liberalism and the new Conservatism to Social Democracy will go on through Fascism and Communism, through revolution and terror.

1934. As I revise proof, the headlines of another well-known "daily" strike my eye. "General Strike in France: Troops ready in Madrid: Czechs beginning Currency Battle: Soviet denounces Japan's War Plans: Vienna Fascist Coup." The time has come for those who believe in freedom for common men to turn to a programme of action, with a view to establishing a Protectorate of Liberty. An interval, but not a great one—a short time in which to act—still separates this country from revolution.

GEORGE ALLEN & UNWIN LTD
LONDON: 40 MUSEUM STREET, W.C.1
CAPE TOWN: 73 ST. GEORGE'S STREET
SYDNEY, N.S.W.: WYNYARD SQUARE
TORONTO: 91 WELLINGTON STREET, WEST
WELLINGTON, N.Z.: 8 KINGS CRESCENT, LOWER HUTT